URBAN POVERTY IN AFRICA

URBAN POVERTY IN AFRICA

From understanding to alleviation

Edited by
SUE JONES and NICI NELSON

INTERMEDIATE TECHNOLOGY PUBLICATIONS 1999

Intermediate Technology Publications
103/105 Southampton Row, London, WC1B 4HH, UK

© the individual authors; this collection IT Publications 1999

A CIP catalogue record for this book is
available from the British Library

ISBN 1 85339 474 2

Typeset by Dorwyn Ltd, Rowlands Castle, Hants
Printed in the UK by SRP Exeter

Contents

Notes on Contributors	vii
Introduction	xi
NICI NELSON	
List of Acronyms	xiv

PART ONE: Urban Poverty: Some strategic considerations

1. Urban Poverty in Africa: A historical perspective — 1
   NICI NELSON
2. Defining Urban Poverty: An overview — 9
   SUE JONES
3. The Role of the Government of Urban Areas in the Creation of Urban Poverty — 16
   MICHAEL MATTINGLY
4. Africa's Urban Informal Economies: Between poverty and growth — 27
   KENNETH KING and SIMON McGRATH
5. The Impact of Structural Adjustment on Welfare and Livelihoods: An assessment by people in Harare, Zimbabwe — 36
   DEBORAH POTTS

PART TWO: Coping with Urban Poverty: Institutional responses

6. Participatory Poverty Assessments: The World Bank contribution and emerging agenda — 49
   DAVID BOOTH, JEREMY HOLLAND, JESKO HENTSCHEL, PETER LANJOUW and ALICIA HERBERT
7. Multi Layered Responses to Urban Poverty: Possible donor agency action — 60
   SUE JONES
8. Urban Poverty Alleviation and Housing Creation — 71
   A. GRAHAM TIPPLE

9. uTshani Buyakhuluma (The Grass Speaks): People's Dialogue and the South African Homeless People's Federation 83
    JOEL BOLNICK
10. Diversity in Practice: An international NGO's experience of micro-finance 91
    HELEN PANKHURST and DEBORAH JOHNSTON
11. Municipal Responses to Urban Poverty: A case study of Gaborone, Botswana 102
    A.C. MOSHA

PART THREE: Coping with Urban Poverty: Livelihood strategies

12. Decision-making in Poor Households: The case of Kampala, Uganda 113
    GRACE BANTEBYA KYOMUHENDO
13. Truck Pushers, Grain Pickers and Grandmothers: Some gender and age aspects of vulnerability in Tamale, Ghana 126
    CAROLYNE DENNIS
14. On Growing up in the Streets: The plight of street children in Nairobi, Kenya 138
    PRISCILLA W. KARIUKI
15. Gender and Urban Poverty in the days of AIDs in Uganda 149
    CHRISTINE OBBO
16. Urban African Livelihood Systems: Straddling the rural-urban divide 160
    JO BEALL, NAZNEEN KANJI and CECILIA TACOLI

Notes 169
References 173

Notes on Contributors

Dr Nici Nelson took her Ph.D. at the School of Oriental and African Studies, London University. She is now a Senior Lecturer in Anthropology at Goldsmiths College, University of London. Her research interests include gender power issues in development and urbanization processes; informal survival mechanisms; HIV/AIDs and changing family structures – all with special reference to Africa.

Sue Jones is a social anthropologist and urban planner, who has worked in both the private and public sectors in the UK and overseas for donor agencies since 1975. She has mainly been concerned with developing multidisciplinary development projects involving health, education, employment, infrastructure and environmental resource management, including a number of urban poverty projects in India, Jamaica, Kenya, and Botswana. She worked on a World Bank-funded urban development programme in Jordan. Her particular concern is with mechanisms that ensure community-based responses are fed into the strategic level and affect policy and resource allocations.

Michael Mattingly teaches at the Development Planning Unit, University College, London in the fields of urban planning, urban management, and land management. In addition, he provides training, teaching and consultancy in training in a variety of countries around the world. He is currently engaged in research in environmental planning and management to benefit the poor. Earlier in his career, he worked as a professional urban planner, including several years with governments in East Africa.

Kenneth King is the Director of the Centre of African Studies and Professor of International and Comparative Education at the University of Edinburgh. His research interests over the years have focused on aid policy towards all subsectors of education; on technical and vocational education and training and on the special character of microenterprises and the informal economies of Africa. He is currently working on a DFID-funded research project called 'Learning to compete: small enterprises in the age of globalization' which has a particular focus on South Africa, Ghana and Kenya.

Simon McGrath is a Research Fellow of the Centre of African Studies and the Department of Education and Society at the University of Edinburgh. His research interests are in analysing the development of education and training policy and practice, including the role of external agencies, and the relationship of such developments with broader socio-economic contexts. He is currently involved in the 'Learning to Compete' project, funded by DFID and working in Ghana, Kenya and South Africa.

Deborah Potts has been a lecturer in Geography at SOAS since 1979. She has specialized in Africa, in particular southern Africa, and urbanization and migration theories. Since 1985, she has undertaken, with a Zimbabwean colleague, three major surveys of migrants in Harare. In addition, she has done fieldwork in Malawi, South Africa, Namibia and Botswana. An important focus of her urban-based research on Africa has been the impact of structural adjustment on the urban poor. Other aspects of her research include land tenure and land reform in southern Africa.

David Booth heads the Poverty and Social Policy Unit at the Overseas Development Institute in London. A sociologist, he was formerly Professor of Development Studies at the University of Wales Swansea.

Jeremy Holland is in the School of Social Sciences and International Development (formerly CDS) at Swansea, where he co-ordinates the Social Development Resource Centre funded by DFID.

Jesko Hentschel and Peter Lanjouw are economists working at the World Bank on poverty-analysis issues. Hentschel was the task manager for the Ecuador poverty assessment and is currently interested in the use of combined methods for evaluating health-service delivery. Lanjouw is co-author of a number of influential articles and books on household- and village-survey data in South Asia.

Alicia Herbert works for the International Development Department (formerly DAG) at Birmingham University, where she is the principal research officer on a major evaluation of DFID's support for poverty reduction.

Dr Graham Tipple has worked on housing and development issues in developing countries for over 20 years. A town planner by training, he lived and worked in Zambia and Ghana before joining the Centre for Architectural Research and Development at the University of Newcastle upon Tyne in 1982, where he is now a Reader in Housing Policy and Development and Director of CARDO. He has acted as a consultant for the World Bank, UNCHS, ILO and several UK consulting engineering companies working overseas. He is joint editor of *Housing the Poor in the Developing World: Methods of analysis, case studies and policy* (Routledge, 1991) and is currently completing a book on user-initiated extensions to government-built housing for Liverpool University Press.

Joel Bolnick is the co-director of The People's Dialogue, an NGO whose sold function is to support the activities of a social movement for the poor in South Africa – Umfelandawanye (The South Africa Homeless People's Federation.)

Dr Helen Pankhurst worked as the Regional Programme Officer at ACORD for over four years. She is now Head of the International Programmes Department at Womankind World-wide.

Dr Deborah Johnston is an economist, who has worked mostly in Southern Africa. She worked briefly for Acord on their micro-finance programmes and policy.

Professor Aloysius Mosha is a town and country planner currently with the Department of Environmental Science, Urban and Regional Planning Programme. He has practised and taught planning in Tanzania, Zimbabwe and Botswana. His research interests include urban governance and management, urban finance, urban poverty, housing and urban agriculture.

Grace Bantebya Kyomuhendo trained as a social anthropologist and is a lecturer in the department of Women's Studies in Makerere University. Her research is focused on women and children's health, and women and the labour market.

Carlyne Dennis has undertaken research in Africa on re-unification in Cameroon and a long period of research and teaching in Nigeria on rural industrialization, women's work and social theory. She has since worked in India, Indonesia, Zimbabwe and Lesotho. Recently she has completed research on NGOs in Ghana. Her interests include decentralization, social sector policy on planning, gender analysis and planning.

Priscilla Wanjiru Kariuki is Professor of Psychology at the College of Education and External Studies, Unviersity of Nairobi. She received her B.A. in Social Work and Social Administration from Makerere University of Uganda and an M.A. in Educational Psychology from the University of Nairobi, where she was also a Research Fellow with the Child Development Research Unit. She obtained her Ph.D. in Educational Psychology from the University of Alberta in Edmonton, Canada in 1980. Her main areas of research include social, cultural and psychological concomitants of development, especially as they affect children, women and families. She has been involved in multi-disciplinary research on street children in Kenya. She is currently working in a collaborative research study (with Nici Nelson) entitled 'The changing status of women and children in Kikuyu families in Kenya'.

Christine Obbo is a Ugandan anthropologist, was for many years a professor at American universities and is currently a research associate at the Centre of African Studies at the School of Oriental and African Studies at the University of London. She has published a book, *African Women*, and many other articles on gender and social change, and gender and AIDS. She is writing a book on gender, knowledge and ownership of the HIV epidemic.

Dr Jo Beall teaches Social Policy and Planning in the Department of Social Policy at the London School of Economics. She works on issues of poverty and social exclusion in southern Africa and South Asia and has worked extensively in South Africa, India and Pakistan. Over the last ten years she has worked with national and local governments, a range of international development agencies and NGOs. She is on the editorial board of Oxfam's journal *Gender and Development* and *The Journal of Southern African Studies*.

Dr Nazneen Kanji is an independent social development consultant and teaches in the Social Policy Department at the London School of Economics. She has lived and worked extensively in Eastern and Southern Africa and has carried out research on the social impact of economic reform, including a study on the gendered impact of the structural adjustment programme on urban households in Harare, Zimbabwe. Over the last ten years, she has worked with government, NGOs and donor agencies in mainstreaming gender issues in development.

Dr Cecilia Tacoli is a Research Associate at the International Institute for Environment and Development. Her main research interests are gender and international and internal migration, patterns of urban change in the South and livelihood systems. She currently co-ordinates a research programme on 'Rural-urban interactions, livelihood strategies and socio-economic change' conducted in collaboration with partner institutions in Africa, Asia and Latin America.

Introduction

NICI NELSON

In December of 1996 I convened a symposium on African Urban Poverty for the African Studies Association UK. At the end of the day, everyone agreed that we should publish the papers. Sue Jones and I, as the co-editors, have been concerned to compile a volume which includes more conventional analyses of structural contexts, with anthropological examples of urban poverty and considerations of alleviation policies and programmes.

No one book can cover a complex topic completely, much less one dealing with an issue as complicated and multifaceted as urban poverty in Africa. The editors recognise that such topics as structural adjustment and rural-urban linkages require a book on their own. These issues are only considered here from particular angles, in the chapters by Potts and Beall, Kanji and Tacoli. While efforts were made to cover the continent, some regions are not included and while we wanted to cover a wide range of topics there are important gaps, such as education.

This book has a tripartite structure. The first section, entitled 'Urban Poverty: Some Strategic Consideration', explores issues of the structural contexts of urban poverty. Nelson, in the first chapter, gives a brief historical overview of the characteristics of African urban poverty as well as approaches to dealing with it, while describing the general themes addressed by the contributors. Jones goes on from there and sets out the current thinking about disaggregating the category, the urban poor. Mattingly spells out the ways in which municipal authorities have contributed to urban poverty in Africa's cities by failing to provide quality public agency action to facilitate the creation of wealth in urban areas. King and McGrath explore a similar issue, putting forward suggestions on how national governments could and should contribute to the small-scale economy to make it capable of lasting growth. Potts raises the issue of how urban migrants perceive the impact of ESAP (Economic Structural Adjustment Programme) and emphasises the structural importance of rural-urban linkages when the economic constraints of ESAP begin to be felt.

In the second section, entitled 'Coping with Urban Poverty: Institutional Responses', Booth (et al.) examine the accumulated understanding compiled by poverty assessments and participatory poverty assessments undertaken at the instigation of the World Bank during the years 1993–7, which translated both macro-statistical and grassroots understandings into forms that policymakers can and must relate to. Jones explores the multi-layered approaches to poverty alleviation currently being developed that could be (and have been) supported by donor agencies such as DFID (Department for International Development) (in the UK). Tipple puts forward the thesis that the creation of housing by governments can act as a method of poverty alleviation, not just a way to provide a social benefit for the poor. Bolnick, describing the work of an NGO called Peoples' Dialogue, demonstrates how an NGO acting on behalf of the homeless in South Africa has struggled to utilize a political window of opportunity and has managed (within limits) to tap the resources of the national government to help the poor build their own houses. Pankhurst describes the rationale, the principles and the operation of micro finance programmes in the Horn of Africa organised by one NGO, called ACORD, which like the People's Dialogue capitalize and build on the productive initiative of poor people themselves. Lastly Mosha, writing about Gaborone City, describes the way one municipality responded positively to the alleviation of urban poverty.

The third and last section entitled 'Coping with Urban Poverty: Livelihood Strategies', explores aspects of grassroots survival strategies. Bantebya Kyomuhendo examines the way in which poor families in Kampala constantly strategize to obtain resources and to allocate them for survival, with special reference to women's health-seeking behaviour. Dennis examines social groups vulnerable to poverty in Tamale, Ghana. The analysis centres around street children and the fostering of children under conditions of increasing economic insecurity for children and old women living on their own. Obbo's chapter describes the strategies used by poor people with AIDS in Kampala, including well-established strategies of friendship, fictive kinship, religion and ethnicity as well as other more *ad hoc* solutions such as informal networks which help them deal with their disease both in illness and eventually even after death. Kariuki, examining the words and perceptions of street children, makes it clear that their lives and strategies are logical responses to the problems they face living on the streets. The book is completed with a consideration by Beall, Kanji and Tacoli of general livelihood strategies and the significance of rural-urban linkages for the urban poor in Africa.

Various themes weave through the contributions. The strongest theme is the strength, initiative and courage of those whose lived experience is urban poverty. Linkages of various kinds is a second important theme. Urban-rural linkages are developed in the contributions of Potts; Dennis; Obbo; Beall; Kanji and Tacole as are the linkages between the formal (or large-scale) and informal (or small-scale) sectors of both the polity and economy (by Mattingly, King and McGrath, Pankhurst and Johnson, Bolnick, Jones, Booth, Dennis and Beall, Kanji and Tacoli).

On issues relating to developmental policy and initiatives, a very important theme in most of the submissions is the recognition that the various categories of the urban poor themselves consistently demonstrate strength and initiative in dealing with their situations – whether they are old women in Ghana, people with AIDS in Uganda, the homeless seeking to provide their own shelter in South Africa, or employed Zambians coming to terms with an erosion of quality of life caused by ESAP. Failure to achieve stated aims will be the ignominious end of development programmes which have not taken into account the fact that it is the urban people experiencing particular, historically-specific forms of urban poverty who know best and who surely are the most appropriate 'experts' to design and implement projects. Directly and indirectly, this assumption is supported by the chapters by Potts, Jones, Pankhurst and Johnson, Bolnick and Beal, Kanji & Tacoli as well as others. At the same time and in related vein, it is made clear in many of the chapters, especially the ones in the third section, that the 'urban poor' are not one 'lumpen' mass. On the contrary they are highly differentiated, and different categories of people experience complex and situationally-specific conditions and processes of poverty.[1]

This book describes the contexts and structural conditions of some of the types of poverty found in Africa's cities. The analyses and descriptions try to come to terms with the complex reality which is urban poverty on the African continent, raising the initial question of how these situations have arisen.

List of Acronyms

ACORD	Agency for Co-operation and Research in Development
CBO	Community-based Organization
Danida	Danish International Development Agency
DFID	Department for International Development
ESAP	Economic Structural Adjustment Programme
GCC	Gaborone City Council
HBE	Home-based Enterprise
HHH	Household Head
HIES	Household and Income Expenditure Studies
IDS	Institute of Development Studies
IIED	International Institute for Environment and Development
ILO	International Labour Office
IMF	International Monetary Fund
ISTED	Institut des Sciences et des Techniques de'Equipement et de l'Environnement pour le Developpement
MSE	Micro and Small Enterprise
NGO	Non-governmental Organization
NORAD	Norwegian Agency for International Development
ODA	Overseas Development Agency
ODI	Overseas Development Institute
PA	Poverty Assessment
PLWA	Person Living With AIDS
PPA	Participatory Poverty Assessment
PRA	Participatory Rapid Appraisal
SAP	Structural Adjustment Programme
SED	Small Enterprise Development
SHHA	Self-help Housing Agency
SIDA	Swedish International Development Authority
SME	Small and Microenterprise
SWAA	Society for Women and AIDS in Africa
TASO	A local Ugandan NGO to help people living with AIDS
UNCHS	United Nations Centre for Human Settlements
UNDP	United Nations Development Programme
USAID	United States Agency for International Development
WHO	World Health Organisation

PART ONE:
URBAN POVERTY:
SOME STRATEGIC CONSIDERATIONS

1. Urban Poverty in Africa: An historical perspective

NICI NELSON

Introduction

A rather apt phrase in a Netherlands publication by the Ministry of Foreign Affairs (Ministry of Foreign Affairs, the Netherlands 1994: 6) captures nicely the rapid process of global urbanization. 'The world is changing from a global village to an urban globe.' It is certainly true that by 2010, half of the population of the southern world will live in towns.

Africa has traditionally been one of the least urbanized regions of the world. That is not to say there was no urbanization. Sixteenth century cities in West Africa compared favourably with their European counterparts. For example, the Yoruba cities were of similar size to those in Europe. Benin cities of Benin and Timbuktu had 20000 inhabitants, the size of Cologne, the largest city in Europe at that time. Many historians of the region feel that the depredations of the slave trade and the consistent extraction of wealth by precolonial and colonial European powers on the continent prevented the expansion of African economies and cities.

In the modern era, other regions of the world have urbanized much more rapidly. At the end of the twentieth century, Africa's rate of urbanization (the percentage of the total population living in cities) is low on a global scale, being only 30 to 40 per cent. However, the growth of urban populations has been very rapid. Since World War II, Africa's cities have expanded rapidly. Between 1960 and 1990, the large capital cities have grown at an average of 7 to 8 percent per annum, a rate which has made it next to impossible for urban authorities to provide low-income housing, urban services or sufficient employment (Stren 1978, Nelson 1997a: 338). Dakar had expanded to 16 times its pre-war size; Lagos to 25 times and Accra to a mere 10 times its size before 1940 (Hart 1982: 122). While growth of big cities has slowed, it is predicted that in the run up to the millennium, cities will continue to grow at a consistent 5 per cent annually. Most of this increase is caused by in-migration.

While Africa has been written about as a place which is rural and backward, a discourse of poverty is relatively recent. Part of the problem has been to find a usable definition of poverty. There are *absolute* ways of defining poverty (e.g. establishing a minimum necessary to maintain a person's life efficiency) and *relative* measures (e.g. poverty is measured against the average living standards of a particular society, or by comparison with other societies) (Illiffe 1987: 1). There are conceptual difficulties with using relative measures, especially those which cross different cultural boundaries, such as using European standards to establish reasonable occupancy rates per room in low-income housing which fail to take into account different climates and patterns of social usage. Certainly in the early days of anthropological interest in urban life (the early 1960s) anthropologists (and some sociologists and social geographers) working amongst members of the lower strata of urban hierarchies, avoided the term 'poor' (seeing it as judgemental and a relative term with little comparative validity) preferring instead to emphasize the socio-cultural adaptations to urban life, the hard work and the enthusiasm of their informants. Southall (1967: 00), a pioneer in the field of urban anthropology, was a good example of this tendency. Later urban anthropologists working in Africa, including the present writer, maintained this culturally relativist stance into the decade of the 1980s, thus laying themselves open to the accusation that they had ignored urban poverty. Still, it is possible to say with Bromley and Gerry that 'of all the social sciences social anthropology has played the greatest part in initiating interest in Third World poverty' (1973: 3). Their many seminal studies of social relations in low-income urban neighbours generated a rich and detailed description of the lives of those poorest members of the cities. It has been only recently that anthropologists and other social scientists have directed their attention to survival and coping strategies, an approach which implicitly recognizes poverty, vulnerability and socio-economic inequality. Their insights into social structure and culture have surely expanded the understanding and definition of poverty contributing to a definition of 'poverty' beyond the narrow limits of income measures generated by economists (who have always recognised the category of the poor). Kenyan anthropologist, Judy Bahemuka (1998) calls for a multi-variable approach to the definition of poverty, including such indicators as literacy levels, health strategies, nutritional status of children, the quality of water and housing available. Most practitioners in the field would agree that increasing income or material assets is only one part of alleviating urban poverty; improving human rights and improving basic services are also crucial. (IIED 1995) In the last 3 decades feminist anthropologists have highlighted the gender component of poverty, emphasizing the gender-specific vulnerability of women in towns (Mandaville 1979, White 1990, Brydon and Chant 1989, Nelson 1997a).

There is a second reason why there has been relatively little discussion of poverty in Africa in general and African cities in particular. Partly this is explained by a conceptualization of Africa as a last Arcadia. This is what Illiffe refers to as the 'myth of merrie Africa' where there was no economic differentiation, resources were freely available and more than adequate, and the extended family took care of less fortunate individuals (1987: 3). During the colonial era, in point of fact, those migrating to the cities were defined as the fortunate, the progressive and the upwardly mobile, no matter how difficult their lives might have been when they arrived there.

As Guyer observes, Africa was for a long time regarded as a continent immune from the kind of catastrophic famines which affected millions in Asia. Circumstances, and perhaps perceptions have changed, as Africa has now been associated with intractable under-nutrition and malnutrition (1987: 2).

Wratten makes the point that southern development literature has focused on the inequalities between the poorer rural sectors and the richer urban areas. Late 1950s development theory was marked by an emphasis on modernization, a process in which the urban centres would absorb the poor from the countryside and become the engines of this modernization. This conceptualization of the city rendered urban poverty relatively invisible. Even Gutkind and Wallerstein, in their path-breaking look at the political economy of Africa (1976) made no reference to poverty, urban or otherwise.

Urban Poverty in Precolonial Africa

Little has been written about urbanization in Africa in the precolonial or pre-imperialism stage of its history (Gutkind and Wallerstein, 1976). Certainly almost nothing has been written about poverty in cities, until Illiffe's ground-breaking examination of poverty in Africa (1987). He convincingly demonstrated that there was poverty in urban areas. There were interesting similarities and differences in the causes of poverty at this time compared to the period post-dating the impact of colonialism and global capitalism. According to him, poverty existed in both rural and urban sectors, despite the plentiful supply of land. People were impoverished by the use of political power which limited their access to land. Early visitors to precolonial cities, such as Lagos and the cities of Ethiopia, described well-developed precolonial traditions of begging. The thriving economies of the cities (residences of the elite and merchants), provided a wide range of low-paid, unskilled occupations for the poor (petty trading, porterage, heavy manual labour and low-skilled manufacture). The poor were essentially those who had suffered personal misfortune, were incapacitated, aged, solitary and/or who had lost their access to land. The experience of the poor differed from place to place. For example, in Rwanda and Burundi, the 'really poor' were orphans, famine victims, debtors, victims, and the dispossessed and women outside of marriage (who were probably barren). The poor were generally cared for by the institution of clientship. In the precolonial era the 'poor of precolonial Africa were bred in the countryside but seen in town' (Illiffe 1987: 164). Poverty in Nigerian cities is well recorded in mission records from 1845 to 1900 (ibid.: 82). The largest categories of the poor were those incapacitated by guinea worm or leprosy, unwanted slaves, abandoned children and childless old people (ibid.: 166).

Urban Poverty in Colonial Africa

In colonial times, the urban areas were seen as engines of progress and development and rural-urban migrants as wealthier and more fortunate than the stay-at-homes. No colonial administrator and few contemporary scholars analysed the colonial economy as one which exploited African workers or created poverty. Some more recent work, especially that done with a political economy slant, stresses these points (von Zwanenberg 1975, Hart 1982). Other work concentrated on vulnerable groups, such as single women, who were often poor both absolutely and relatively (White 1990, Nelson 1997b).

Certainly it is true that once the worst of the living conditions of the early colonial period were remedied, the average African townsperson was healthier and better nourished than people in the rural areas (Illiffe 1987: 173). The Africans who did migrate to the new colonial towns found it easy to get work, on a temporary circulatory basis. They frequently maintained their rural farming base under the management of their wives and stayed in town to earn money for improvements, bride wealth or consumer goods. Thus they accumulated the surplus which permitted them to become an African sub-elite in the colonial social structure (Stichter 1982). Just as in the pre-colonial period, the city offered the means, not based on land, to accumulate a surplus. In addition, it also offered opportunities for survival of poor and vulnerable migrants in the small-scale, informal sector. Development funds generated by colonial taxes increased the productive capacity of the urban economies. 'There were certainly disproportionate amounts spent in urban infrastructure and urban consumption . . . village life is a dead end. That is the main source of rural-urban inequalities' (Hart 1987: 140).

By 1940, in-migration had outstripped the capacity of the economy to provide jobs and the authorities could not ignore urban poverty. Even the employed were often poor. Only 10 per cent of urban dwellers could save and the bottom third depended on rural subsidies and ate poorly (von Zwanenberg 1975, Illiffe 1987: 171). Conditions worsened in 1940, with inflation. Colonial forms of poverty (proletarianism, unemployment, prostitution and delinquency) were added to incapacitation, hunger and servitude.

From Understanding to Action

In the 1950s, development planners saw cities as engines of development. This assumption was characteristic of modernization theory, which focused on wealth creation, assuming that poverty would be resolved by a 'trickle-down'. 'Gains from national economic growth would create economic benefits for the poor'. (Bahemuka 1998: 7) This proved overly optimistic.

In the 1970s, Lipton (1977) held that power wielded by urban groups biased the allocation of resources to the city, impoverishing the countryside. This was a common development view in the 1970s and 1980s. Challengers to his theories point out that his rural/urban dichotomy is too simplistic, may be more valid for Asia than for Africa and does not explain the existence of urban poverty (Gilbert and Gugler 1984, O'Connor 1991). Since the 1980s, the disparities between rural and urban incomes has narrowed significantly (Jamal and Weeks 1988). ESAP policies have had a more negative impact on urban economies than rural (Becker et al. 1994). There is even evidence that in severe economic depressions, reverse migration is taking place (Simon 1992).

The issue is still under debate for it is obviously not a simple one. It is clear that cities are crucial to the overall economic development of any country (Simon 1992). At the same time, it is also clear that true urban industrial prosperity cannot be created by policies which depress the development of rural areas (Lofchie 1997: 36). As the 1990s draw to a close, shouldn't we be abandon such a dual-sector view of a national economy in favour of one which sees it as a complex, interrelated whole?.

From Understanding Urban Poverty to Alleviation Policies

To paraphrase Marx; after one understands the world, how does one undertake to change it? Development initiatives, by definition, aim to change the world, basing their actions on common assumptions about the structures and processes of the world. The twentieth century has been a century of self-conscious 'development' in Africa, mainly from the top and from the outside. What approaches to action and the articulation between action and understanding have prevailed in the last 100 years?

During the colonial period, the goal was to eliminate what was seen as Africa's 'backwardness', not poverty. Groups which were defined as health hazards or nuisances, such as beggars and prostitutes, might be seen as poor and the solution to their presence in the progressive city was expatriation to the rural areas.

At the end of colonialism, modernization-based policies resulted in large-scale, capital-intensive investment, most of it intended to encourage manufacture in towns. This investment was to result in a 'trickle-down' both from the urban rich to the urban poor and from the town to the country.

In the 1960s, disillusion with modernization resulted in a shift to an emphasis on rural development. Development agencies promoted a basic services approach which delivered the basic services deemed necessary for their survival. In keeping with the prevailing 'urban bias' assumptions, most such initiatives were directed to the rural areas (Bahemuka 1998). Not until the 1970s did the World Bank begin basic needs provision for the urban poor. Such projects were top-down in nature, conceptualizing poor people as recipients of aid determined from the metropolis.

The late 1970s and 1980s saw two different approaches to urban poverty: structural adjustment and participatory development. ESAP was the IMF (International Monetary Fund) and World Bank's solution to the debt-crisis of the 1970s and has been applied to most southern countries since then. It is a programme designed to stimulate the economy, eliminate government waste and restrictive legislation in order to open local economies to global capitalism.

How did a more participatory approach to the solution of the problem of urban poverty come about? The modernization development approach was based on a conceptualization of urban poverty (or poverty in general) as a form of social pathology and, in my opinion, subsequent ESAP approaches have hardly shifted from this view. It took the work of certain radical political economists in Latin America in the 1970s to initiate a re-conceptualisation of the urban poor (Pearlman 1979) These political economists defined the poor as integral to the socio-economic and political system and not as separate from and marginal to development processes. If the poor didn't actually create their own poverty (see Lewis's Culture of Poverty theory and Vincent's critique) (Lewis 1966, Valentine 1968) they were merely dependent recipients of aid. 'The poor are part of the total system but they have no control over the system and little possibility of changing it' (Bromley and Gerry 1979: 13). This perceptual shift placed the urban poor as significant actors in urban and national systems, albeit as relatively helpless ones.

While analysts like Bromley and Gerry certainly integrated the poor conceptually as part of the system, there was still a sense in which they were being constructed theoretically as dependent because of their structural marginalization. The above quote goes on thus:

> The poor are too busy surviving to think of organization or mobilization and their dependent vertical linkages within the socio-economic system are much more significant than their horizontal linkages and potential solidarity (ibid).

It took another theoretical shift to see the poor, not only as a functioning part of the system but also as proactive and capable of agency. In the 1980s, more radical thinkers on, or practitioners of, development began to develop less patronizing approaches to the urban poor (Chambers 1983,

Nelson and Wright 1997). Local and northern NGOs and certain Scandinavian bilateral agencies began to implement these approaches. Gradually, over the last two decades, greater interest in these approaches has surfaced (see Booth and Jones in this volume). Increasingly popular micro-finance schemes in urban areas are examples of these approaches (see Pankhurst and Johnson in this volume) All of these approaches aim in various ways to understand poverty from the experiences and perspectives of the poor (Bahemuka 1998: 5). The more radical initiatives build logically on this understanding by engaging the poor themselves in the provision of services (from the design to the implementation stages) thus transforming 'recipients of aid' to stakeholders in a total system (Nelson and Wright 1997). The major problem with this type of development is that most of these initiatives have been poorly funded and thus there are major constraints on scaling-up even the most successful projects.

By the end of the 1980s and into the 1990s, it became clear to the World Bank that the social cost of ESAP programmes was too high for the urban poor to pay on their own. The tough measures designed to improve national economies had their harshest impacts on the poorest urban inhabitants. The threat of urban riots was realized in a number of African cities as the cost of food rose with the lifting of food subsidies. Health and education services were cut back or made to 'pay their way' so that the urban poor could no longer afford health care or schooling. For the first time in several decades, child mortality rose and percentages of children in school dropped. As a result of a rethink of their approach, a number of programmes, often referred to as social development funds, were instituted to help mitigate the suffering of the urban poor. Many of these funds are now being channelled through the aforementioned NGOs running micro-level projects in consultation and in co-operation with the urban poor themselves (see Pankhurst and Johnson and also Bolnick in this volume). Larger bilateral and multilateral agencies have gradually recognised that micro-level involvement often means that such projects are more effectively designed and implemented in the long run. This collaboration could be a fruitful way of combining grassroots insights and efficiencies with more substantial funding.

In the run-up to the millennium, where are these various approaches to alleviating urban poverty taking us? At a national level, many governments are pursuing robust policies to strengthen the economy and in some cases to improve urban management (see Mattingly and Mosha in this volume). At the same time, many micro-level workers are learning more and more about the complexities of urban poverty and devising sophisticated ways of giving sensitive and effective consideration to the real needs of the poor, often using funds from larger agencies.

Macro-level policies are concerned mainly with making adjustments to the structures of the state and the economy. There is little or no consideration of the day-to-day needs of the urban poor. While, in the long term, a strong economy is a necessary condition for improving the lives of the urban poor, it is not sufficient and certainly, in the short term, it can be woefully inadequate. The types of initiatives being run by the NGOs fill these short-term needs, however the NGOs lack both resources and political clout at the moment (note Bolnick's example of the People's Dialogue low-income housing initiative and the South African government's ambivalent response).

What is needed in these first years of the twenty-first century is greater articulation between these two levels of African societies. Governments need to pursue their macro-level policies in the interests of a stronger economy while consulting those at the grassroots who are informed about the complex and often contradictory impacts of these policies on the lives of the most vulnerable. Micro-level workers must consult, be consulted and articulate with the structures of government. The days of seeing the economy and the society as consisting of two separate sectors are long past (as King and McGrath recognize in their call for macro-level policy articulation to nurture the small-scale sector).

In this way the initiative, courage and strength of purpose of the urban poor celebrated by so many of the submissions in this volume will be given greater scope. Under these conditions of analysis and action, perhaps the alleviation of urban poverty will be more than just a dream of justice.

2. Defining Urban Poverty: An overview
SUE JONES

There has been a shift, in recent years, in the understanding of the process of development. . . . It involves, ultimately, a fuller view of human beings **(Sen 1997).**

There has been much reconsideration of the definitions and causes of urban poverty, over the last few years.[1] The aim here is to identify all these various approaches as a backdrop to the discussions by practitioners in this book.

The Current Debate about Urban Poverty

Most writers refer to the renewed debate about poverty, and urban poverty in particular, since the 1980s and the increased difficulties faced by poor people in countries in the South, especially in Africa. Some see this as a result of structural adjustment and the World Bank's reconsideration of its responses. Others see it as part of a longer term reconsideration of poverty, prompted by more in-depth understanding of the circumstances of the poor and their needs being provided by participatory and qualitative assessments.[2] Clearly, Robert Chambers has led this debate about putting the last first and has promoted the view that poor people have the right to define their poverty themselves and design measures to solve their problems (Chambers 1997).

In many respects, these two approaches are informed by different perspectives on poverty. To say that this is the difference between the perspectives of economists and social development practitioners is simplifying the issue too much, but it does make the point. Put more crudely, the interest can be seen to revolve around measuring poverty rather than understanding its causes (Satterthwaite 1995a: 5).

Whether, therefore, the World Bank is the motivator for a reconsideration of urban poverty is debatable. It has, however, been reflecting on the impact of structural adjustment and the new categories of poor that have emerged as a result – the new poor, the borderline poor, the chronic poor (Wratten 1995: 13). But possibly the Bank is a moving force because it has the capacity, as it had in the 1970s with slum upgrading and site and service programmes,[3] to promote large-scale responses to urban poverty, which are taken seriously by governments.

Whoever is responsible, there is noticeable glee amongst those concerned with urban poverty that it is back on the agenda. But, in fact, poverty has never gone away. It has been steadily and frighteningly on the increase during the 1980s and 1990s (Satterthwaite 1997: 5), while the attention of policy makers has been focused elsewhere.

What should we make of this intensified debate about urban poverty? Firstly, it has focused attention on action in the field, which is of increasing concern to those working with poor people, rather than those involved in macro-level debates. It has shown the need to involve poor people and to identify, with them, what is happening informally – how people are actually coping with their poor circumstances.

While the importance of the informal economic sector is generally conceded (with such hard-to-ignore examples as the *Jua Kali* in Kenya), the significance of other aspects of the informal sectors, such as informal housing provision and informal service provision is not so easily accepted.[4] But PRA (Participatory Rapid Appraisal) proponents have shown that without an assessment of how the informal systems operate, then one does not have a full picture about poverty, its characteristics and causes. This inevitably affects action proposed and the design of interventions.

Those who have recently joined the debate about urban poverty see the latest shift in World Bank thinking and its use of participatory poverty assessments as a significant change. Unfortunately, those of us who have watched development thinking over time have a more jaundiced view. We have seen a rather interesting tennis game since the 1950s swinging between technical/implementation/programme action and strategy/policy/institutional/management level support. Cynics might say that we are back on the track of looking for specific action to address urban poverty because of the clear shortcomings of macro-level strategies to alleviate it.

However, let's go with the enthusiasts who see some changes on the horizon. What are the current key considerations in defining urban poverty?

Current Definitions of Poverty

The first point, which is probably the only point of agreement, is that poverty is generally defined in terms of a lack or deficiency in some form (Wratten 1995: 12). Beyond that there is much debate.

Poverty defined internationally as a lack of income

It generally now seems to be agreed[5] that poverty is about much more than just income. For a start, many poor families do not earn a regular income and their needs are met with more than just cash inputs. However, most countries still operate on the basis of setting a poverty line (mainly based on income, even though this is now defined in a more sophisticated way). Although this provides a simple tool for bureaucratic decision-making about welfare support, it is not necessarily the objective, scientifically rigorous mechanism that it is promoted as.[6] It is also only a partial and limited perspective on poverty. It shows little regard for a wider range of issues facing the urban poor, in relation to social, health and education conditions.

Identifying figures for poverty at national levels

Such limited assessments also lead to serious under-assessments of the overall number facing poor conditions in countries in the South. As against the World Bank estimates (in 1985) of 330 million 'poor' people living in urban areas, Satterthwaite estimated (in 1990) that at least 600 million in Africa, Asia and Latin America live in 'life and health-threatening homes and neighbourhoods' (Satterthwaite 1997: 5).

Also, the tendency of quantitative assessments is to see urban poverty as a problem concentrated in the capital city. The size and scale of problems in such slum and squatter settlements is very visually evident. However, as identified by Satterthwaite (1995a) two thirds of the urban population in countries in the South live in urban centres with less than one million inhabitants. (Moser, Herbert and Makonnen 1993)

There are also significant groups of urban poor living in peri-urban areas and with different problems to those in inner city slums. Again, it is not simply a case of defining the poor in quantitative terms. It requires a recognition that different types of urban poverty exist.

Poverty defined in terms of basic services

An understanding and assessment is also required of the different ways in which people can be, or can be seen to be, poor. Since the 1970s and the World Bank Urban Development programmes,[7] people have been defined as poor in spatial terms and in relation to a lack of services which other urban area residents have access to – education, health, good housing conditions, water, electricity, appropriate sewerage, land ownership and secure tenure etc.

This is certainly a way of defining the poor – going into slum areas you can immediately identify this as a need. But this basic services approach to urban poverty has come under heavy criticism as a top-down solution, imposed on the poor. It is a technical response. It presumes that their problems will be solved by injections of facilities and services.

It also presumes that all poor people will have equal access to resources provided (when the reality is very different) (Jones and Francis et al. 1996). Most particularly, there have been a range of issues around the management of facilities and the sustainability of the action which have not been resolved by basic services approaches.

I would, however, take issue with some of the criticism about basic services provision. Very often the poor themselves identify this as their need – wanting a house without a leaking roof, provision of water so that women (usually) do not spend most of their day collecting it or the provision of a toilet in their yard to avoid possible sexual harassment if they use open areas. Who are we to tell them that this is only a technical response, if this is what they can immediately see that they need?

Instead, some distinction is needed here. Where basic service provision is seen as an end in itself it has been a very crude response to urban poverty problems. In contrast, where provision has been more sensitively provided, as a means to an end, identified by the urban poor themselves and used as a focus for community decision making, participatory action and ownership by poor people, it has had more of an impact and a different role.

There is also the argument that urban poverty is a series of interlinked difficulties. As an example of this reinforcing cycle of problems that the urban poor face – their circumstances mean that they are likely to eat poorer food, which means poorer health and therefore less likelihood of finding (or keeping) a job, which leads to less income which means more of the family (including children) having to work and only able to afford poorer housing which affects health which is further undermined by poor food – and so the cycle continues. A strategy that provides a range of basic needs support (in an effective way) may be a means of unlocking these cycles of poverty. There is a case for tackling urban poverty in this co-ordinated way (Wratten 1995: 29) and as part of action to address multiple deprivation (Satterthwaite 1995b: 6). Basic needs provision itself can also help to unlock the cycle of poverty. Moser (1998: 11) gives the example of housing as an asset, because it can be rented.

This is not to disagree with Robert Chambers (1983 and 1997) and others, who have promoted participatory appraisals and have criticised needs-based urban poverty responses where they are unlinked to poor peoples' needs. Basic needs approaches cannot provide effective responses if they are not designed by, with and for poor people. They also have to reflect the fact that poor people may see their position and problems in much more qualitative terms. Chambers and other writers have been promoting a range of qualitative techniques for assessing urban poverty (examples are provided in section three of this book).

Qualitative definitions of poverty

Pryer et al. (1997) summarized alternative and more qualitative definitions of poverty as follows:

- Vulnerability, powerlessness, isolation and humiliation (Chambers)
- Entitlement (Sen)
- Deprivation (Townshend)
- Social Exclusion (European Council) (See also Arjan de Haan 1996)

All of these suggest a deeper and more complicated definition of poverty. This is reflected in the various and participatory ways in which qualitative assessments help to define poverty.

Definitions that disaggregate the urban poor
Greater sensitivity is not only needed for overall definitions about poverty and the causes of poverty. The urban poor are not just a 'lumpen' poor. There are considerable and extensive differentiations between them. A number of indicators have been used to make these distinctions, such as levels of literacy (especially for women), types of housing, levels of education reached (by girls as well as boys), levels of indebtedness, percentage of income spent on food, types of food eaten, child labour etc..[8]

I have always found it interesting to look for one key provision as an indicator of the degree of poverty or an indicator of increased wealth, such as shoes in Kenya or cooking pots and cooking facilities in India[9]. Food, both its quantity and quality, seems to be the first area of economy when times are hard and one of the first areas of expenditure if circumstances improve.

Definitions of poverty by the poor themselves
Poor people themselves distinguish between the poor and the very poor. They can often make considerable distinctions among poor people in their localities (Jones and Francis et al 1996, Jones and Matrix Consultants Development 1995: Appendix 5). As an example, in one slum area, poor households identified how the more 'well off' poor households were able to afford proper storage containers. They could also ensure that they were at the front of the queue at the times when the water supply was turned on. Since the communal water tap was turned on only for a short time and at low pressure, they often monopolized what water there was. Without a qualitative assessment undertaken with the poor directly, such an issue (which has a fundamental impact of a water project on the living conditions of the poor) would not have been raised.

The difficulty of geographically or spatially-based urban poverty solutions is that they may not distinguish between the 'better off' and those poor people in greatest need. For this reason, targeting action for specific groups of urban poor has been proposed.[10]

Identification of the poorest and most vulnerable groups
Increasingly, qualitative assessments and action in the field (generally by NGOs and CBOs) have identified a range of vulnerable groups, who face particular poverty problems and have separate needs[11]. Some identified groups include street children, widows, permanently disabled heads of households, female-headed households, unemployed youths.

Some of these groups, such as street children, are not geographically based (except on the streets!) and require a different approach from locality based initiatives.

Household level definitions of poverty
Disaggregating the urban poor raises another area of sensitivity, especially as regards gender issues. Poverty cannot just be considered at the household

level. There can be significant differences at the household level. For example poorer households may send boys to school, but keep girls at home to help, or substitute for the mother if she has to go out to work. These distinctions within households are not always static. Moser (1998) has shown how a household's decisions and responses to their needs can change over time and be affected when the family hits a crisis. Her point is that assessments need to be multi-layered, considering poverty at the intra-household, household and community levels. When considering such issues as possible employment etc. there is also a need to consider city wide responses (see Mattingly, Chapter 3 of this volume).

Defining the poor as active managers
Moser (1998: 1) makes a similar case for the urban poor to the case for the rural poor, so historically made by Chambers (1983). The poor are not just passive in their circumstances but are active 'managers of complex asset portfolios'. The various coping strategies used (Part Three of this book) illustrate how much they manage all their assets as well as they can and how fundamentally this management can be affected by crisis and shocks (Amis 1995: 149).

Family members can be making daily, even hourly, decisions, in order to have sufficient resources to meet their needs. They are often making the most astute assessment of costs, how much services cost, how wealthy or poor their neighbours are or how much land costs in their area. Could you tell me, at this moment, how much your weekly shopping costs? What is the current price of a range of basic food items? What was your weekly shopping cost last year compared to now? What are your weekly service bills? What is the current price of land in your area? What is the going hourly rate for a labourer, a maid or a waiter? If you ask poor people (especially the women) most of them can tell you immediately. And some people still see the urban poor as unaware and unintelligent.

The links between the urban and rural poor
One of the coping mechanisms for the urban poor is support from relatives in rural areas (and *vice versa*). Obviously these arrangements differ from country to country, but increasingly links between the rural and urban poor are being recognized as one dimension of urban poverty coping strategies. All these mutual and reciprocal relationships should be considered when assessing the circumstances of the urban poor.

Conclusion

If we look at all these different ways of defining poverty, we have a vast array of issues to take on board. I can understand when those with a technical or macro-economic perspective say that social development supporters will only be satisfied when the poorest person in the poorest household in the poorest area of the poorest city is helped by a project.

But this is a parody and can be easily addressed. If donor, NGO or government activities have not substantively and effectively addressed the needs of the poorest people as part of their poverty alleviation, they will certainly have brought improvements to an area. They may have benefited a number of people in a poor area and they may have changed the status of an area and increased support to it, even if they have not addressed the issue of poverty.

This is the issue that urban poverty specialists are trying to put back on the agenda. Most responses proclaimed as urban poverty initiatives are, in fact, about urban management or urban development, not about how poor people cope within these urban circumstances.

So urban poverty professionals may be pleased that the debate has been raised again. But what does it mean? Certainly there is more sophisticated and sensitive analysis of urban poverty and widely accepted techniques have been specifically developed for participatory assessments with the poor. Out in the field, practitioners[12] are working at the micro level, trying to address a range of poverty needs with the people. At the macro level, national policymakers are providing more robust national poverty policies, using more sensitive means of analysis.

But it is uncertain what is happening between the analysis and the reality. Are the responses and resources being redirected to meet the challenge? Or do we now have a burgeoning market of specialist urban poverty researchers, PRA experts and academic analysts, while the urban poor (even though they are more sophisticatedly defined) still see no action or benefit?

3. The Role of the Government of Urban Areas in the Creation of Urban Poverty

MICHAEL MATTINGLY

If poverty 'implies deprivation of human needs that are not met' (UNCHS (United Nations Centre for Human Settlements) 1996: 108), then the performance of public agencies can be measured by the extent of deprivation with regard to housing with basic facilities or health care. Moreover, it is suggested that without adequate public agencies, a population cannot rise above poverty (Wolf 1996, Reynolds 1985 cited in Aron 1997:16, Olson 1996 cited in Wolf 1996). When public agencies are inadequate because of deficient legal systems, corruption, bureaucratic obstructions, and the quality of infrastructure (Aron 1997:16), the negotiations necessary for operating an efficient society are not made.

The implication is that governments are more than just instruments or actors to be brought into the battle against poverty. To the extent that they lack public agency action of quality, cities and towns will lack wealth, and the wealth they have may be badly distributed. There is ample evidence that this has been a pervasive feature of urban areas in sub-Saharan Africa.

Urban Poverty and the Government of Urban Areas

Urban places provide preferred locations for the manufacturing and service industries of developing countries which should be the major contributors to their wealth and to that of sub-national regions. In sub-Saharan Africa, even though employment in the modern industrial sector is insignificant outside of South Africa, added value for industry runs to five times that of the rest of the urban economy and ten times that of the agricultural sector. Urban productivity is three to four times greater than rural productivity. (Institut des Sciences et des Techniques de l'Equipement et de l'Environnement pour le Developpement (ISTED) 1998:7) Cities and towns have key roles to play in developing the wealth of their rural surroundings. Large cities may be a support for agricultural development, rather than a drag upon it (Lee-Smith and Stren 1991:25). Studies in Kenya (Collier and Lal 1980 cited in Lee-Smith and Stren 1991) showed that rural poverty is reduced by innovation closely linked to urban jobs which transfer cash and educational skills to rural areas. The urban poor are to a large extent people who have been driven into urban areas by rural underdevelopment in the first instance (Lee-Smith and Stren 1991:25). Urbanization in sub-Saharan Africa has led to specialization in food production with a high added value, for example through market gardening, increasing the productivity of the rural sector (ISTED 1998:11). In turn, this further expands the urban economy, for cities and towns are the bases for marketing, financial, and technical services to these rural activities, as well as local consumers' and producers' markets for products of nearby rural activities. Furthermore, urban areas accommodate the populations which cannot find employment in efficient rural production. Half of the present 100 million urban residents of sub-Saharan Africa are rural people who have come to town, or their children (ibid.:13).

Poor performance of these functions in cities and towns is thus likely to affect negatively both urban and rural production and, as a consequence, urban and rural wealth. However, these urban functions are not carried out efficiently and effectively without key inputs and supports requiring collective, negotiated action, which in most circumstances public agencies are called upon to perform.

Inadequate service infrastructure critically reduces the ability of manufacturers to exploit the economies of scale offered by urban areas (Lee and Anas 1989), while poor living conditions lower production capacities in services and manufacturing (World Bank 1991, Harris 1992). Such living conditions result because the concentration of activities making these economies possible carries costs which are substantial and which cannot easily be reduced by individual actions/decisions, as in the case of air pollution.

Governments are the principle sources of organization for the collective actions needed to exploit the benefits and reduce the costs of spatial concentration. While other institutions can provide some of the means, they almost always lack the capacity to work with the breadth of territory, concern, and mandate of governments. Where collective action is weak or simply not taken, these costs must be countered on an individual basis, if they are countered at all. While economies of scale are lost in some cases (e.g. water provision), in others corrective action becomes almost impossible (e.g. creating shared open space). Greater wealth is then consumed to counter these costs or they must be suffered as deprivations by those too poor to do otherwise.

Therefore, if urban government is not adequate, the production of wealth in a city or town will be held back, as well as that in adjacent rural areas, and all in the urban area will be the poorer for it, including those migrating from nearby. Moreover, the costs of concentrated living, normally relieved by governments doing what individuals cannot, will be a greater burden upon urban residents. Yet inadequacy is not the whole story. Even when governments are weak, their regulations and licensing can obstruct efforts to increase wealth and their support or interference can be biased to favour those who are not poor. Furthermore, they can fail to distribute to the poor their fair share of public assets, particularly housing and land.

Wealth Creation and the Government of Urban Areas

Urban benefits not captured

If the economies of scale for production which urban concentrations make possible are to be utilized, governments must properly organize the collective services that are necessary. The World Bank concluded that 'the major constraints to urban productivity have their origins largely in weaknesses in the public sector' and that not enough attention has been given to critical responsibilities of local institutions of government (1991:23) The point was not lost in regard to Africa. Halfani (1996) argues that African cities have been marginalized in the process of global accumulation because of their lack of service infrastructure. Production costs have been much higher than necessary – and therefore products less competitive – because of grossly inadequate or failing urban services. Bubba and Lamba (1991) argue that the availability of urban services affects productivity in Nairobi. Planning studies for the towns of Mvuma, Gokwe, Shurugwi and Chivhu of Midland Province of Zimbabwe conclude that they face shortages of water which will require rationing and act 'as a major brake on new industrial investment' (Government of Zimbabwe n.d.:170). Rogerson (1996:180) identifies five key areas of concern for policy and strategic intervention to support informal economic activity, which like others he reckons is an undeveloped source of urban wealth in the Pretoria-Witwatersrand-Vaal (PWV) area of South Africa. Two of these are the provision of infrastructure and services, and urban management, both responsibilities of governments.

Inadequate provision of those services critical to manufacturing – energy (most often electricity), transport, education, water, and communications – has been a common problem in urban Africa. The World Bank's research in Lagos found that large manufacturers were burdened with costs 30 per cent higher than would be the case if government water, electricity, transport and postal services were reliable. For smaller companies the burden was even greater (Lee and Anas 1989). Although essential urban services for Abidjan (water, electricity, affordable housing, public transport, serviced land) were provided by successfully managed state or joint companies during the 1970s, these have all since suffered from slackness in their management and the inability of the government to finance its responsibilities, so that companies have failed or become ineffective (UNCHS, 1992b:77).

Taiwo reported in 1991 that the volume of water available for use in Lagos would serve only 2.1 million people, or 30 per cent of the metropolitan area's 6 million population (1991:5), without even considering the needs of industry. Kulaba reasoned that the working days lost – hundreds of thousands of them – to the production of companies in Tanzania because of breaks in water and electricity supplies have resulted in substantially lower production and profits (1989). Stren and White (1989) document at length how water provision in cities and towns of Nigeria, Kenya, Tanzania, and Mauritania has been or has become woefully inadequate. These are stories of inadequate investment, poor maintenance, bureaucratic delays and incompetence, and insufficient staff skills.

Traffic congestion in Lagos is legendary. But many other cities such as Nairobi and Ibadan have long experienced excessive costs of moving labour, materials and products during manufacturing and distribution because of packed roads. A major additional cost has been the wear and tear on vehicles coping with damaged road surfaces and stop-start driving. At the same time, pervasive low quality mass transport produces long, uncomfortable and therefore tiring journeys to and from work which sap productive capacity. *The Economist* reported that Maputo's bus service had just 25 vehicles, one eighth of the total it had five years before, and that a 1983 study showed that on an average day in Brazzaville, Congo, just half the bus fleet was mechanically sound enough to leave the garage, and half of those had broken down by the end of the day (1990:20). Mass transport facilities and services in Nigerian cities are generally held to be poor and inadequate (Bolade, 1989).

Accounts of other key services are little different. For instance, Onokerhoraye (1982) in a detailed study of Ilorin, concluded that the number of primary schools in the city fell below that needed for Nigeria's universal free primary education programme. Similar conclusions have regularly featured in the urban planning reports prepared throughout sub-Saharan Africa (for example, Kumasi Metropolitan Assembly 1996). Beyond mere buildings and grounds, there are widespread shortfalls in teaching staff to be considered.

Good urban services are of little value if an industry cannot locate where it has access to them. When land – itself a basic factor of production – is largely or completely in the ownership of a government and is badly allocated, there are shortages of the right kind at the right place at the right time. This can not only discourage investment, but it can unnecessarily raise land costs which then reduces productivity at the workplace. Higher land costs also create pressure for higher wages to meet higher housing or transport costs or force workers into the less healthy environment of lower cost housing, which in turn can reduce their productivity. Schmetzer (1990) reports that an acute shortage of land existed in Lusaka in 1985 because of poor management of government-owned land by the responsible agencies. Delays of three years were experienced in processing applications, and only 842 plot leases were issued in 1985 for a demand of 7 000 to 8 000 new dwellings every year (ibid.). During the mid-1980s, officials in Kano lamented to the author that mis-allocation to speculators of all government land designated for industrial use had led to such high asking prices that investors in new industries sought sites outside the city. It must be added that local bureaucracies in many African cities take years to issue property titles (*The Economist* 1990:26, Mabogunje 1993). The absence of a title discourages investments in building.

Urban costs not reduced

At the same time that it is failing to bring about economies of scale, a government may not properly organise those collective actions which reduce costs associated with urban concentrations. These include the provision of open spaces, refuse collection, sanitation, drainage, control of air pollution, and other public health measures. Consequently, there are demands upon the wealth of individuals to meet these additional costs that are greater than if these provisions are organized collectively. More of the wealth produced is then used to counter the costs of urban concentration than if collective actions are taken. Moreover, where such costs cross an affordability threshold, or where effective action by individuals is virtually impossible at any price, the action will not take place at all. This results in further reductions in wealth produced because poor health and low motivation lowers worker productivity.

Without collective action, open space cannot be provided, air and water pollution cannot be checked, traffic congestion cannot be prevented, proximity to nuisances of noise and odours cannot be minimized. Firefighting is more critical in a concentrated physical environment. Sanitary and solid waste collection and disposal cannot be left to individuals, nor can storm waste drainage. Houses are crammed together in ways which shut out light and air and thus breed debilitating and fatal diseases, psychological as well as physiological. Faulty building construction threatens those who use the spaces inside as well as those who travel the roads and paths overshadowed by structures. Desperate or greedy individuals push their activities and buildings into roads, paths and other spaces meant for shared needs.

Stren and White (1989) have documented at length how growing urban populations in Africa receive fewer public services on a per capita basis. Their account ranges over water provision, waste disposal, transportation, housing, urban planning, and building construction regulation. It depicts uniformly low levels of service management and consequent provision, even where successful strategies have created improvements. It has been particularly difficult for governments to achieve the provision of basic infrastructure in new housing areas. Like the Lusaka Urban District Council which no longer had the funds in the late 1980s to provide services in subdivided areas (Schmetzer 1990), governments have not earmarked enough resources. Consequently, virtually all cities of Africa have for many years contained substantial areas of housing which lack basic services.

Dar-es-Salaam illustrates the point. There was an overall decline in expenditure on services of 8.5 per cent for 1978 to 1986 while population grew by an estimated 10 per cent per year. An annual expenditure in the mid-80s estimated at US$5.80 per person accounted for urban roads, public transport, water provision, and public health facilities which were in an appalling state by any developing country's standards (Kulaba 1989). This amounted to a fall in public service expenditure per person in the 1980s of 10 per cent per year in real terms, about five times faster than the decline in the Tanzanian GDP (*The Economist* 1990:22). In Nairobi during the same period, the annual per capita expenditures were declining rapidly and with them the state of the services themselves (Lee-Smith and Stren 1991).

Commenting on the Pretoria-Witwatersrand-Vaal (PWV) region of South Africa, Tanner (1990), a consulting municipal engineer, maintained that most municipalities did not have enough funds to maintain existing services adequately. Few had full electric lighting; usually only the main roads were tarred. Residents complained that refuse removal was erratic, garbage piled up in open spaces, water and sewage pipes burst onto road surfaces, houses flooded because of poor stormwater drainage, parks, playgrounds and halls were absent or inadequate. UNCHS (1992a:22) reported that the fast and continuous growth of the population of cities in the former Zaire has everywhere been accompanied by the slow and interrupted provision of infrastructure services. Mbuji-Mayi was an illustration of this: there were only 13 400 individual water connections and 44 standpipes for a population of 500 000, while only 20 km of roads were surfaced with asphalt. Abiodun (1997) calls it double-taxation of the citizenry because they have to provide their own water, electricity and security services in Lagos.

Obstructions by governments
Governments may hamper the production of wealth or add costs with their regulations and licensing. Land use and building regulations figure prominently here, as does the licensing of traders and petty commodity producers. These costs may be in terms of both money and time, and they may block a productive activity altogether. They result in a further erosion of wealth creation.

There may be sound reasons for regulations and licenses. They may be instruments for achieving essential collective actions. Building codes, for example, aim to protect occupants and the passing public from dangerous construction. However, where a balance of public interests is needed, there has too often been blind pursuit of bureaucratic objectives and/or individual gain. In too many cases, procedures and standards established by a colonial government have been maintained without adequate regard for their relevance and affordability in current circumstances.

In Cameroon for instance, a building permit which should take a maximum of six weeks to obtain requires one year, creating a severe impediment to the process of creating housing. Most of the requirements for a building permit in Cameroon are unnecessary anyway because of the type of structures which the great majority of builders are capable of erecting (Njoh 1992). Seemingly simple procedures for obtaining a building permit in Tanzania's Survey Plot Programme are, in actual fact, complicated and time consuming, involving nine agencies (Mghweno 1984, cited in Njoh 1992). A UN study showed similar delays in Ghana and Nigeria (United Nations 1973, cited in Njoh 1992). An NGO which has been upgrading slum houses in Nairobi has found official standards require a total investment of ten times more than it was spending (*The Economist* 1990:22).

Building regulations of this sort have been ubiquitous in Africa. Equally ubiquitous have been planning policies which restrict the uses to which urban land can legally be put and which determine if land can legally be used for urban purposes in the first place. For decades, it has been standard in African urban plans to forbid manufacturing in residential areas, to limit commerce to a few selected sites and to define city limits beyond which construction was not allowed. These policies are violated wholesale in ignorance, for profit, or for survival. Consequently, substantial areas of housing and countless manufacturing and service businesses have been rendered unlawful. Illegality has subsequently blocked access to formal lines of credit and has frequently been a basis for governments to refuse the provision of basic services.

What is more, it has been the excuse for large-scale destruction of housing stock and businesses thus deemed illegal, a capital loss that no African city or town could afford. Nelson (1997) gives a vivid account of unlicensed beer brewers in Nairobi's Mathare Valley who suffered significant losses of capital when police levied fines and confiscated materials and equipment. Unlicensed street traders have been a favourite target of African local authorities (*The Economist* 1990:22), whose actions destroy hard-earned capital.

Wealth Distribution and the Government of Urban Areas

The result of ineffective and ill-judged government of an urban area is that its residents are likely to be less wealthy and that the poor among them are likely to be poorer. This is not all. Governments can intensify urban poverty by distorting the distribution of the effects on wealth production identified above, as well as the distribution of the net wealth which comes into public ownership.

Biased distribution of services

Governments of urban areas may skew the provision of services to favour the better off. This means that the poor are less able than others to take part in productive activities and to enjoy economies of scale in countering the costs of urban concentrations. Generally it has been observed that governments have tended to favour the more wealthy and powerful with housing, roads, water supply, drainage, and electric power (for example, World Bank 1991, McNeill 1983:123). In Africa 'services supplied to the rich gobble up most of the municipal budget' (*The Economist* 1990:21).

South Africa, of course, made this a clear policy for many years. The incidence of poverty in the PWV region is now greatest among the black community, and deep poverty is concentrated in the informal shacklands (Rogerson 1996:171). The apartheid government provided the predominantly white towns and suburbs of the PWV with good infrastructure; black townships and informal settlements have poor infrastructure and social facilities (ibid.:170). In other parts of Africa, it is typically the houses of the poor which are not given services when illegal buildings are denied services. The urban poor cannot afford to make the status of their lands or houses legal (Bubba and Lamba 1991:52).

Throughout Africa the poor have received less water, often at a higher price and with more effort. Communal standpipes have been typical and long queues at them have been a common sight. In Nairobi, 83 per cent of high-income households had a water source within their compounds as compared to only 17 per cent of low-income households (Government of Kenya 1986:38, cited in Bubba and Lamba 1991:52). The poorest, who are in informal settlements, obtain water from vendors at communal standpipes, if any, where they may be charged up to three times the normal price (Lee-Smith and Syagga 1989:16, cited in Bubba and Lamba 1991:52, Jones and Matrix 1995:10).

Recent privatization of government services in Africa has favoured the better-off (Stren and White 1989:38). Well-administered contracts, cross-subsidization, effective regulation of prices and quality, and government provision to those the private sector does not reach have not been adequately achieved in African urban areas. Privatized provision in the Ivory Coast illustrates this point. Once lauded for its quality and efficiency, it has failed to match the number of new connections with the rapid rise of spontaneous settlements around Abidjan and other cities. In these low-income areas, water from private vendors fetches five times the normal price. The government tried to subsidize water provision to the poorer areas, but during the economic recession of the late 1970s, the subsidy programme was steadily reduced (Stren and White 1989:41).

The failure by governments to provide efficiently can result in some of the population being deprived altogether of a service. Wealthier homes have their own gardens, while the poor have to go without, as Mehta and Macharia (1997) report regarding Nairobi, echoing countless African urban planning studies. Refuse collection simply may not take place in the neighbourhoods of the poor (Stren and White 1989), but the rich can buy their own service. There are occasions when there is, in fact, no water for use by the poorest.

The same can be said for the needs of production. Self-employed services and manufacturing, on which so many of the poor depend, cannot be carried out if costs of adequate and reliable services become unaffordably high because they are not collectively provided so that they benefit from economies of scale.

Biased regulations and licensing

Government regulation of urban land and the construction of buildings can disproportionately reduce the wealth of the poorer population, because they are the most likely to infringe the minimum requirements and least likely to have the political or financial power to obtain licenses or to avoid fines, demolition, or being removed. Demolition of housing is particularly damaging because residences are commonly the greatest unit of accumulated wealth in the ownership of all but the richest. Another result is that it is the poor who are most often prevented by the illegality of their homes or businesses from obtaining credit to improve either. Okpala estimates that over 60 per cent of urban residents in African countries dwell in circumstances where they are constant victims of actual or threatened evictions by public authorities, and that most are people whose poverty has made impossible the observance of planning and/or building regulations (1997:1).

The result of such government regulations and restrictions – even where they are motivated by the best of intentions – is that much, if not most, of the informal-sector shelter and income-earning activities are illegal and are fettered and hindered, despite a revival of policies to support informal-sector business. In urban Africa, the poor make up most of those engaged in informal-sector activities; and the poor obtain a major portion of their goods and services from such activities (Bubba and Lamba 1991).

Biased distribution of public assets

Finally, governments are custodians of urban assets belonging to the public at large which they can allocate with a bias, creating or reinforcing differences in wealth levels. The more obvious substantial assets are land and housing; one less obvious asset is information.

African governments have usually been well endowed with quantities of urban land. This was the legacy of colonial powers who took land for public control of its allocation and use, or who claimed rights to hold tribal lands in trust for public aims. Some countries, Nigeria and Tanzania among them, later nationalized all land, and in others like Lesotho and Swaziland, a ruling family claim custody.

These very substantial assets have been widely misused to consolidate political power and to achieve personal gain. The result has been to concentrate the benefits of land ownership among those who already had the greater wealth. Kombe reports that the allocation of state land in Tanzania has mainly served the economically and politically powerful (1996:31). Of the land in Apapa, Victoria Island and Ikoyi, 92 per cent belongs to just 20 per cent of the population of Lagos (Agbola 1987, cited in Njoh 1992:25). As a rule, government site and services schemes in urban areas have benefited the high- and middle-income groups rather than the low-income groups, as noted by Nwaka (undated:15) in Nigeria, UNCHS (1987) in Kenya, and Dubresson (1997) in Abidjan.

A detailed picture is provided for Mubuji-Mayi in Zaire. In spite of the nationalization of land at the beginning of the 1970s, much of the land is allocated by the traditional chiefs. These – and local administrators who manage state lands – are generally in collusion with the *nouveaux riches* among the miners and diamond merchants, such that they share the profits from the sale of plots which the latter acquire and develop. Where the administrative services build housing estates, the distribution of the properties is carried out by the Registrar of Land Titles, who systematically reserves a portion of the plots for himself, the local chief, his surveyor colleagues, the governor of the region, the city commissioner, and other senior officials, the security services, and certain traders and diamond merchants. Though some of these go to relatives, the majority are placed on the market through channels which have become monopolistic, leaving most people with little or no access to these plots (UNCHS 1992a).

Sites earmarked or even used for community purposes have often been grabbed by the elite. Public open space in Nairobi, whose greatest beneficiaries are those too poor to have green space to enjoy with their housing, is steadily being taken for development by private sector interests. An international hotel was placed in public gardens in the city centre and recently there has been a fight to ward off proposals for the erection of a business complex in an adjoining major park (Mehta and Macharia 1997). Appropriation for personal use by those more rich and powerful has been a common fate for primary school sites in Kano, Maiduguri and other Nigerian cities, especially in poorer areas where the potential for organized community resistance is weakest.

Colonial and newly-independent governments provided housing to key workers in both the public and private sectors. This practice – arguably necessary to support the growth of productive activities – extended well beyond the time when private sector capacities became sufficient to build for the middle- and higher-income families. When the urban poor finally became the aim of housing allocations from the public purse, the result was usually well off the target. Illustrating a typical situation, members of the Nairobi City Commission have often been accused of biasing the allocation of land intended for the poor by using their influence to obtain it for themselves and their friends (Bubba and Lamba 1991:49). Low-cost housing provided by governments has almost always ended up in the possession of middle-income households either because of corruption or because the poor have not been able to afford the charges (ibid.:52).

Much of the need for information (to which the poor have little or no access) is created by the operations of governments. The processes of revenue generation, of regulating business, land use, building construction, of providing services, and of allocating publicly-owned assets need to be understood by citizens if their benefits are to be enjoyed and their penalties avoided. Moreover, government activities provide opportunities for commercial contracts which must be understood if competition for them is to be open. Then there is knowledge of decision-making regarding all operations – taxation as well as service provision, regulation, and asset management – which, if limited, can protect those favoured with benefits, both legal and illegal.

Governments of urban Africa do not have a good record of providing information to the general public, much less to the poor. Schmetzer (1990) found that land allocation processes were not understood by most people. Often the new urban migrants and poorly-educated masses who use illegal land subdivisions and informal housing do not even know of the existence of land use laws and building construction regulations. Njoh (1992) concluded that their lack of knowledge of the official procedures for obtaining a building permit in Cameroon was a formidable barrier to most builders.

Conclusion

Individually the weaknesses and biases of governments given attention here can be found throughout the world. What is arresting is the role in the creation of urban poverty of their persistent, common and combined presence in cities and towns of Africa.

There is ample evidence that, for some time, to be poor in a typical African city or town is to be poorer because of the failures and distributional biases of governments. Since such a large portion of urban African is poor, and such a large portion of migrants from rural areas are poor, and given the expectations of few economic opportunities for them to rise unaided out of poverty, the quality and performance of the government of urban areas is a matter for grave concern. As a contributor to poverty, a government will find itself very strongly challenged to carry out the interventions which are being called for to relieve urban poverty.

4. Africa's Urban Informal Economies: Between poverty and growth[1]

KENNETH KING and SIMON McGRATH

Economic growth is the prime means of creating income and employment opportunities. Where markets for products are expanding, poor people are able to establish sustainable livelihoods for themselves either by increasing their existing production and finding new products to market, or by finding employment opportunities with new or growing enterprises. Without growth – with stagnant or even declining incomes – the poor will only be able to make insignificant improvements in their livelihoods at the expense of other poor people (DFID 1997: 29).

For the small-scale economy[2] to be genuinely capable of contributing to lasting growth in Africa, it must be formalised. Links must be incorporated that are capable of transmitting macroeconomic signals and generating incentives for expansion. Such links may consist of more comprehensive credit systems, reliable regulatory systems and functioning institutions. Accordingly, the small-scale economy and the informal sector become more amenable to economic measures – no longer 'just' a means of livelihood for poor groups in the population, but also an important pillar of the country's economic future (Swedish Ministry for Foreign Affairs 1997a: 119).

Introduction

These two recent reports on international development from the UK and from Sweden underline the potential interrelatedness of small and micro-enterprises (SMEs) in Africa with the broader macro-economic context of development trajectories and growth strategies. Micro and small enterprises are intimately connected to larger enterprises, whether positively through linkages or negatively through exclusion and isolation from the larger industrial economy. The productivity of the small-scale economy is fundamentally bound up with the fortunes of the economy as a whole. Development co-operation policies also directly and indirectly impact upon SMEs, and new trends in the donor community in the 1990s make it likely that for those countries with appropriate national small-enterprise policies, there will be increasing evidence of sector programme support from external sources. In particular, both national and donor strategies for the promotion of SMEs are more than ever coupled with concerns about vocational and enterprise skills (Working Group for International Cooperation in Vocational and Technical Skills Development 1997).

The impetus for this chapter was a desire to revisit the growth potential of Africa's small-scale economy at a time when from many different quarters it began to be said that the African tide was turning, and that in a substantial number of countries real GDP growth was positive, and even foreign direct investment was picking up (Holman 1997; Swedish Ministry for Foreign Affairs 1997a; Killick 1998). At the same time it was assumed that the era of structural adjustment would have affected the small and microenterprise sector, for good or for ill, and equally would have had an impact on the institutions that have supplied skills both to the larger and to the small-scale economy. Finally, during 1997 and 1998, it was becoming clear that within the donor community the increasing emphasis on poverty eradication and pro-poor growth was possibly going to raise questions about existing policies for small-scale pro-capitalist development.

At the very beginning, it should be said that there are one or two really major differences in the discourse about poverty, growth and the informal or microenterprise sector now as compared with the 1970s when the term, 'informal sector' was first coined. One of these was a tendency then to discuss and debate the informal sector as if it was fundamentally an urban phenomenon. Monograph after monograph in the 1970s was about the *urban* informal economy, or about the *casual poor of third world cities*.[3] Even now this tendency has continued in some quarters and not least in the ILO (International Labour Office) which played such a key role in the internationalization of the concept of the informal sector after the Kenya Employment Mission of 1972. As recently as the ILO's *World Employment Report 1995* and its account of the African informal sectors, it can be noted that the concern is only with 'the urban informal sector'. This rather suggests that the ILO continues to see the informal sector as a basically urban phenomenon reflected in its still having an 'urban and informal sectors unit' as a part of its World Employment Programme in the early 1990s. In the report, there is another very short section on 'rural employment'. but this says nothing beyond one line on 'rural non-farm employment'; and thus the report implies, perhaps unintentionally, that rural microenterprise is something very different from its urban counterpart.

More importantly for the link between the urban informal sector and poverty, the 1995 *World Employment Report* goes on to assume that in Africa 'informal sectors are still dominated by low productivity survival activities' (ILO 1995:92–3). In this chapter, without minimizing the scale of *urban* poverty, we find it more valuable to look at the poverty debates across whole countries and not just their urban sectors, and we find it equally important to look at the linkages between poverty and growth in the current conceptualization of development policy.

The New Development Debate

There is an increasing perception that we are entering yet one more new phase in international development co-operation (King and Buchert 1998, King and Caddell 1998, McGrath 1998). As Riddell (1997) has argued, debates about development have gone through a number of stages in the fifty years since the United Nations and Bretton Woods institutions were set up. At the heart of the changes in development discourse has been the relationship between poverty and growth. As another recent Swedish policy paper admits this is by no means straightforward:

> But the interaction between economic growth and social and human development makes it almost impossible to distinguish between assistance that is designed to eradicate poverty and assistance that promotes growth (Swedish Ministry for Foreign Affairs 1997b:43).

At the risk of oversimplification, the period up to the end of the 1960s was one in which 'development' was seen as relatively unproblematic. Economic growth would lead to the eradication of world poverty. However, at the end of the Keynesian golden age, leading agencies and analysts of development began to perceive that development had not been taking place in this simple way. Thus, they began to focus directly on poverty eradication through the basic needs approach.[4] The 'discovery' of the urban informal sector was very much a part of this basic needs approach. The assumption that economic growth should necessarily lead to poverty eradication was seen as one of the primary development fallacies.

However, by the late 1970s fashion was beginning to change again as economists and politicians of the right began to develop a powerful critique of welfarism both within the economies of the North and in the conditions of aid to the South. Their prescription was to let the market work unfettered. In effect, a version of the poverty-eradication-through-growth-maximization paradigm was restored, although growth was now seen as a more complex business which needed to be planned for through the radical structural adjustment of economies, states and welfare systems.

By the late 1990s it has become clear that the power of this neo-liberal vision is waning. The World Bank has begun to play down its anti-statism and its critics have developed a considerable arsenal of evidence against the alleged efficacy of structural adjustment. Across sub-Saharan Africa as a whole, there is still insufficient data to conclude that either poverty or growth have been adequately addressed via adjustment. There are now signs that a new consensus on development co-operation may be emerging. In documents such as the recent British development white paper (DFID 1997) poverty is once more the primary focus, as it is in the policy papers of several other bilateral and multilateral agencies (e.g. Danida 1998, Finland 1996, etc.). However, it is apparent that at present there is a major concern with achieving coherence in the interplay of poverty and growth policies, both in the assistance community and in national governments.

Small and Microenterprises: for Poverty Reduction and/or Growth Maximization

The current focus – especially of assistance agencies – on poverty eradication/alleviation also raises serious questions about sectoral development strategies for small-enterprise. Because the beneficiaries of small enterprise policy could arguably be identified both as the poor and as the emergent entrepreneurs, it has been possible to suggest that donor support to small-enterprise development (SED) could have multiple goals. Thus the previous UK administration's SED policy had the following rationale, and was aimed at both urban and rural activities:

> Small and micro enterprises are an important source of off-farm employment and self employment for the poor. Growth and productivity increase in this sector thus make a significant contribution to poverty reduction. Moreover, some micro and small enterprises expand into medium and even large scale enterprises through investment and skill acquisition, and thus contribute to the vigour of private sector development (ODA 1995: 2).

Indeed, in the quarter of a century or so since the informal sector was formally identified, small and microenterprises have been the focus of a range of both national and donor rationales for growth and for poverty alleviation. With few exceptions, such policies have sought to cover both urban and rural populations.

Small and microenterprises have been seen by some constituencies, and particularly by many Northern NGOs, as a haven of the poor. NGOs have been more frequently involved with income-generation schemes for community groups, and especially poor women, than they have been identified with the support of economic growth via individual entrepreneurs. This widespread NGO hesitation about the individual entrepreneur has not generally been shared by what could be called the 'technology NGOs' with their different strategies and priorities (Jeans 1998).

Beyond the NGO support to survivalist or subsistence microenterprise, there has been a growing concern about emergent enterprises. In several African contexts, the policy dilemmas in encouraging this segment not only relate to the long-standing debates about the characteristics and determinants of success or 'graduation' amongst microenterprises, but they also acknowledge that successful enterprises emerge into a situation where they often face very severe competitive challenges from established white, Asian or other formal small- and medium-sized industry (Rogerson 1998a, King 1996). In other words, the emergent entrepreneur debate is linked in some countries in sub-Saharan Africa to discussions of level playing fields, positive discrimination and securing niches in modern industrial areas where there are sometimes very few indigenous entrepreneurs. Significantly, there has been relatively little attention given to the characteristics and modalities of Asian success in graduation from very much smaller or even microenterprises several decades earlier. Given the almost exclusively urban location, at least in East Africa, of this Asian transition from microenterprise to modern industrial firm, there would seem to be a case for analysing 'the Asian miracle in East Africa'.

The second major strand of the pro-small and microenterprise literature is that which sees it as the uncertain beneficiary of wider international trends, including structural adjustment. In these accounts, a series of decisions taken by or imposed upon the formal-sector firms has led to outsourcing, informalization of the workforce or the complete collapse of formal firms. In these references the SME sector appears very much as the knock-on sector, dependent to quite a significant extent for its health and vitality on trends that are beyond its direct control.

It is essential that a clearer picture be developed of whether the different strands of small and microenterprise support policy are compatible with each other and under which circumstances. Equally, it is necessary to address whether each of the major policy strands can be adopted for small and microenterprises in general or whether different policies must be adopted for different segments. Moreover, it is vital that strategies for support to and intervention in the small and microenterprise sector should be consistent and coherent with programmes focused on large and formal enterprises.

In many African urban environments, it continues to be the case that whatever we may have said above about the knock-on effects from the formal to the informal sectors, the two remain geographically very distinct, at least in the major cities. The small, formal industrial areas of Africa are in many senses a world away from the ever-increasing scale of the urban informal economies. Indeed, we have argued elsewhere that the informalization of African cities has continued apace, but without really touching the so called modern industrial sector (King 1996).[5]

Continuum or Segmentation? Describing the Small and Microenterprise Sector

Since the 'discovery' of the informal sector, much effort has gone into definition both from academics (see Mead and Morrison 1996) and policymakers (see Visser 1998). There are almost as many definitions and names for this area of economic activity as there are writers about it. The degree of informality and the size of employment have perhaps been the two most readily accepted criteria on which classification has rested. Whilst the search for definition can be sterile, it is also important to have some useful sense of what is being talked about. On this occasion it seems worth highlighting three different types of enterprises which are thrown up by the debate:

- Formal and small:- These enterprises are the classic small enterprises of the literature on Northern economies but are also to be found in the South. Such enterprises conform to regulations to a significant extent, exhibit high levels of human capital and are integrated into the structures of the formal economy. They are often excluded from discussions of the informal sector and poverty alleviation but are potentially significant players, particularly as sources of skills or as part of the glass ceiling for the next category.

- Informal and small:- Those elements of the informal sector which are given descriptions such as 'successful' or 'sustainable'; 'emergent' or 'entrepreneurial'. It is in these enterprises that informal-sector incomes can outstrip those in the lower reaches of the formal sector (Mead 1998). Though outside formal-sector structures, often the owner-operators of such enterprises have had significant exposure to both formal education and training and to formal employment. Such enterprises are seen as central to the poverty-growth debate as important producers of goods, services and employment. This does not mean of course that they are necessarily part of any industrial growth project of their respective states. Quite the opposite, it has been argued (Mkandawire 1998), though they have gained from a very small number of positive discriminations in their favour (e.g. Trade Licensing Act in Kenya).

- Survivalist:- these are the enterprises in which the equation between poverty and informal sector is most apparent. Engaged primarily in commerce but also in basic and low-quality forms of production, those running these enterprises are typically at the level of subsistence, with the income earned being one of a number of resources that must be combined together in order for survival (Mead 1998).

The extent to which these types represent discrete segments with significant barriers between them (and with the medium and large formal sector too) or simply modal points along a continuum is one that continues to be debated. Mead (1998) points to the ability of enterprises to move along the continuum. King has shown how, over time, there has been often quite dramatic movement from subsistence to enterprise status with associated transfer from the roadside to the ownership of factory premises (King 1996). Rogerson (1998b), however, emphasizes the massive disparities between the segments and the particular racial nature that the division between the first two categories has historically taken in South Africa.

This is an important debate in that it highlights the need to look carefully at the intended targets and beneficiaries of specific policies. Crucially here it is necessary to consider whether targeting a policy on current realities is to reinforce inequalities (Rogerson 1998b) or whether it is possible actively to target those with potential – basing interventions both on where they are now and on where they might be in the future (Mead 1998).

In the light of the current uncertainty about the relationship between poverty and growth, the decision on which types of enterprise to target with which kind of intervention is a major challenge for policymakers and practitioners. Should the principal focus, for instance, be on those who have the greatest potential to employ others (Jeans 1998) or should it be on the poorest of the poor? A decision on this will have serious implications for the kind of interventions to be contemplated.

There has been a long standing concern that small and microenterprise growth has taken place through involution rather than evolution; that is, by growing the number of enterprises rather than growing the amount of employment in existing enterprises (Jeans 1998, Mead 1998, Rogerson 1998a). This is taken to be indicative of an expansion of survivalist rather than sustainable (self) employment. However, Mead points to a growing realization that the picture is more complex.

He notes that the health of the economy as a whole has a strong relationship with the health and nature of the micro and small enterprise (MSE) sector:

> in good times, a relatively high share of the new MSE jobs are closer to the 'growth' end of the spectrum, reflecting a response by entrepreneurs to profitable business opportunities. When the state of the macroeconomy is less favourable, by contrast, the opportunities for profitable employment expansion in MSEs is limited; people will be forced to seek their living in alternative ways. In such circumstances, a larger proportion of the employment growth would reflect decisions by entrepreneurs to start new enterprises, a higher proportion of which would be closer to the survivalist end of the spectrum (Mead 1998).

We need to consider how an awareness of such a dynamic can best be taken account of in programmes of support to and intervention in the small and microenterprise sector but also in programmes which aim at influencing the vitality of the economy as a whole.

What has been intriguing about this most current literature on definitions of formality and informality, and about continua from survival to growth, is that it does not generally seem to be conducted in terms of the urban-rural distinctions which we mentioned at the beginning for the ILO. Indeed, it is much more commonplace now to emphasise the rural dominance of microenterprise numbers, as in the following survey of micro and small enterprises in nine countries of East and Southern Africa:

> Three quarters of the enterprises are in *rural areas* (localities with less than 2 000 people). This is important since much of the early work on

MSEs focused on urban areas, leading to a substantial underestimation of the magnitude of the small enterprise universe as well as a distorted focus of policy and projects (Mead 1998:2).

Formalizing the Informal Sector: A Developmental Project

As was stressed in the quotation at the beginning, what the small-scale economies of Africa currently mostly lack is any sense of being part of a larger project of the state for their support, development and incorporation as part of an industrial strategy. There are valuable illustrative elements of a more inclusive vision in South Africa's policies for skills development (Department of Labour 1997).

One of the core elements in their ambitious green paper (on skills development) is a new system of learnerships. A key challenge in the new policy will be to ensure that the new training instruments will no longer operate primarily in the traditional industrial sector, e.g. in seeking to halt the declining number of apprenticeships, but should apply across a variety of employment and self-employment sites, including the small and microenterprise sectors. This has meant thinking how to deliver to small and microenterprises the crucially important work experience and other requirements of these new learnerships.

There are certain to be difficulties in arranging this; but what is clear about the South African proposals, even from the discussion in the green paper alone, is that in contrast to many other countries in Africa where there are effectively two training systems, the so-called traditional or informal apprenticeship and the so-called modern, the intention is clearly to have a single national system, if at all possible. The aspiration is to plan for both the urban and the rural at one and the same time.

There is thus the aim to develop learnerships across all sectors. This led the Green Paper to anticipate that there will need to be 'special arrangements for target groups' if they are to be satisfactorily included in the national scheme. This means that those specially disadvantaged by South Africa's apartheid history, or by gender, location or disability can look to state training participation schemes managing the planned levy funds to ensure their participation in the emerging national system.

Enough has been said to suggest that this formalizing and inclusive aspiration, though hugely ambitious, should attract research attention from its earliest stages. Whether a common national qualification currency will be sufficiently persuasive to draw all skills into a single system is still unclear. But what is important with this South African initiative is that it will, like the Swedish quotation with which we began this account, send out signals about the small-scale economy becoming part of a nationally accredited system.

The Small-Scale Economy as a Central Part of the National Economy

More than 10 years ago the Danish Association of Development Researchers put on a meeting that summarises rather accurately one thread in the debate about the small-scale economies of Africa (Danish Association 1987). They may contain the bulk, numerically speaking, of the economically active population, both male and female, in many countries, but the employers and workers in these informal economies most certainly do not feel themselves to be in the situation captured in the title of the Danish volume: *The Informal Sector as an Integral Part of the National Economy: Research needs and aid requirements.*

Most probably those in the informal sector do not feel themselves to be part of any developmental project of the sort described by Mkandawire (1998). Whether, by contrast, they would prefer to feel themselves to be part of a new poverty focus of their state is doubtful. If they are in Kenya, Ghana or South Africa, the very idea of a poverty focus or framework for their government may seem rather surprising. But if that focus were to involve any sense of their options for upward mobility being somehow foreclosed, they would likely have none of it.

The previous (1975) white paper of the UK Government captured very nicely the danger of a policy that was carefully shaped for the poor of the rural areas (or for that matter of the urban informal sectors of Africa):

> We must beware of adopting policies which while intended to meet the needs of the poorest people, and especially those in rural communities, imply that poorer people and people living in the country can expect only a standard of education lower than those who happen to live in towns. There is a need for education about education (Ministry of Overseas Development 1975:22).

This points to the dilemma at the heart of much of what we have been discussing here: the danger that targeting can slip into ghettoization or, conversely, that non-discriminatory policies will leave existing power imbalances in place. It is to be hoped that the renewed attention being given to both poverty and growth in the African context can be the catalyst for careful re-examination of principles and practices that affect, both directly and indirectly, the majority of African workers – those located in small and microenterprises, whether in rural or urban areas.

5. The Impact of Structural Adjustment on Welfare and Livelihoods: An Assessment by people in Harare, Zimbabwe

DEBORAH POTTS

Introduction

When Zimbabwe finally achieved its hard-fought-for independence in 1980, fashions in development economics had changed radically from those which informed the development strategies of most other sub-Saharan African governments at independence in the 1960s. Rather than active intervention by the government to direct the nature of economic development, the international financial institutions were arguing that prices should be determined by market forces, and that economies should be liberalized and opened to the forces of global competition. Heavily indebted, most African countries were forced to follow these strategies in the 1980s. However Zimbabwe chose to follow the 'old' interventionist development path throughout the 1980s. Having inherited a grossly racially divided society the political pressures for intervention were undeniable. In comparison to most other sub-Saharan African countries, Zimbabwe did well in the 1980s, with GDP per capita growing slowly, accumulating food stocks and significant improvements in African health, education and marketed agricultural production. Nevertheless, the external and domestic pressures to introduce market reforms and liberalize the economy were growing (see Stoneman 1996, Potts and Mutambirwa 1998) and by 1990 the government finally acceded and introduced its Economic Structural Adjustment Programme (ESAP).

In common with other such programmes ESAP meant that within a few years subsidies on food (including the staple, mealie-meal) and controls on many other basic products were removed; import controls were dropped exposing local industries to external competition; the currency was devalued; the private sector was encouraged to take over the provision of services – even in sectors such as low-income housing; the public-sector wages bill came under huge pressure; and cost-recovery measures were introduced in public services, including health and education. The macroeconomic indicators of Zimbabwe's performance in the early 1990s were disastrous: GDP growth and real incomes plummeted and inflation soared. Since the introduction of ESAP coincided with the start of a terrible two-year drought, the relative contributions of the two factors to the economic collapse are hard to disentangle, but both played a part.

In April and May 1994, a sample survey of residents of Harare, Zimbabwe's capital city, was conducted. The survey included open questions about how residents perceived ESAP to have affected their lives. The approach was specifically qualitative and responses were taken down verbatim. Interviewers were careful not to make any suggestions about the nature of the impacts (e.g. positive or negative) or the topics (e.g. employment, transport, health) which might be discussed. The hope was that this approach would give us an indication of the issues which were most significant to the people themselves – which they naturally thought of when the topic of ESAP came up – and that the research would let their voices speak about structural adjustment, rather than prejudging the topics to be analysed.

Whose Voices?

Since government policies affect different people in society in different ways, it is important to establish the nature of our sample. The results reported here are based on a random sample survey of 203 people resident in high-density, low-income areas of Harare. Most lived in Kuwadzana, a post-independence site and service settlement, and the rest in Mbare, Highfields and Glen Norah – older areas of formal housing originally built by the colonial regime. The research was part of a wider survey on rural-urban migration, and all the respondents were adult migrants who had come to Harare since 1990. Only one individual from any one household was interviewed, but their relationship to the household head (HHH) was not specified, so that a wide range of household members was covered, including heads, spouses, adult children and various other kin. Since many migrants stay with relatives in town before establishing their own household (if they choose to do so), the respondents' household heads were not necessarily migrants, recent or otherwise, themselves.

The gender, age and household status of the respondents is shown in Table 1, and their marital and age status in Tables 2 and 3. As can be seen

Table 1: Household status and gender of migrant respondent (%)

Relation to HHH	All resps. %	Male %	Female %
HHH	56 (114)	79	21
Spouse	21 (43)	5	95
Son/daughter	12 (25)	48	52
Brother/sister	7 (14)	64	36
Other relative	2 (4)	0	100
Others[1]	1 (3)	0	100
All respondents (%)	100 (203)[2]	55	45

Notes: 1. 'others': two employees (domestics), one unspecified.
2. In all tables: bracketed figures = number of cases; number of cases may vary due to some missing values for certain categories of data. Percentages may not add to 100% due to rounding.

Table 2: Marital status of migrant respondents

Marital status	All resps. %	Respondent HHHs[1] %
Never married	33	27
Married	56	56
Divorced	5	7
Separated	2	3
Widowed	4	6
All respondents (%)	100 (199)	56

Notes: 1. This column disaggregates those respondents who were also heads of household.

Table 3: Age profile of migrant respondents

Age band	All respondents %	Respondent HHHs[1] %
18–24	34	18
25–29	24	25
30–34	17	21
35–39	9	13
40–49	9	16
50–59	9	4
60+	0	0
DK	3	4
All respondents %	100	56

Notes: 1. This column disaggregates interviewees who were also heads of household.

the sample covered a very broad range of household members, and therefore the views expressed can be regarded as reasonably representative of residents of Harare's low-income housing areas, although the fact that they were recent in-migrants should be taken into account.[1]

Employment Profiles: a Key Role Still for the Formal Sector

A particularly interesting and important characteristic of our sample was that nearly all of them either had a *formal sector* job, or lived in a household headed by someone with a formal job. Employment rates among HHHs in our survey were extremely high: 96 per cent of respondent HHHs were working and 94 per cent of the HHHs of 'dependent' respondents and, of these, 92 per cent and 100 per cent respectively were in the formal sector. Two specific aspects of this characteristic might be noted at this point. First, low-income households in Harare in 1994 were much less reliant on the informal sector for their primary subsistence than is the norm for most sub-Saharan African cities, particularly since the era of structural adjustment (King 1996 and this volume, Potts 1997a, Rogerson 1997). The pattern found in this survey confirms that found in others in the recent past. Second, whilst people with formal sector jobs may often be in an advantageous position compared to most of those in the informal sector,[2] in times of rapid inflation such as have occurred in Zimbabwe since ESAP was introduced, they can be more vulnerable to price rises in the short- and medium-term, being unable to effect increases in their incomes at short notice (or indeed, sometimes even after long periods of negotiation with employers). The self-employed in the informal sector, on the other hand, can adjust their prices, and hence incomes, very quickly in line with inflation.

Formal-sector employees in Harare have managed to obtain some major wage rises during the 1990s but these have always lagged far behind the price rises which made them necessary, and have usually far from compensated for them anyway. Households reliant on such incomes therefore suffer massive squeezes on their budgets, relieved every now and then and for short periods by sudden upward jerks in their incomes. They will thus spend most of their time 'falling behind' inflation and inevitably will find it very difficult to budget when major items of household expenditure are increasing rapidly in price, whilst incomes remain mainly static.

The small number of HHHs in our sample working in the informal sector was disproportionately female as is common in urban Africa: 56 per cent of this group were women but they accounted for only 21 per cent of all HHHs. The informal sector did contribute in other ways to some households' economies: 18 per cent of HHHS had a secondary income and this was usually derived from the informal sector. However most of the adult dependents (i.e. respondents who were not HHHs) who were not ineligible for work because they were homeworkers or students, were actually unemployed (see Table 4) – only 22 per cent were working, and only 25 per cent of these were in the informal sector. Nine 'dependent' respondents also

Table 4: 'Dependent' migrant respondents' activity status

Activity status	'Dependent' respondents %
Ineligible for work:	59 (53)
Housewife[1]	45 (40)
Education	12 (11)
Other[2]	2 (2)
Eligible for work:	40 (36)
Working	9 (8)
Unemployed	31 (28)
Total	99 (89)

Notes: 1. Includes 86% of spouses of HHHs, plus three other married female respondents.
2. Includes unable to work (1); 'not wanting to work' (1)

reported that they had some income from secondary activities. Overall though the role of informally generated income in our households was quite limited. It seemed quite surprising for example that 86 per cent of female spouses classified themselves as 'housewives' – that is they were neither working nor seeking work.

The income levels of the sampled households were generally very low too. The average primary income of all HHHs (including the heads of 'dependent' respondents' households) was Z$907 per month:[3] nationally, low-income households in 1994 were designated as those earning under Z$1,200 (Auret 1996: 53) although the industrial minimum wage was only Z$800. Secondary incomes from HHHs made a significant further contribution in the minority of households where these were available, averaging Z$622 per month, but any earnings by other household members were generally very small.

Personal Assessments of ESAP

When asked to rank how ESAP policies had affected their lives, our respondents were overwhelmingly negative: 90 per cent felt that they had been disadvantaged compared to a mere 2 per cent who felt better off (see Table 5). Most thought they knew what ESAP was – that is they were aware that the government had introduced a series of policies which affected controls on trade, currencies and prices and so on which had, in turn, had various effects on the economy. Several respondents in fact tried to engage the interviewers in a debate about ESAP in general: many wanted to know why such apparently (to them) disastrous policies had been implemented. It is interesting to note that the government was definitely perceived as the progenitor of the policies, and therefore carried all the blame when it was felt things had gone wrong. There was little if any recognition that international financial institutions had any role in deciding domestic economic policies.

People were asked to explain the reasons for their rankings, if they did not give them spontaneously, but no further prompting was given. Their answers have been analysed to see what sort of issues were being offered as

Table 5: Rankings of impact of ESAP (%)

Impact of ESAP on respondent	% of responses
Made things better	2
Made things worse	90
Made things both better and worse	1.5
Nothing has changed	1.5

Note: Percentages do not add to 100% mainly because of a small number of respondents who could not rank the impact of ESAP.

Table 6: Explanations of perceptions of the impact of ESAP on Migrant Respondents

Type of Comment	%*	Number
Negative impact of which:	93	159
1. Prices and affordability issues:	57	97
of which:		
Accommodation problems	14	24
Food (e.g. not enough; consumption reduced)	5	9
Clothing (e.g. cannot afford to clothe children)	5	9
Devalued Zimbabwe dollar	4	6
Taxes too high	4	6
Transport costs	3	5
2. Job-related	23	39
3. Education problems (e.g. children had to leave school; high fees)	16	27
4. Adverse effect on rural linkages	9	16
of which:		
'Forced to live separate from family to make ends meet'	4	7
'Had to join family in Harare to cut expenses'	1	2
'Cannot go "home" regularly because of high transport costs'	2	3
'Cannot afford to support rural relatives properly'	1	2
Neutral impact	4	6
Informal sector and second job-related comments	8	14
of which:		
1. Positive	2	4
2. Negative	6	10

Note: * 171 respondents made specific comments about the effect of ESAP on themselves personally. The percentages indicate how frequently specific issues were included in these comments.

explanations for their perceptions. A number of topics came up very frequently and were obviously those found to be most significant. Table 6 indicates the frequency with which the main issues and problems identified were mentioned in the set of explanations – many people of course identified a number of issues, rather than just one.

Our respondents' unprompted answers made it quite clear that rising prices relative to incomes were by far the single most important problem caused by ESAP as far as they were concerned, which were in turn leading to their own living standards falling. Again and again their responses reflected adverse changes in their livelihoods and thwarted ambitions. Illustrative comments by household heads bemoaning their new difficulties included that they were now 'failing to support the family properly', that their 'salary was no longer sufficient' or 'did not last the month', that they could no longer 'dress and educate the family properly', had 'cut down to make ends meet' or that they could 'no longer achieve anything because of low pay'. A number of respondents felt that their problems were being compounded by tax rises and/or the devaluation of the dollar. As one said, 'the dollar has lost so much value I have to cut off other needs to get food', whilst another, less specifically, complained that her 'ambitions had been hampered by the continual devaluation of the dollar'.

In their explanations people often mentioned specific items in their budgets which had been adversely affected by ESAP-related price rises. By far the most common item was accommodation. Rising rents was part of the problem. Just over half the respondents were living as lodgers and obviously private landlords and landladies would increase rents in line with inflation. The choice of phrase often used however was that individuals and their families simply could not afford '*decent* accommodation' – about a third of those worried about housing said this. Although this comment was not followed up by the interviewers, it could be taken to indicate that such households could not afford the sharply increasing rents and had substituted inferior housing. In a rather different position were the 38 per cent of respondents who lived in owner-occupier households. There has been a very significant shift in low income housing policy since independence to site and service schemes where the plot and building costs have to be paid up front or borrowed from a private building society (Potts and Mutambirwa 1991, Rakodi 1995). This combination of privatization and cost recovery is exactly what structural adjustment is all about. Repossessions from those who cannot keep up payments have become a major issue (Potts 1998). The minimum deposits demanded when stands become available for waiting list applicants often disbar even those who might just have made the instalments (Kasete 1997), and the whole approach excludes most of the poor. It is in the context of these policies that the following perceptions of ESAP become understandable: about half the people who mentioned accommodation complained that they could not afford their house instalments or to complete their houses or, in particular, had not been able to afford the deposit for a stand. As one respondent commented, 'I have been denied the chance of getting a house as I have a low income'.

Nutrition had also come under pressure because of ESAP, according to our sample. The food category in table 5 specifically excludes comments which only indicated that food prices had risen – these are included in the general 'prices and affordability' comments. Only explanations which clearly demonstrated that people felt that their nutrition had been adversely affected by ESAP were included.[4] For example:

- We are failing to buy enough food for the family
- We are not able to eat a balanced diet
- Not getting sufficient food as there are no jobs
- Have cut down on basics – sugar, mealie meal and meat
- Can no longer afford enough food for the children

People also indicated that clothing had become unaffordable and pointed out that many people had turned to the second-hand sector. As will be seen below, this perceived disadvantage was however seen as a positive side of ESAP by some others.

The next most significant set of issues for our sample after price and affordability problems were related to difficulties in either finding, or keeping, a job. The generally parlous state of the job market was mentioned by many, but 23 respondents had either lost a job due to ESAP, or felt that the new economic climate meant that they simply could not find one. As one remarked: 'I cannot find a job regardless of qualifications'. In a third of the remarks about jobs 'retrenchment' was specifically mentioned – this being the term which by 1994 had become common in Zimbabwe to mean job and factory cutbacks and closures caused by the newly liberalized economy. Illustrative remarks include:

- I have been retrenched from work and am now doing part-time jobs
- Companies are not taking on workers or are retrenching
- I have failed to get a job and my relatives have been retrenched therefore our accommodation is poor
- Companies are no longer employing so life is hard
- I have been retrenched and can't get another job
- I was retrenched and given no benefit
- I have been retrenched from work and am now a vendor

Education problems caused by ESAP-related costs were important issues for our respondents too. Many complained that the increased costs of education had meant that either they or their children had had to leave school, or could not stay at the school of first choice, or had not been able to do their exams. The imposition of much higher fees due to ESAP was clearly causing real difficulties. Hardly anyone mentioned that their health had been adversely affected by ESAP, which seems curious given that another survey has noted that ESAP has impacted on people's health in Zimbabwe's urban areas (Bijlmakers et al. 1996). Our sample did feel that hospital fees were a problem when talking about Harare in general, however (Potts and Mutambirwa 1998). Charges for public health consultations for adults in Harare in 1994 were Z$16 (Bijlmakers et al. 1996).

Table 6 also shows that for a small sub-category of migrants the adverse affect of ESAP was primarily explained in terms of problems with rural-urban linkages. The curtailment of visits and remittances was specifically mentioned, which can be easily understood in the context of falling incomes. For some, the main problem was that they were living *apart* from their family, against their wishes, because it was cheaper to keep some family members in the rural areas. Increased poverty seemed a real issue for these families. On the other hand, two respondents felt that ESAP had caused problems by forcing them to *join* their families in Harare in order to cut down on the expense of keeping two homes, although in neither case did serious poverty seem to be the main problem. One of these cases was a woman who had joined her owner-occupier husband in Harare because the 'modern' house which they had been building in the communal area could not now be completed. The other was a teacher who had been transferred from the town of Mutare to join his wife in Harare.

ESAP and the Informal Sector

A large number of studies in sub-Saharan Africa have shown that urban households have tended to increase their reliance on and participation in the informal sector in response to the job losses and falling real incomes associated with structural adjustment (e.g. Potts 1997a, Rogerson 1997, Tripp 1990). As already indicated, the role of the informal sector in Harare does not seem to be nearly as significant. Nevertheless some people did refer to this sector or to 'second jobs' (nearly always informal) they had taken up, in addition to their formal-sector jobs. In most cases their feelings about informal employment in the ESAP era were negative, often because their customers' new poverty seriously limited the demand for their goods. For example people said:

- I do supplementary work, but people aren't paying
- I do not get as many outside jobs – we mostly depend on my salary
- Clients aren't paying
- People are not buying lots of vegetables now as parents are not living with their children
- Orders have decreased because customers have been retrenched
- People are not buying my commodities
- My income is very low – people are not buying my products

Only four people felt positive about their informal-sector jobs. One pointed out that he could charge higher prices when he needed to, another that ESAP had 'taught him to be resourceful and people [from the high density area] come to my informal business rather than go into town'. The other two were women who praised 'the free market' which let them sell their things 'wherever we want as long as we have a licence'. Their profiles were remarkably similar. Both were unmarried women aged 30–34 (one was divorced) who were born in towns – one in Gweru and one in Bulawayo – and who had come to Harare in 1992 and 1993 respectively. They both had two jobs: a formal-sector job (licensed street vendor and shop assistant) and an informal job which involved selling second hand clothes. Their respective monthly incomes were Z$350 plus Z$800, and Z$500 plus Z$500. They both stated, unlike most other respondents, that they planned to remain in Harare all their lives. Clearly both of these women, one of whom lived in Kuwadzana and the other in Mbare, were exploiting one of the key niches which had opened up with trade liberalization – the trade in second-hand clothes. Not only was it now easier to bring the clothes in from other countries,[5] but the demand for such clothes had increased as people could no longer afford new clothes. Furthermore, they could set their prices to reflect their costs: as one remarked when explaining why ESAP had improved her life, 'I can now go to neighbouring countries to buy things and sell them at my *own* prices'.

Even for women, however, there is some evidence that ESAP in Zimbabwe (in contrast to structural adjustment programmes elsewhere on the continent) is *reducing* their involvement in this sector. Although Rakodi (1994: 15) reports an apparent increase in informal sector participation for female spouses and female HHHs in Harare from surveys conducted in 1991 and 1993, she says that this could be due to a methodological change in the survey between the two dates. Reduced participation was found by Brand et al. (1995) in a survey specifically of Harare informal sector traders. They report that between 1992 and 1993 22 per cent had stopped a trading activity, whilst only 5 per cent had started up new ones. According to them, 'ESAP had resulted in more competition and lower returns, leading to a decision that further effort was cost-ineffective' (ibid.: 153). Too much competition in certain trades, on the other hand, suggests that the rate of new entrants had increased, but perhaps this was a temporary 'surge'. Kanji and Jazdowska (1993) also found that women (also in Harare, in Kambuzuma) had experienced reductions in their informal sector activities and income between July 1992 and January 1993. This was largely ascribed to falling demand due to their customers' increasing poverty under ESAP. The general tenor of the comments on the informal sector made by our sample certainly seems to support this picture.

Case Studies

So far the qualitative data on Harare residents' perceptions has been offered as isolated comments. When these comments are put in the context of individuals they become more understandable and 'real'. This section offers three contrasting case studies:

> Mrs X, a married women in her early thirties, was looking for a job. Her husband was an accountant who earned Z$900 per month and they were owner-occupiers in Kuwadzana. She had an informal part-time job selling vegetables and eggs. She had migrated to Harare in 1991 from Mahusekwa communal land where she and her husband had 6 acres of land, 7 cattle and a modern house. They produced 10
>
> *continued over*

bags of maize in 1993–4. In her opinion ESAP had made things worse not only in Harare, where workers were losing their jobs and food prices, transport and health costs were high, but also in the rural areas where 'retrenched workers were overburdening rural folk so that there was not enough food and land to go around'. She found it hard to support her household on her husband's salary, even though the monthly loan payments were low at Z$120 due to the age of the scheme, plus Z$20 for services. She and her husband would probably eventually return to their farm but intended to stay in Harare for at least ten years.

Mr Y was a single male lodger in his early twenties. A soldier, earning Z$500 per month, he had been transferred to Harare from Gweru in 1990. He had been born in Gokwe communal area, but had no land there. He paid Z$100 per month in rent for one room. His feelings about ESAP were universally negative: the rural areas were burdened because fertilizers had become so expensive, it was now more difficult to get jobs in Harare than Gweru and parents were having to send their children away to the rural areas to cut expenses, and he complained that he could no longer visit his family regularly because of high transport costs.

Mr Z was one of the few who had positive perceptions of ESAP. A married man aged 30–34, he stated that it had given 'young people a chance at work – as older workers were retrenched'. He worked as a security guard for a low income of Z$400 per month, and had no secondary job. His wife and children had been left in Mutoko communal land, his birthplace, where he planned eventually to return to farm. He was also positive about the impact of ESAP on the rural areas, saying that people there 'could sell crops at high prices, and get free fertilizers from the government'. On the other hand he felt that ESAP had had a negative impact on him personally because his 'wages were very low and he had to borrow his bus fare at the end of the month'. Perhaps the man who had formerly had his post had been retrenched: whatever the case, his perceptions appear to reflect a desperate dog-eat-dog attitude.

Conclusion

Structural adjustment, according to its proponents, is meant to improve a country's macro-economic performance. It is not possible here to elaborate the debate about Zimbabwe's macro-economic development in the 1990s; suffice it to say that after negative growth rates in the early part of the decade, these picked up in 1994 and after a bad year in 1995 have since been positive, but this may have been due to better rains rather than government policy (Potts and Mutambirwa 1998, Potts 1997b). Furthermore from about 1996 the government has started to unpick some aspects of the structural adjustment package: for example, trade and currency liberalization have both experienced setbacks as some restrictions have been re-imposed. The IMF suspended loans in response.

It is clear however that ESAP and its follow-up, ZIMPREST (Zimbabwe Programme for Economic and Social Transformation), have had a terrible impact on urban livelihoods in Harare. It should be noted that urban people have not suffered these conditions without protest. Small-scale food riots in the early stages of ESAP were followed by much more organized industrial action in 1996 and 1997 which forced through some quite major pay rises for parts of the public sector. In January 1998 full-scale urban riots which were met with brutal police action, also occurred when the price of mealie meal shot up by 21 per cent followed by another 24 per cent rise in one week (*Guardian*, 1998). Government popularity in Zimbabwe's urban areas had been under pressure for a long time and this may be at least one reason why the government started some backtracking on 'adjustment' policies.

In many ways the evidence of our survey simply proves that in the 1990s the urban poor of Harare have joined their continental counterparts in experiencing deteriorating urban incomes and conditions in the era of structural adjustment. Nevertheless, at least one aspect of the livelihoods of our sample suggests that, in 1994 at least, Harare did differ from most of sub-Saharan Africa because the role the informal sector plays in the survival of the urban poor is rather different. For household heads in particular, the sector was playing a relatively minor part, and even when other contributions to the household income are taken into account, the share of formally-earned incomes was clearly generally predominant. Furthermore, other surveys in Harare have suggested that people are being discouraged from entry into the informal sector, or are leaving, because conditions of trade are deteriorating under ESAP. Falling incomes leading to reduced demand are one problem cited. This could, however, be an advantage in particular sub-sectors of informal trade, as evidenced by the tiny minority in our survey benefiting from the second-hand clothes trade. They were essentially occupying a niche made possible by everyone else's increasing poverty – but whilst their new form of employment clearly advantaged them it is hard to see its development as progress for urban society as a whole.

Increased competition and falling incomes are typical of the informal sector in other African cities in the context of SAPs, yet the sector has 'boomed'. The explanation may well lie mainly in the differing severity of economic conditions – whilst undoubtedly Harare's low-income residents are really struggling with the impact of ESAP, they have not had the rug pulled from under their feet in quite the way typical of, for example, the poor in many sub-Saharan African cities like Lusaka, Accra, Dar es Salaam or Lilongwe (e.g. Blunt 1997, Jeffries 1992, Tripp 1990, Chilowa and Roe 1990) where informal-sector activities have become a virtual *sine qua non* for economic survival and monthly incomes from formal jobs frequently cover only one week's food needs (Potts 1997a). In such circumstances there may be little choice about participation in the informal sector, no matter how small the returns. Another factor limiting the sector's growth in Harare may be the level of official harassment it experiences – it is probably true to say that increasing acceptance of the *Jua Kali* sector (King 1996) as in many other parts of Africa is as yet far off in Zimbabwe where it still tends to be regarded as unfortunate and unsightly (Rakodi 1995). However, if unemployment and economic conditions for the poor do not improve in the near future it is certain that this sector will further develop its role in urban Zimbabwe.

The evidence presented in this chapter suggests that the vast majority of residents, in the parts of Harare where most people live, regard structural adjustment as a disaster for their own livelihoods. Almost every aspect of their day-to-day lives has been disadvantaged: incomes have fallen, jobs have been lost, prices have rocketed, education and health have suffered, people's personal ambitions and plans have been wrecked. Very few perceived any advantages. For most ESAP can be summed up, as it often is in local media, as 'Ever Suffering African People'.

PART TWO:
COPING WITH URBAN POVERTY: INSTITUTIONAL RESPONSES

6. Participatory Poverty Assessments: The World Bank contribution and emerging agenda

DAVID BOOTH, JEREMY HOLLAND, JESKO HENTSCHEL, PETER LANJOUW and ALICIA HERBERT

Introduction

In terms of fundamentals, we may not know a great deal more about African urban poverty than we did a decade ago. What is certainly true, on the other hand, is that the relationship between whatever research-based understanding we have and discussions about policy (within national governments, international agencies, NGOs, etc.) has been transformed beyond recognition. Knowledge about poverty – both in the shape of better statistics and also, more unexpectedly, in the form of ethnographic and other grassroots evidence – now informs policy discussions with a directness that would have seemed remarkable in the 1980s.[1]

The principal reason for this shift is, of course, the much higher profile that poverty reduction has acquired as a general objective of policy in Africa. However, an important contributory factor is the build-up over the decade of a body of experience in translating statistical and grassroots understandings into forms that policy makers can, and feel obliged to, relate to. This chapter focuses on what is by far the largest single source of such experience, the comprehensive series of Poverty Assessments (PAs) and Participatory Poverty Assessments (PPAs) undertaken at the initiative of the World Bank during the years 1993–97.

The Bank's PAs, and especially the sub-set that included a strong participatory component or free-standing PPA, have set a new standard for the establishment of positive linkages between knowledge and policy for poverty reduction. However, the record of the African PAs is both varied and problematic. The different national assessments illustrate more or less well certain basic principles to do with the 'value added' from combining statistical and other evidence in a participatory framework that is capable of influencing poverty. Some of the assessments, but not all of them, are useful in signalling an emerging agenda of policy work that probes more deeply into the roots of poverty in Africa, urban and rural. This chapter highlights both kinds of contribution of the World Bank's experience and suggests something about the possible future shape of poverty-assessment work on the continent.

This chapter draws most of its evidence and analysis from a report prepared for the Working Group on Poverty and Social Policy of the Special Program of Assistance for Africa (Booth et al. 1998). The argument develops in five steps. We begin in the next section by identifying and distinguishing the main points about the added value from participatory and combined approaches. Illustration is then provided in the form of a discussion of major insights obtained from the first round of African Poverty Assessments. Attention shifts in the following section to the insights to be expected from new (or old but neglected) emphases and emerging themes. Finally we consider the implications for policy.

Participation and Combined Methods: The Basic Rationale

It is worth distinguishing three distinct elements in the standard case for participation and combined methods in poverty-assessment work. The decision at the World Bank to include a participatory dimension in a number of African PAs reflected each of these arguments to some degree, and we believe it is important to keep each of them in the picture with its own specific weight.

Participation as stakeholder involvement

The most basic, and in many ways most important, argument for participation in PAs is that these should be participatory in the sense of involving both primary and secondary stakeholders in a *process* that is capable of influencing policy and practice. Involving a range of stakeholders in poverty-assessment activities not only improves data quality and deepens understanding but makes it more likely that poverty reduction will figure centrally in national policy agendas and their implementation (Norton and Stephens 1995). By helping to give the poor a voice, bringing new actors into the policy dialogue and encouraging those who decide priorities to engage actively with these discrepant perspectives, a good PPA alters the terms on which policy is decided.

Experience broadly confirms that this is true. To a greater or lesser extent, the Bank PAs that had a participatory component or a separate PPA involved efforts both to 'consult the poor' and to involve government and other secondary stakeholders in preparatory workshops and follow-up activities. Although these efforts varied considerably in their effectiveness in securing some local 'ownership' of the results of the PA, a review of their findings does suggest that the depth and breadth of stakeholder involvement was a factor in both the quality of the assessment (more involvement produced more insights) and its effectiveness as an influence on policy (Norton 1997, Robb 1998).

The meaning of poverty and the views of the poor

Consulting the poor and other stakeholders through a PPA is thus principally about maximizing influence on policy processes. However, it is also seen as an important means of widening the *scope* of a PA, in the sense of increasing the range of data-types and forms of analysis that are recognized and considered legitimate by policymakers.

A certain amount of fog tends to surround discussions of the meaning and measurement of poverty, and to some the whole field still seems awash with non-communicating paradigms (Chambers 1997). With this in mind, it seems helpful to identify clearly a number of distinct claims. Compared with conventional methods and procedures of poverty assessment, PPAs are helpful in:

- 'bringing to life' the poverty profiles and evidence on trends constructed from household-survey and other aggregate statistics using income- or consumption-based measures – communicating more effectively *what it means* to be poor;
- suggesting the importance of indicators of deprivation that usefully *complement* income/consumption measures, though they are no less susceptible to standardized data collection – examples including nutritional status and educational attainment, drawing on the arguments of Sen (1985) about the multi-dimensional nature of well-being and deprivation;
- indicating the importance of *locally-specific* and possibly in commensurable dimensions of well-being and deprivation – bearing in mind the warnings of Jodha (1988) and Chambers (1995) on the lack of any necessary correlation between consumption-based and local conceptions of well-being; and
- promoting a *more dynamic* or explanation-oriented approach to poverty-assessment work by focusing on what the poor perceive to be the main constraints under which they live, such as limited access to important markets and services, a narrow asset base and other sources of vulnerability – as in Chambers on coping (1989) and the need to consider poverty as a complex (1982).

The first three points are about three different ways of enriching the poverty profiles provided by narrowly 'money-metric' approaches. The last point goes further. It is concerned with moving on from better poverty profiles (and trend analysis) – important from the point of view of assessing policy *priorities* – to the formulation of better explanations of poverty and deprivation, the key to better policy *instruments*. This distinction is important to the shift of emphasis we explore further on in the chapter.

Triangulation and the limits of single-stranded methods
The *process* and *scope* arguments for participatory methods in PAs are distinct but mutually reinforcing. By giving expression to the many different dimensions of deprivation and to what poor people themselves say about what causes them to remain poor, PPAs have the potential both to give us a fuller understanding of poverty, and to make it more difficult for poverty to be ignored or sidelined by politicians and other decision makers.

Additional force is provided by the third major argument behind the advocacy and success of PPAs. This concerns the *superior validity and reliability* of understandings that make use of data of different kinds or exploit a variety of methods or investigative styles – the principle of methodological triangulation.

One suggestion here is that local participatory enquiries not only provide important complementary understandings of poverty by highlighting dimensions that would be left out by a poverty assessment based entirely on statistical data; they also prove a check on the robustness of the conclusions drawn. They can, depending on the case, serve to 'ground-truth' findings from household-survey data or to point to anomalies that call for further investigation.

On the other hand, knowledge of the results of major surveys provides one means among others by which the participatory research team insures itself against freak observations, misinformation and its own biases. Other checks are provided by the range of different stakeholders and written sources consulted, and the deployment of a variety of data-collection methods by a multi-disciplinary team.

Insights from the First Round of Poverty Assessments in Africa

This chapter does not attempt a full survey of the contribution of participatory and combined methods to PAs, but provides illustrative material, with a special emphasis on neglected and emerging themes. Several more comprehensive studies exist, focusing particularly on process (Blackburn and Holland 1997, Robb 1998), method (Carvalho and White 1997, IDS (Institute of Development Studies) 1994) and substantive issues (Hanmer et al. 1997). There have also been short policy-oriented summaries of the main thrust and contribution of the early PPAs. Two of these provide a particularly good point of departure for our discussion (Norton and Stephens 1995, World Bank 1996, but see also Salmen 1995, World Bank 1994).

Norton and Stephens noted that PPAs up to the time of writing had most commonly focused on enriching the descriptive poverty profile by adding the poor's own perceptions of their predicament to the standard quantitative measures. They had also added value by highlighting:

- service-delivery issues from the vantage point of the poor;
- the bearing of land, labour and capital markets on the lives of poor people;
- the salience of particular aspects of the economic and regulatory framework of some countries
- changes in the effectiveness of different survival strategies and safety-net arrangements; and
- the importance of community-level organizations (1995:10–13).

Looking closely at 11 of the 18 African PAs then scheduled, the report of the Task Force on Poverty in sub-Saharan Africa (World Bank 1996:75–6) identified the major contributions of the PPAs to the method and scope of the assessments in the following way. They had enriched the poverty profile by illustrating local understandings of poverty and vulnerability. And they had shed light on three areas of key importance to the implementation the Bank's anti-poverty strategy by:

- eliciting the perceptions of the poor on the accessibility and relevance of services and infrastructure;
- improving analysis of constraints to the realization of market-based opportunities by the poor; and
- supporting policy analysis of emergency and safety-net provision.

The Task Force was particularly struck by what the PPAs had revealed about the priorities of the poor for public action. Its report highlights how different country PPAs drew attention to:

- a sense of isolation, from services, markets, government institutions and information;
- the key importance of water supplies;
- security of life and livelihood as a primary concern;
- access to curative health care as a consistently high priority; and
- the relative importance in urban areas of access to employment, skills and education, and small-enterprise credit.

It is worth noticing about these summaries that while they illustrate well how PPAs have generated findings that are relevant to current policy priorities, they agree in reporting that the main emphasis was on enriching the statistical poverty profile and on prioritizing constraints as perceived by the poor. Issues relating to the accessibility and quality of government services emerge very strongly. Compared with the general prospectus of participatory and combined methods as an input to poverty-assessment work, there is comparatively little emphasis on the development of more complex causal stories involving vulnerability and the assets of the poor. Gender and other intra-household relations emerge fairly strongly, but mainly as a profiling issue.

The somewhat more recent survey of PPAs undertaken for our study does not suggest a radical departure from the above. However, there are some significant new strands that begin to emerge along with the established themes. Looking at the full range of PAs now available, the following strong concerns emerge from the participatory components or from the dialogue between the different methods deployed:

- local visions of poverty relating to prevailing community norms (non-material notions of dignity and self-respect);
- inherent or socially-constructed characteristics of individuals as sources of differential vulnerability (gender, age, childlessness, health status, disability, and individual pathologies such as drunkenness);
- hunger and dietary inadequacy as a distinct dimension of deprivation;
- the seasonality of access and vulnerability;
- intra-household poverty dynamics (existence of distinct income streams, and differentiation of income-poverty and other attributes by gender);
- physical isolation as a key factor in access to services and markets;
- the decline of traditional – and insufficiency of alternative – safety nets;
- Community-level poverty versus household or individual poverty.

Various of these generic findings are illustrated with reference to two country examples, Zambia and Tanzania, in our report to the SPA Working Group (Booth et al. 1998: Annexes 4 and 5). These case studies also illustrate, however, the way the latest poverty-assessment work is beginning to move beyond this somewhat heterogeneous catalogue of 'insights from PPAs' and towards lines of work that a) are more systematic about exploring the roots of poverty and vulnerability, and b) exploit more deliberately the potential of combining methods in a single design.

While the kinds of findings summarised above do demonstrate significant value added, we think it is a mistake to rely solely on themes such as these in advancing the case for participation and combined methods. Increasingly, there is a more compelling case to be made, drawing on a broader range of examples.

An Evolving Agenda: The Asset Framework

In three important ways, our report suggests, the trend of poverty assessment work is towards consolidation, systematization and a real coming-of-age. In the first place, the promise that poverty assessment will turn into a nationally and even locally-owned activity seems to be on its way to realization in a number of countries. A second tendency that is clearly observable is the deployment of an increasingly rich suite of methods and techniques. This is accompanied, we suggest, by a more deliberate exploitation of the comparative advantages of, and sources of synergy between, what are best called 'contextual' and 'non-contextual' methods.

The third dimension that is highlighted in the report is the attention given in some of the more recent PPAs to the more dynamic or explanatory side of poverty analysis. It is on this last dimension that we concentrate here.

Thematic selectivity in poverty assessments
In the reporting of the early PPAs, we have seen, there was a strong emphasis on 'ground-truthing', and injecting new dimensions into, the construction of poverty profiles. Subsequently, a good deal of prominence was given to identifying the priorities of the poor in relation to public policies. It is important to stress that neither of these concerns is about to become irrelevant. We have indicated that local-participatory and other 'contextual' investigations have an important continuing role in both qualifying and improving survey- and consumption-based poverty profiles. Also, the contribution of PPAs and poverty-monitoring systems as voter-satisfaction barometers for politicians, or training grounds for planners, is going to remain an important part of their role.

In the long term, however, an equally important contribution may lie in the ability of PPAs to bring to the fore, and articulate as policy-relevant, the dynamic processes behind vulnerability and persistent poverty. This involves looking in a more comprehensive way at the assets of the poor and at a wider range of limitations to access, including those arising at intra-household and community levels. It entails addressing issues that may not easily be recognised as relevant to policy, and do not sit very easily within current policy frameworks, but which nonetheless cry out for consideration at this level.

There are a number of reasons why questions about the causality of poverty should have been given less prominence than they deserve in the PA experience to date. Between the production of PPA field reports and the consumption of 'insights from PPAs' by professional decision-makers, there is obviously selectivity at various levels. Not all of the Bank's PPAs generated useful insights into assets and vulnerability, or into the dynamics of gender relations, but several did, including some of the earliest (e.g. Ghana, Zambia, Cameroon). Why do such concerns figure relatively little in the overall PA report, where this is produced as a separate document, and very little indeed in the sort of policy-oriented summaries of results reviewed in Section 3 above?

The reasons are no doubt complicated and not identical in any two cases. However, it is clear that they begin with the notorious difficulty of reflecting locally-specific results in analyses that must of necessity generalize. They include the pressure on writers of country synthesis reports focusing on policy messages to highlight findings that have immediacy for policy makers – priorities, barriers to access to services, etc. They probably culminate in the need for general overviews of PA/PPA findings to demonstrate relevance to the prevailing strategic perspective on poverty reduction, and not put this at risk by inserting more complicated and uncertain messages. These constraints are likely to remain, and they need to be taken seriously.

The argument that follows is based partly on a review of some of the more recently produced PPAs (Tanzania, South Africa) and partly on the accumulating weight of a related analytical literature – on food security and entitlements (Sen 1981), stores, investments and claims (Swift 1989) and the asset-vulnerability framework (Moser 1996, 1998). In the light of this work, we suggest that a more systematic approach to the dynamics of poverty might justifiably undertake a double task.

One is to pick up and give a more explicit policy twist to those asset/vulnerability and access issues that were present, but remained somewhat submerged for the reasons just explained, in the first round of PPAs. The other is to build these into a more comprehensive conceptual framework for analysing the assets of the poor. The distinguishing feature of this framework is that it brings together a range of conventionally-recognised economic assets with a number of 'sociological' factors, conceived as forms of capital.

The framework just described needs to be sufficiently flexible to incorporate considerations of access to markets – for inputs and outputs, labour (including demand-side issues of economic opportunity) and finance. These are key considerations in examining the ability of individuals, households and communities to manage or convert their asset stocks. However, the unifying notion is that treating the assets of the poor as capital – as stocks that can be created, stored, exchanged and depleted – provides a powerful entry point into causal explanations of poverty. This in turn has the potential of enriching considerably the range of discussion about poverty-reduction strategies and strategems.

Intangible assets

The interpretation of PPA and other contextually-derived evidence within an asset framework underlines most notably that there are 'intangible' assets – now known respectively as social and political capital – which are critical for poverty and vulnerability analysis. Social and political capital are intangible in the sense that they arise from and are only observable in social behaviour. In its most famous usage (Putnam 1993), social capital refers to the prevalence of norms of civicness, and to the vibrancy of the horizontal ties of associational life at the level of the community. However, in some contexts social capital is taken to include important relational variables at the household level. Political capital – referring to stocks or reserves of power – can also be used to analyse powerlessness at several levels that are important for understanding poverty, including societal, community and intra-household (especially, gender and age) relations.

Without attempting to be completely exhaustive, a more comprehensive framework for analysis of the dynamics of poverty might therefore include access to and exclusion from means of increasing or sustaining each of the following:

- poverty-critical dimensions of natural and produced capital, including common-property resources and physical infrastructure;
- human capital (nutrition, health, local knowledge and education);
- social capital, at the household, community and societal levels; and
- political capital and powerlessness, both within and beyond the household and local community.

In our full report, the meaning and potential significance of each of the above groups of asset/access issues are discussed with reference to a range of African poverty assessments. In one of the annexes, an attempt is made to show how the concept of political capital can be used to organize and synthesize observations about gender relations in Zambia drawn from the PA and other sources. Another annexe, referring to the Tanzania PPA, illustrates the entry of social capital – measured in terms of the density of associational life at the level of the rural community – into a central place in poverty-assessment work.

Even though it is based entirely on rural data, the Tanzania PPA's social capital study (Narayan 1997, Narayan and Pritchett 1997) calls for special comment. It represents a significant breakthrough for the design of poverty-assessment work, demonstrating in particular the nesting of a specially-designed survey within a larger survey of a more conventional type, permitting the econometric modelling and testing of hypotheses derived from general analytical literature and nuanced by focus-group enquiries in the same sites.

The substantive conclusions from this work are also quite striking. After controlling for a range of other variables that might be expected to explain away the relationship, and giving due consideration to the possibility of reverse causality, the investigators conclude that village-level social capital is a powerful determinant of levels of individual income. The quantitative effect is, moreover, large: a one standard deviation increase in village social capital is associated with a 20–30 per cent increase in expenditure per village inhabitant. This is equivalent to *tripling* either the level of education, or the stock of non-farming physical assets. The most powerful intervening variables seem to be the levels of use of improved agricultural inputs and credit (Narayan 1997; 98–100).

The policy implications of this finding are important and touch upon areas that have been little explored in previous PAs. It is suggested that more attention needs to be given in development policymaking to not unwittingly destroying or 'mining' social capital – e.g. through the adoption of an unduly technical and bureaucratic approach by sectoral ministries. There may also be a need to look again at the arguments against a demand-led approach within poverty-oriented social funds. Although there are indications that the importance of social capital varies inversely with the effectiveness of the state, it seems unlikely that these conclusions simply reflect some quirk of the Tanzanian data or unique features of the national society. In the context of the argument in this section, it represents a singularly powerful, but not isolated, example of the potential for re-orienting poverty-assessment work within an asset/access framework.

The Role of Poverty Assessment in Policy and Practice: Engaging with the Strategic Consensus

Since the beginning of the 1990s, strategic thinking on poverty has been dominated by the policy 'consensus' summed up in the Bank's three-pronged formula: labour-intensive growth, priority to human capital investments, plus safety nets (World Bank 1990). There may be a few holes in this consensus (Lipton 1997), however, the formula remains for many practitioners a serviceable instrument, concentrating on a few well-researched, easily-grasped and generally-acknowledged focuses for intervention.

On the other hand, it has to be admitted that a merely three-pronged fork has serious limits. Although quite broad in economic terms, the Bank's formula is now generally recognised to be extremely restricted in its ability to convey the importance of non-economic issues and 'intangibles' of all kinds. The recognition given to safety-net issues is an exception, but a very partial one.

The issues not picked up, although they are increasingly of concern to donors and the Bank, are of various sorts. They include most obviously both non-income dimensions or correlates of poverty such as insecurity and lack of leisure, and the gender dimensions of these and other inequalities (Blackden and Morris-Hughes 1993, Elson et al. 1996). Less obvious, but just as important in the light of the foregoing argument and current research in and around the Bank, the three-pronged formula now begins to look narrowly economistic in its handling of capital-asset and access factors that impinge powerfully on the incidence of poverty as conventionally understood.

There are two challenges here. One is the challenge to policy thinking, to find means of bringing the strategy formula into line with the latest research and PA work without rendering it unserviceable (for example, by over-complicating it). The other is to improve the volume and sharpness of the policy analysis that is generated or supported by asset/vulnerability enquiries – to think through the implications of, say, the critical importance of women's political capital, and to begin to translate these into coherent proposals that have at least the immediacy for policymakers of, say, social safety-nets. On the second level, as well as on the first, a great deal remains to be done.

Conclusions

The relationship between knowledge about poverty, including urban poverty, and policy discussions in and about Africa is now far closer than it was a decade ago. To the extent this is so, it owes much to the cycle of national Poverty Assessments and Participatory Poverty Assessments initiated in 1993 by the World Bank. This chapter has drawn on a recent evaluation of PPA experience to reflect on two main themes: the basic rationale of an approach that combines different methods in a participatory framework, and the way the scope and focus of poverty-assessment work in Africa have been evolving.

The suggestion has been that the best PPA work has contributed, along with influential tendencies in the research literature, to the emergence of a broader perspective on the dynamics and causalities of poverty. What is distinctive about this approach is captured well by the notion that the poor are constrained by their access to or exclusion from a range of assets: natural and produced, human, social and political.

The major challenge posed by this conclusion has to do with strategic policy and its relationship to research-based knowledge. We have suggested that this needs to become more of a two-way relationship. The Bank's three-pronged strategy must be opened up to the inclusion of a limited number of new priorities, especially in the area of non-economic assets and forms of exclusion. At the same time, more work needs to be done by researchers to follow through the possible policy implications of the major recent findings in this area.

7. Multi Layered Responses to Urban Poverty: Possible donor agency action

SUE JONES

Introduction

This chapter provides a practical example of how to translate urban poverty analysis into a framework for action that could be acceptable to a donor agency. It is primarily based on work undertaken with a Kenyan consultancy, Matrix, for the Overseas Development Agency (ODA, now DFID) in 1995 that sought to provide a situation analysis of urban poverty in Kenya. It does, however, draw on other urban poverty experience that I have gained from a World Bank project and work for other agencies, such as the EU. Over time, it became clear that there were similar issues arising in each of these cases, even though they were in very different localities. This chapter draws out these general issues.

The Current Level of Urban Poverty Responses

It is surprising that more donor agencies have not responded to governments' poverty concerns by developing larger programmes to address urban poverty specifically[1]. They have evidence of how serious (and increasing) urban poverty problems are. The forecasts are of great concern. 'Within the last forty years, the absolute number of the urban population has increased almost five fold from an estimated 300 million to almost 1.5 billion'. Also, 'in the 1960s and 1970s slum and shanty town dwellers represented on average 30–60 per cent of the urban population in developing countries, present estimates suggest an average of 50 per cent and rising to 79 per cent in some cities.'[2] Various agencies have made commitments to poverty alleviation their core concern.[3] It is generally recognized that urban poverty is a complex interlinking of problems and deprivations faced by poor people which requires concerted efforts (and resources) in order for change to be brought about.[4]

So why do we not see more concerted effort, strategies and models by donor agencies to address urban poverty? A number of reasons can be identified for this:

o The effects of Michael Lipton's persuasive argument about 'urban bias', especially in Africa[5], still undermine any promotion of urban poverty responses.
o The urban development programme approaches developed in the 1970s by the World Bank were not seen as a success in addressing urban poverty.

- The sheer scale of the problems and action can be off-putting. It is now also recognized that area-based responses have severe limitations (primarily because the economic sphere in which the urban poor try to find an income is often city-wide and outside the poor urban area in which they live.)
- Certainly the complexity of possible responses – concerned with health, education, housing, infrastructure, ownership and tenure, social capital, community action and more complicated qualitative issues, such as entitlement, rights, access, social exclusion,[6] can be like entering a labyrinth. On more than one occasion I have seen a group of professionals, academics and government staff become so mesmerized with the intricacy of interlinked urban problems that they did not move from analysis to suggested action.

An additional reason why urban poverty programmes are not promoted, is because it is difficult for donor agencies and governments to act in a coherent way. These institutions are effectively organized in terms of sectoral responses and departmental responsibilities. Urban poverty cuts across these divisions. It also demands intensive management of its various components. Who, within donor agencies, would lead such interdisciplinary efforts?

But there are indications that agencies are trying to take a more interdisciplinary, even partnership approach with other stakeholders. This paper suggests a possible approach for multidisciplinary donor agency action, built round a framework that has emerged from trying to find practical responses in a range of countries and using the case of Kenya.

The Situation Analysis Study[7]

In 1994, the concern of our team[8] was to undertake a situation analysis of urban poverty in Kenya and identify possible action that the ODA (now DFID) could support, based on qualitative and quantitative assessments. In brief the process used was to:

- Review existing studies and assessments,
- Review existing action and proposals by other agencies – government, donor agencies, NGOs and local CBOs,
- Undertake some additional qualitative assessments, as required,
- Identify the key problems in this urban sector,
- Evaluate possible responses to the problems and then identify where the donor agency might make a contribution or add value to existing efforts,
- Identify a possible framework for further action.

This is a standard approach for such assessments. A number of general lessons can be drawn from this assessment (and similar experiences another studies) about the process of assessing urban poverty and developing an urban poverty response. These are highlighted within the following discussion.

I will look firstly at defining urban poverty, secondly at identifying key problems and thirdly at the process of deciding on possible action. Given the complexity of urban poverty, the possibilities for action are enormous. The concern has to be to find ways of targeting specific problems, effectively co-ordinating action and organizing action on such a scale that it has a real impact on urban poverty. The key to an approach for each of these stages is multilayered action.

Defining Urban Poverty in the Local Context and with Local People

Defining urban poverty requires a consideration of a series of layers – previous analysis, the action of other current players and stakeholders, disaggregated definitions of poverty and definitions of urban poverty problems by poor people as well as professionals.

Finding the range of existing data and studies about certain aspects of urban poverty[9] and local skills to undertake further studies
In our case, Matrix had already undertaken a quantitative study, which provided a base of information. Looking at this and other studies we could then decide on the additional information that needed to be gathered and the focus for qualitative work. While there is considerable criticism of the shortcomings of survey data[10], they can provide useful triangulation material along with more qualitative assessments.

Times are also changing. Some qualitative assessment of urban poverty is likely to have been done already in-country. For example, participatory poverty assessments undertaken for national poverty policy development and UNICEF's situation analyses, which provide qualitative evidence about the situation of women and children, can often provide significant amounts of information. Local skills in qualitative and participatory techniques are likely to have been developed to do these studies. There would be local expertise available, in that case, for any further studies.

Identifying micro-level studies and action and putting these into the macro-level picture
Given the increasing influence of PRA and qualitative techniques, there are likely to be more qualitative assessments undertaken by academics and researchers. These may be partial and in specific localities, but should be pulled in to any overall assessments. Strong use can be made of anecdotal work in broad assessments.

As with studies, so with action. In a recent debate with practitioners and NGOs dealing with urban poverty[11], one of their key concerns was that they are taking action and making a difference to the lives of poor people by working together at the micro level (household, community, locality) but they cannot get wider recognition or feed their activities into government/policy-level considerations. Undertaking an assessment can play an important role in helping to feed lessons learnt at a microlevel into the broader context.

It is also important to check what other agencies etc. are doing. Poverty reduction has become so 'popular' with agencies, that there can be some territoriality about poverty action. At the same time as this study was underway, action that could be taken by NGOs to address urban poverty was being considered in a major way. Fortunately the team undertaking this NGO study were more than willing to share their initial findings about possible poverty reduction action. This is not always the case. This was important so that any proposals could take this into account, rather than duplicate their efforts.

Using qualitative studies to expand the understanding of poverty and to help define the urban poor more sensitively
Having established that information about urban poverty was already available and who was taking action to support the urban poor, we could then see where the gaps in understanding were. A key concern was to provide a fuller picture of the very poor and to ensure that key vulnerable groups had all been identified. Some key groups, such as female-headed families, unemployed youths, the elderly, widows and the long-term unemployed, are now generally recognized as particularly vulnerable groups.

However, careful consideration has to be given to the circumstances within a country. As an example, in Kenya, single-female-headed households have been recognized for a long time as a special vulnerable group.[12] But there is a new dimension to this problem. Times have become so difficult, economically, that there is now an emerging group of street mothers who live on the street with their families since this is now the only place left to them to bring up their families. Also, since one member of the team had personal and specialist knowledge of the problems facing the disabled urban poor, the study gave specific focus to the particular needs of this client group. In previous studies, issues of personal security and safety had been a high priority and so these needed to be considered.

Asking people themselves to discuss their needs and problems as a way of ensuring that different categories of urban poor are disaggregated and their special concerns identified
Street children's definitions of their own problems illustrate the need for a full assessment in order to have a substantive understanding of the different circumstances of urban poor people. In focus-group discussions with different groups of street children, they indicated the differences between

those who are on the streets and go back home to slums etc. at night and those children who are live on the streets twenty four hours a day. The plight of this latter young group of survivors, especially in terms of the abuse and physical punishment they can receive from anyone and the total lack of security of their lives, especially at night, is not only heart-rending but also brings up issues any urban poverty response has to be aware of.

Identifying the way in which deprivation is interlocked and the key indicators of poverty in the local context
Even if an assessment of the short falls in meeting basic needs – housing conditions and tenure, supply of electricity, water, health and education services – is only identifying the immediate manifestation of urban poverty, it is important to see how the short falls are interlocked and cause further problems within the local context.[13] In Kenya, most of the inner city slums in Nairobi have severe shortages of land – these were areas demarcated during colonial times which have been much more intensively used since then with families moving into the area. There is chronic overcrowding in poorly ventilated and minimal accommodation. Fifteen people comprising several families can be sharing one room and all paying rent. In the worst slums there are cases of people sleeping in shifts and children sleeping under their parent's bed. (Jones et al. 1995: 4). Before we did the study, we would not have connected the problem of toilet provision to land in such a close way. But this is what the study illustrated very clearly. In such circumstances up to 50 people can be using one pit latrine. When these are full, they may not be emptied and reused but are urgently built over to provide additional accommodation.

It is also important to identify, with poor people, both the costs involved in the various services and also how services operate informally. For each study I undertake, building up a profile of the costs for poor families of such activities as sending children to school or for using health services is important.[14] From such discussions, it can become apparent that 'free' services involve poor families providing what, to them, are significant amounts of cash. Also services that government officials say are provided in the area may have broken down, may only operate at particular times or may be monopolized by those with greater influence in the area.

Building up a profile of coping strategies, as a way of showing the complex process of how poorer people, families and communities survive on a day to day basis
We were fortunate, in this study, because a useful piece of work on coping strategies in one urban poor area had been undertaken by a local anthropologist for another donor agency study. This provided details which we summarized into a framework about household economies, income-diversification strategies and supportive networks[15]. What became clear, in

such a detailed consideration, was the overriding issue of food and the considerable difficulties that many people faced in getting basic nutrition each day. It was here that I was told about a local lunch – 'air burgers' – i.e. you open your mouth and try to swallow air because that is all that you are likely to eat.

Checking findings with other key stakeholders – such as local government officials, NGOs and field workers involved in poverty action
Other stakeholders can often reinforce poor people's assessments and add their own experiences, which give greater validity. This also serves as a check on comments made by poor people. Having a detailed assessment of how services and facilities actually work can also provide evidence that contradicts myths about the urban poor. As an example, in Kenya we discussed with local officials why they did not provide water connections to poor people that they provided for middle-income areas. Their reply was that such people could not afford the Ksh 180 (US$4) connection charge. However, when we went through with them, step by step, how much water poor families need per day (as a minimum) and the market cost, they could see that poor people were already paying three times the price (up to Ksh 600 (US$14)) that middle-income people were paying (Jones et al. 1995: 11).

Moving from Analysis to an Identification of Possible Action

Considering possible action in response to poverty issues identified in the analysis, again requires a layered approach to assess each of the urban problems, decide on priorities and consider possible action and the value the donor agency can add by taking action.

An unexpected participatory approach to problem identification, utilizing local knowledge
Because of circumstances our survey was delayed. This proved to be a very valuable (and humbling) delay. Not wanting to lose our survey team (since, these days, good qualitative facilitators/researchers are in high demand), we decided to brainstorm some ideas about key problems facing the urban poor. We had envisaged that this would be based on secondary data. However, we found ourselves with an excellent source of primary data – our researchers. They had been used by a range of bilateral, multilateral and academic institutions to undertake qualitative assessments of the poor. Not only did they already have this detailed knowledge, they also had witnessed a range of agencies considering possible action. Such experience is a huge (and often untapped) resource. This knowledge became a cornerstone in our thinking.

Undertaking a key problems process approach
We began by brainstorming all the urban issues, then seeing how these could be grouped into key issues. In the Kenya case, three issues emerged – community-based support, capacity building and policy/strategy development. From there, we considered the different broad strategy options that could be adopted. For example, practical action on the ground could focus on private land slums, on larger slums in Nairobi, poor areas outside Nairobi or on the newer slums in Nairobi where there is greater insecurity.

Then we looked at the scope of action that could be taken, followed by a consideration of limitations to action (i.e. the likely constraints that could undermine effectiveness). Following this, we considered possible approaches that any donor agency could take and then refined this to see where our specific donor agency could add value or where action responded most closely to their own objectives.

Establishing a Framework for Donor Agency Action

Based on this assessment, various options for action had emerged under each heading. The task then was to see how these could be developed into a framework for action.

The need for a multi-layered institutional response
The problems have to be tackled not just at the community level. Often urban poverty action has operated only at the community level where the problems are evident, but is that where attention should be focused? Is that dealing only with the symptoms? So many of the problems facing the urban poor are a result of lack of access because of their inability to demand what other urban residents receive and an inability to deal with officials and the negative attitudes of officials towards poor people. How can community based approaches respond or have an effect on these strategic and structural problems? How effective can it be to empower people if there is no change in government attitudes or response to their needs? This has resulted, at times, in calls for institutional and policy focused programmes. But is a focus of resources at policy level providing effective support to poor people who need action and (initially anyway) very basic support?

To resolve the contradictions that face urban poverty practitioners today, the suggestion that emerged from this study (and emerged from other urban poverty assessments[16]) is that:

○ The response has to be based on the disaggregated needs of the urban poor.
○ Most particularly, it has to identify the poorest and most vulnerable categories of people and provide action that is both flexible enough and targeted to respond to their needs.

- It also has to produce action on the ground – to give poor people the confidence and the faith that their circumstances will change and this has to be done in a way that is based on their participation and their design.
- The response has to deliver at the community level, still providing practical help (if action is only at policy/strategy level it is unlikely that the poor will see any action, or see how it relates to their needs).
- But it also has to deal with the problem that action on the ground may have no impact at policy (and more importantly financial allocation) levels.
- It needs therefore to be targeted at the macro as well as the micro level – at the strategic level influencing policymakers so they are responsive to the concerns and needs of the urban poor.
- But the approach also has to look at the meso level, increasing the capability of whoever is helping to deliver support and services to the urban poor, whether this is a government official, NGO, local politician or a community representative.
- Again it is useless to address urban poverty through generating community action and increasing the sensitivity of policymakers, if those who provide practical support and deliver services have a negative attitude towards poor people and their capacity to decide on their own futures.

So, any action has to operate at three levels:

Community-level action	↔	Service-Delivery Capacity-Building	↔	Policymakers/ Strategic decision-making

A programme approach was suggested, which would ensure greater impact on these interconnected problems, with the added value of tackling urban poverty at different levels. In addition a process approach was suggested, focused on delivery of some short-term action as an initial phase. This is particularly important at the community level so that poor people can see some results fairly quickly and can be involved in developing a more detailed action programme.

Unlocking the poverty cycle – taking action on the ground
Recognizing that the poor need to see changes in their circumstances, and that the problems they face are interlinked and huge, how can we take effective action?

Firstly we need to ensure that the wide range of urban poverty needs are at least identified, even if they cannot be addressed. Building on the checklist of key variables provided by Satterthwaite (1997: 13–14):

Action to specifically support different vulnerable groups/the poorest people

- Different very poor clusters – e.g. street children, pavement dwellers, scavengers
- Gender dimensions of poverty – e.g. widows, single female headed households
- Particularly vulnerable groups – e.g. unemployed youths, disabled, elderly

Increasing income and assets

- Employment creation
- Micro-credit
- Training
- Legal tenure

Levels of basic services

- Housing (tenure and finances)
- Infrastructure/environmental services – water, electricity, garbage collection, drainage and sanitation
- Health care
- Education, including day care, adult literacy and vocational training
- Transport

Level of access to decisionmakers/decisionmaking and to justice/rights

- Access to justice
- Access to credit/micro-finance
- Access to delivery system of urban services
- Increased security
- Access to decisionmakers/achieving recognition

Special action needs to be taken to support the very poor, who are unlikely to benefit from general urban poverty action. For more general urban poor needs, it is important to focus on their most pressing needs, and find entry points to give support. This can be action related to health, education, income generation or a community hall, as long as this is one of the key priorities identified by the urban poor themselves. The point is that they can see a difference and can be involved in changes through initial action. They are then taking control of a process which has generally been organized to marginalize them. They are working in a context which often sees them as passive recipients if not lazy losers. Very small-scale action can be expanded into a more strategic response later.

The issue is not whether providing services works or not. It is about understanding urban poverty issues from the point of view of those most affected by such poverty and working with them on mechanisms to unlock some initial action and change attitudes. It is also about being flexible. Once some immediately identifiable needs/problems have been addressed, it is highly likely that the poor will see far deeper problems to address. It is also true that once some action has an impact it unlocks further support for the urban poor.

Packaging community action together with a programme of capacity building and policy-level support has several advantages. It is at a sufficiently large scale to attract donor agencies' funding and allows micro-level action which the urban poor can see for themselves, but ensures responsive policy decisions and provides mechanisms for macro-level and micro-level communication and changes in attitude towards urban poverty problems.

The proposed framework

As if that task were not difficult enough, such a package has to be simple. This brings me to the last component of such a multi-layered approach. Of most importance is some sort of poverty strategy which sets out the objectives and the contribution of this approach to poverty reduction. In other words, there has to be a recognition of the limitations of any single action/project/programme on the complex problem of urban poverty.

In the case of Kenya, the strategy was an initial framework around which action would be based. To guide this development, a Project Manager was appointed. Since then, a whole series of people have been developing action and would be able to provide more personal perspectives.

This process provided the framework for urban poverty action that was informed by a far more sensitive understanding of urban poverty issues within local contexts. It means that the framework for urban poverty action was based on the identified problems and needs of various urban poor groups. Its intention is also to provide a supportive context for urban people to do what they are excellent at – finding ways of making best use of whatever resources they can, but ensuring that they are given the opportunity and on an equal basis to other urban residents. The following schedule summarizes the approach.

DEFINING URBAN POVERTY IN THE LOCAL CONTEXT AND WITH LOCAL PEOPLE

- Review a range of existing national data and studies
- Identify local resources with skills to undertake studies
- Identify micro-level studies and action

- Identify the gaps in information
- Consider quantitative additional information needed
- Focus on qualitative studies to expand the understanding of poverty and define urban poverty more sensitively

- Ask poor people themselves to discuss
  - their needs
  - different categories of poor
  - the special concerns of vulnerable groups
- Identify the ways in which deprivation is interlocked in the particular local context
- Identify key indicators of poverty in the local context
- Build up a profile of coping strategies
- Check findings with other local stakeholders – local government officials, NGOs, field workers

MOVING FROM ANALYSIS TO AN IDENTIFICATION OF KEY URBAN POVERTY PROBLEMS

- Take a participatory approach to problem identification
- Undertake a key problems approach

ESTABLISHING A FRAMEWORK FOR DONOR AGENCY ACTION

Consider a multi-layered response in three directions:
- Community-level action
- Service-delivery capacity-building
- Policymakers/Strategic decisionmaking

For community-level action, consider the need to respond, focused on:
- Specific action to support the poorest/most vulnerable groups
- Entry points of action responding to urban poor needs
- Possible basic service support
- Possible qualitative concerns and increased access, security, rights

SET OUT THE FRAMEWORK AS THE POVERTY STRATEGY

8. Urban Poverty Alleviation and Housing Creation[1]

A. GRAHAM TIPPLE

Introduction

A dwelling is important to a person in poverty not only as a place of shelter and domestic life but also as the means to make an income. Housing has been traditionally regarded as a welfare good and so investment therein has been abandoned in times of economic hardship. Recently, however, there has been a change of emphasis. We have recognized that housing is a productive sector in which to invest so that individual lives and the economy as a whole can be improved.

In this chapter, I intend to bring out some of the issues discussed in a much longer document I wrote and which has been published as UNCHS/ILO (1995). I will refer especially to the situation in Sub-Saharan Africa where the need for urban housing is particularly acute.

In an earlier paper, I made a very rough estimate of the need for dwellings in sub-Saharan Africa (Tipple 1994b). This was calculated by first estimating the population growth and then assuming that each new household will need a new dwelling.[2] According to the United Nations population forecasts shown in table 1, between 1980 and 2010 about 422 million people will be added to the region's urban population. The growth in the first ten years of the new century alone is likely to add 162 million.

The next stage of this extremely crude calculation is to divide the population into households because these are the units in which people live. If we assume a mean household size of five, we arrive at the figures in table 2. Thus, about 21 million dwellings were required in the 1990s and a total of 66 million will be required in 2000–10. If a different mean household size is

Table 1: Estimated urban population in sub-Saharan Africa, 1980 to 2010

	Urban Population (millions)			
	1980	1990	2000	2010
Eastern Africa*	25.2	47.5	86.2	146.7
Middle Africa	16.4	27.2	43.9	67.2
Southern Africa	16.3	23.4	33.2	45.5
Western Africa	32.0	55.5	96.7	162.6
Total sub-Saharan Africa	89.9	153.6	259.9	421.9

*Including Sudan
Source: UNCHS (1987).

Table 2: Estimated additional urban households in sub-Saharan Africa, 1980 to 2010

	Additional households (millions)		
	1980–89	1990–99	2000–09
Eastern Africa (inc. Sudan)	4.5	7.7	12.1
Middle Africa	2.2	3.3	4.6
Southern Africa	1.4	2.0	2.4
Western Africa	4.7	8.3	13.2
Total sub-Saharan Africa	12.7	21.3	32.4
Cumulative total from 1980	12.7	34.0	66.4
Millions of dwellings required per year	1.3	2.1	3.2
No of new dwellings required annually per 1 000 urban population at start of period	14.2	13.8	12.5

Source: Tipple (1994b)

preferred for the calculation, other figures will emerge. For example, if four is preferred, another 16 million more dwellings would be required by 2010.[3]

Probably the most telling data in this table concern the number of dwellings this generates per thousand population. This is a useful measure of the size of the task facing a country uninfluenced by its size. In times of extreme effort in the past, countries have been able to build ten dwellings per thousand population for short periods. Here, however, we see that countries in sub-Saharan Africa would need to build in excess of ten dwellings per thousand people every year for decades to keep up with the need for new housing if each new household were to have a dwelling of its own.

As there will be a need for at least one new job per new household, the employment potential of housing provision becomes not only attractive but also an essential part of creating sustainable urban lifestyles. One of the most helpful characteristics of employment in construction is that it is very highly suited to people with few skills. Thus, it can be said to be self-selecting to the poor. The construction of these millions of new dwellings can either increase employment among the poor and, therefore, encourage poverty alleviation, or it can ignore employment considerations and use high-technology solutions with a subsequent reduction in the ability to address poverty.[4]

Employment Potential in the Process of Housing Provision

The construction sector in industrialized countries tends to employ around eight per cent of the economically active population. In the least developed countries, however, the official figure is only about three per cent (ILO

1987).[5] Unfortunately for employment potential, the formal construction industry in developing countries currently tends to rely on equipment intensive methods. Even where labour is plentiful and inexpensive, highly capital-intensive methods have been used in some countries and represent a commitment which would be expensive to reverse.[6] In sub-Saharan Africa, capital cities increasingly feature high-rise, high-technology office and apartment blocks built with imported materials of extremely high status value. These highly visible projects set the trends which others follow and increase the reliance of the economy on imported materials and technologies at a time when the reverse should be encouraged. It is clear that employment and poverty alleviation are assisted in construction in inverse proportion to the cost of the technology.

Some Asian data can assist us in assessing the employment potential intrinsic in housing supply.

In the Sri Lanka data (table 3), luxury housing with high standard of finishes generates more jobs per square metre but fewer per million rupees expenditure than conventional masonry or traditional earth construction. In sub-Saharan Africa, the picture is similar. High-cost housing construction generates more jobs per square metre but fewer jobs per dollar than low-cost housing, and formal-sector construction methods are less labour intensive than informal (Hughes 1976, Syagga et al. 1989). For each unit of expenditure in informal-sector housing, a fifth more jobs can be created than in formal-sector development. At the same time, as many as six times as many (lower standard) dwellings can be built for the same investment (Sethuraman 1985).

The construction of housing is particularly efficient in providing work to low-income workers (Moavenzadeh 1987). It is technically quite simple, there are few large or sophisticated components which demand heavy machinery or extreme care for their positioning, and most processes and components are amenable to hand working. Building simple dwellings is among the most straightforward assembly operations available. Indeed, this is the basis for self-help housing; if it was not simple, it would not be

Table 3: Employment generated by construction (Sri Lanka)

House type	Area (meter^2)	Cost (Rupees/m^2)	Employment generated (person years) (per metre^2)	(per million rupees expenditure)
Luxury	181	475	0.133	280
Conventional	50	190	0.097	510
Traditional	37	76	0.038	500

Source: Spence et al. (1993)

easily picked up by ordinary people. Small-scale enterprises in house-building are particularly important for maximizing employment in construction and its related sectors for four main reasons. First, they tend to use labour-intensive methods in the absence of machinery and other capital equipment. Second, they have knowledge of local conditions. Thus, they work within local neighbourhoods and can offer a service based on customers' special requirements. Third, they can develop from a very small scale, often in the home, and can give employment to local skilled, unskilled and unemployed labour. Fourth, they can use a variety of local materials and a minimum of imported inputs.

Much of the informal-sector housing in developing countries, and so a great deal of the new housing, is being produced by relatively small-scale enterprises in a multiplicity of single house projects. On the other hand, large-scale projects are dominated by the formal sector with its relatively capital-intensive techniques. However, if small-scale informal construction enterprises could be involved in these large projects, they would tend to use more unskilled labour, fewer imports and less hard currency than their large-scale, formal-sector counterparts. As Mensah (1997) demonstrates, large housing estates controlled by government housing agencies can be constructed by small-scale enterprises if the will is present. In his example from Kumasi, Ghana, the State Housing Corporation (now Company) successfully demonstrated that sub-contracting residential construction to small-scale enterprises, three dwellings at a time, could cut construction times and increase efficiency many-fold over the direct labour employed by the company.[7] So successful were the small firms, that when redundancies were necessary to streamline SHC's operations for privatization, gangs of workers were awarded loans to supplement their end of service benefits to enable them to set up small enterprises. They were then allocated contracts to construct a few dwellings, to get them started (ibid.).

In self-help housing projects where the households are expected to contribute substantial amounts of construction themselves, a surprising amount of paid work can be generated. Laquian (1983) shows that self-help builders use at least a proportion of paid labour through local small-scale enterprises and individual artisans. In El Salvador, each site and service house provided an average of 6.5 work-months labour of which only 2.5 months was 'sweat equity'. In Dandora, self-help house builders employed 8.9 workers on average (ibid.). Ironically, those who use self-help may employ as many or more workers than those who simply have a contractor to do the work.

Traditional technologies often require maintenance on an annual basis. Many originate from rural areas where there are quiet seasons in which house maintenance can be done. Such maintenance requires only locally-available materials and commonly-held skills to accomplish it. This is the approach which produces very low-cost housing initially but requires continual maintenance. It minimizes initial cost at the expense of on-going costs. On the other hand, advocates of 'modern' materials and industrialized technologies claim to produce housing which requires minimal maintenance. They attempt to minimize cost-in-use by opting for high initial cost. However, such technology can present serious problems when maintenance is required especially when it is used in multi-storey buildings for which cranes and scaffolding are required for maintenance tasks.

Apart from in such high-technology projects, most house maintenance tasks are ideally suited to small-scale enterprises which have a high labour input. Thus, the high capital cost/low maintenance approach which has been favoured by governments and the formal sector may be less appropriate if job creation is valued in development strategies.

Employment Generation Through Backward Linkages

Backward linkages in housing supply are demands created in the region in other sectors (for materials, equipment, and their transportation) by the construction of housing. They tend to constitute approximately half the value of the housing (Moavenzadeh 1987, Moavenzadeh and Hagopian 1983) or $500 for every $1 000 worth of housing built. This compares quite well with industrial sectors. These backward linkages are inversely related to the cost of the housing because a larger proportion of the cost is building materials and they are more likely to be locally produced with locally-made tools or machines. Backward linkages are also greater for labour-intensive building operations than for those using capital equipment (Klaassen et al. 1987). In addition, self-help housing and upgrading activities are particularly effective for backward linkage generation as they almost always use techniques and materials at the local and labour-intensive end of the spectrum. Table 4 shows that mud, clay, stone and construction are especially effective at generating backward linkages in the building materials industries. In contrast, the currently popular pre-cast concrete panels and cement-block technologies produce less valuable backward linkages. Unfortunately, such technologies are not without advocates in multinational companies and international development agencies.

The production of building materials can also have great impact on the overall employment generation arising from house-building. Small-scale, relatively labour-intensive building materials technologies are generally associated with large multiplier effects because they tend to use locally manufactured machinery, local fuel, and are marketed and transported by small-scale enterprises (ILO 1984). In contrast, large-scale, capital-intensive technologies generate few jobs per unit output and per dollar invested. This century has seen a move towards high-technology, low labour intensity building materials production through technology transferred on a turn-key basis.[8] Such factories are usually large and capable of

Table 4: Source and labour intensity of various materials

Material	Source of material: Place	Source of material: Sector	Labour intensity in production and processing
Mud and wattle	local	informal	high
Sun-dried clay or stabilized soil blocks	local	informal or formal	high
Stone	local	informal or formal	high
Timber	local	informal or formal	high (skilled)
Precast concrete panels	local or imported	formal	medium
Cement blocks with chemical additive	local or imported	formal	low

Source: modified from Klaassen et al. (1987).

fulfilling demand over a large area, sometimes a whole country. The huge brickworks imported into Zambia from Germany in the early 1970s were capable of satisfying national demand with the ability to export but used little labour. The tendency to import such technologies could be reversed if policies favoured the creation of jobs as a development goal. Furthermore, most currently used imported materials can be replaced by a local equivalent, which in turn can be produced in small-scale, labour-based plants (Hansen and Williams 1987). The difference in employment generation between large plants and small, and between equipment-based and labour-based technologies, can be very great; twenty-fold in the case of brick making (table 5) (CNC 1976).

It is important to look also at the loss of jobs in the informal sector if a government allows, for example, a high-technology brick-making plant to be set up. It is inevitable that at least some of the production of the new

Table 5: Labour generation in large- and small-scale brick production

Method	Output per plant (bricks/day)	Labour input per 10 million bricks (person-years)
Small-scale, traditional manual	2 000	160
Small-scale, intermediate technology	2 000	200
Soft-mud machine, otherwise manual	14 000	76
Moderately mechanized	64 000	20
Highly automated	180 000	8

Source: CNC (1976).

Table 6: Unit production costs, brickmaking

Classification of brickmaking process	Unit production cost (US cents per bricks)	
	Medium wage regime*	Low wage regime*
Capital-intensive, all year round	6.5	6.2
'Least-cost', all year round	3.1	2.3
'Least-cost', seasonal working only	2.9	2.0

* Medium and low wage regimes refer to assumed wages for unskilled workers in middle-ranking and poorer developing countries in 1977.
Source: (Keddie and Cleghorn 1978)

plant will be at the cost of existing small-scale operators using traditional labour-intensive methods. While a centralized plant may generate additional jobs in the inevitable transportation effort to spread the products throughout the region, the additional cost of transporting the heavy, relatively low-value-to-bulk material must be borne by users, and much of it is in foreign exchange (vehicles, fuel, motor spares). Thus, the jobs are comparatively expensive to the national economy.

Higher labour intensity in building materials manufacture tends not to cause inflation. There are significant price benefits from substituting capital goods like machinery with labour. Experience in Tanzania demonstrates that it is cheaper to load gravel with a gang of labourers than with a machine loader even when the latter is being used efficiently. When inefficiency creeps in, for example in bad weather, it is much cheaper to keep the labourers idle and no foreign exchange is involved (UNCHS/ILO 1995). However, earth-based and labour-intensive technologies are still often seen to be the poor relations of higher-technology imported solutions even though the practical results of several decades of research into adapting and improving upon local technologies are available for use. There is a great need for research into social attitudes and into improving the image of traditional materials so that they are not seen as inappropriate for 'modern' lifestyles in developing countries.

Forward Linkages: Shelter as a Workplace

Forward linkages are those in which the house forms an intermediate good, just as a windscreen is the output from a auto-glass factory but only an intermediate good in the manufacture of a car. The scale of forward linkages from housing are difficult to calculate but evidently quite significant. They include the range of maintenance activities and production of the fittings and furnishings which people buy to make their dwelling into a home. However, they are particularly important with respect to economic activities carried out within dwellings and their immediate surroundings.

The use of home as a workplace is relatively common in developing countries. Informal-sector activities carried out in the home range from retailing of food to giving injections, from manufacturing cigarettes to keeping livestock. The activities involve a wide range of skills and resources, and may use small or considerable parts of the living quarters, despite the small space available for all activities. The ability to use space for both living and working is a major attraction of home-based economic activities.

In low-income areas, the complex web of economic linkages present in and between the home-based enterprises (HBEs) allow all but the destitute to eke out a living and have access to some shelter. Dwellings are an important asset to the poor in their provision not only of shelter but also of the means to make an income, either through renting out a room or by establishing a shop or workshop. The distinction between production (economic activities) is reproduction (domestic activities) are not clearly drawn in developing country households (Hays-Mitchell 1993). Thus, there is believed to be a symbiotic relationship between housing and HBEs. Owners may be enabled to consolidate their dwellings through the income earned in an HBE. Many households would not have their dwelling without the HBE and many enterprises would not exist without the use of the dwelling (Strassmann 1987). Thus, housing plays an important part in the existence and operation of the informal economy in many countries.

The largest category of active home-based enterprises are retail outlets. Other types of activity differ between types of neighbourhood: petty retailing and cooked food preparation tend to be common in very poor neighbourhoods; areas with good communications tend to have light manufacturing and a variety of services (especially medical and dental) (Gilbert 1988, Strassmann 1986 and 1987, Raj and Mitra 1990, UNCHS/ILO 1995). Together they provide means of livelihood and employment for many people, especially women who may not be able to leave the home or its environs for cultural reasons.

Sinai (forthcoming) found that about one quarter of households used their rooms for some type of commercial activity, the most common being preparation of food for sale in the house, to shops, in the market or in the streets. Arimah (1994) describes how residents of government housing estates in Ilorin, Nigeria, built extensions in order to provide space for commercial activities. These included, especially, provisions shops, grain milling and grinding machines, and tailoring services. Afrane (1990) found similar use of government housing in Kumasi.

Renting is probably the most important income-generating activity related to housing. Indeed, in Africa it probably provides the majority of the poor with their dwellings. In Kumasi, for example, about 55 per cent of households live in rooms rented from a house-owner. Such owners are not necessarily any better off than their tenants (Tipple and Willis 1991). All over urban Africa, the income from renting a room or two allows many households to afford to own a home when otherwise they could not. Even squatter areas are showing increasing levels of renting (e.g. Schlyter 1987).

Scope for Support to Employment Generation in Shelter Provision

Despite its advantages, the informal sector has been neglected or harassed in much of sub-Saharan Africa in favour of an inefficient formal sector even though its current output is a major part of most countries' housing development. This is partly owing to the unregulated fashion in which informal sector SSE's tend to operate, without labour regulations, regular tax payments, and the urban regulatory framework.

Small-scale contractors are central to the implementation of policies to increase employment potential in the shelter sector, but their participation involves give and take on both sides. If they are to be assisted by the public sector to take a more central role, they must co-operate more with regulating bodies in order to benefit from the change of attitude which public authorities are urged to make. The dilemma of the informal sector is that its participation in the formal economy may involve changes that mean the loss of its economic advantage (Hansenne 1991). How far this will be true is, as yet, unknown but we must monitor progress carefully if we are not simply to advocate the continuation of exploitation as a strategy to gain employment opportunities for the poor.

Large-scale contractors should be encouraged to make better use of labour-based technologies; to behave more like small-scale contractors in technology choices. Government and large formal-sector organizations should encourage labour-based techniques through project design and funding; they should use, and engage contractors who use, labour-intensive methods. The ILO has had enough success in its training programmes and pilot projects in labour-based infrastructure development to give us confidence that shelter can utilize similar techniques. The Namuwongo Market parking area in Kampala, Uganda, demonstrated that cement blocks were as effective as tarmac but generated many more jobs. The labour-based roads contractor training programmes in Kenya, Ghana and Botswana have been successful in creating a cadre of labour-based contractors, in the generation of rural jobs, and in the standard of road constructed (UNCHS/ILO 1995). Experiments in South Africa have also been encouraging, even where the political and security context were less favourable. In Soweto, a land drainage project was designed to replace huge spun concrete pipes with a lined concrete and stone drain that could be constructed by hand (Watermeyer 1993). House-building projects are similarly adaptable, as the SHC experience in Ghana demonstrates (Mensah 1997), or through technologies such as the *pisé* building method (Tipple 1993a). International donors should take a lead here, considering employment and poverty alleviation through the implementation phase as a serious component in measuring project success. However, great care must be taken not to exploit low-cost labour and to include training for any suitable members of the workforce as a project component.

Local government and other public-sector bodies are also urged to adopt a more supportive role towards informal-sector, small-scale enterprises, and labour-based technologies either in their own direct works, when contracting to the private sector, and in their maintenance functions. If shelter and infrastructure are to keep up with demand, partnerships between public authorities and the private sector must become part of local government activity. However, there is a need for a change of political culture away from a hierarchical rule from above towards democratization and empowerment of people and their communities (Rondinelli and Cheema 1985). This will require new skills, moving away from technical functions to managerial and enabling functions, substituting engineering skills for public relations and project management.

In the past, community initiatives in settlement upgrading and servicing have relied on unpaid labour. However, this is neither ideal nor necessary. Under the ILO's distinction between major and minor works (Lyby 1992), all but the most local tasks should involve paid labour drawn from the neighbourhood. Communities have shown their ability to take on contracts for local infrastructure work (UNCHS 1991) and could be encouraged to do the same in house construction. Community contractors share most of the strengths of small-scale enterprises discussed above but also have great potential for instilling confidence and pride in the environment in members of poor neighbourhoods who take part in their activities. They are being encouraged in Sri Lanka (UNCHS 1991) and there seems to be little to prevent their success in Africa.

Under the current enabling approach to housing arising from the Global Strategy for Shelter (UNCHS 1990), greatly increased levels of housing supply are aimed for. While, in the recent past, housing policies have concentrated on helping households to develop their own housing, there are efficiency gains to be made by addressing the relationship between contractors and the housing process. As I have pointed out elsewhere (Tipple 1994a), instead of addressing policy and support to individuals to build a single dwelling (the interface between the householder and the house), attention should be focused on enabling contractors to build dwellings more efficiently (the contractor/house interface) and assisting householders to obtain good work at a fair price (the householder/contractor interface). The contractor/house interface should be lubricated by ensuring that the inputs to housing supply are in place and available to small-scale contractors and that they can obtain access to credit against staged payments, insurance, advice on site management and labour relations, etc. The householder/contractor interface requires potential householders to be informed about contracting, perhaps with model contracts, advice on payment, householders to be empowered to demand good value for money, and the settlement of disputes.

Clearly, while the informal sector is disadvantaged, the cheapest housing available is less efficiently provided than it need be. Legal, institutional and financial measures are required to integrate the informal sector into the mainstream of the economy without removing its competitiveness. Land supply and the regulations governing buildings are important fields for government action to ease the supply of housing by the informal sector. Unless small builders can access land to build on and obtain credit to finance the first few houses, they will not be able to build ahead of demand and will be locked into the *ad hoc*, single house development which is the mainstay of housing supply in most urban areas in Africa but which lacks the efficiency to provide enough housing for all the people. Some form of training, finance, servicing and involvement in government contracts should also be offered to small-scale enterprises (Hansenne 1991, Mensah 1997).

Legislation affecting small-scale enterprises should aim to maximize their efficiency while progressively addressing labour standards issues to prevent exploitation and increase health and safety. Home-based enterprises should be recognized as important contributors to the poorest households' economies and to the country as a whole. The best policy for current home-based enterprises is tolerance and non-intervention (Gilbert 1988) while allowing them to be eligible for small business loans, training assistance, etc. It is proposed, however, that it should be possible to use loans for small businesses to extend the home for business use (Tipple 1993b).

As UNCHS/ILO (1995) suggest, assistance targeted at small-scale enterprises and implementation of labour-based infrastructure works are likely to benefit the poor as they will largely involve the poorest workers. Assistance should also be given to the construction of rental housing through the private sector, especially as rental rooms adjoining owner-occupier houses.

Proposals for specific project measures financed and technically assisted by the international donor community are as follows:

- Employment generation should be included as a main criterion in programme design.
- Mixed uses in the form of home-based enterprises should be promoted initially in pilot projects to allow some assessment of their costs and benefits in a newly-built environment.

There is a need for future research into:

- The costs and benefits of labour-based approaches to urban works and services,

- The implications of home-based economic activities on residential environments and income generation,
- The effectiveness of alternative dissemination paths for research on building materials and technologies, and
- Alternative financial institutions for the working poor.

Clearly, the public sector, NGOs and international donors have an important role as enablers and encouragers in the process of maximizing employment opportunities in the provision of housing and infrastructure in the coming decades.

9. *uTshani Buyakhuluma* (The Grass Speaks): People's Dialogue and the South African Homeless People's Federation[1]

JOEL BOLNICK

The South African Homeless People's Federation

The South African Homeless People's Federation is a social housing movement for the urban poor. It was established in 1994 as the formalized network of autonomous local organizations running housing savings schemes. Its national character, active membership, autonomy and high level of participation make it one of the most important social housing movements in Africa.

The Federation is a close-knit network of community-based organizations from all over South Africa. They are united by a common development approach. All member organizations are rooted in shack settlements, backyard shacks or hostels. All of them are involved in savings and credit managed by the communities themselves. Men are not excluded, but the vast majority of Federation members are women. The organizations are all fighting for security of land tenure and affordable housing for their members. The Federation is decentralized and power and decision-making are the sole responsibility of the organizations themselves.

A number of regional and national groups have developed in response to the Federation's rapid growth which facilitate interaction between the autonomous organizations which make up the Federation and provide support. One of these, the People's Dialogue, is an NGO which initially created space for the Federation to emerge and which now acts as a support arm of the Federation.

The Federation's activities are as extensive as is their outreach to informal settlements throughout the country. While shelter issues remain the Federation's most prominent focus this is by no means their only savings-related activity. The national and regional structures have several other activities that grow out of savings and credit and these, in turn, are replicated at settlement level. The Federation's work includes, exchange programmes (both in South Africa, the rest of Africa, in India and other Asian countries), community-based training and information gathering, technical- or construction and planning-related support, uTshani Loans, micro-enterprise activity and land identification. Constraints of space mean that this article can only address three of these activities in detail: the housing savings schemes, the community-based training and enumeration and the uTshani loan scheme.

Housing Savings Schemes

In the Federation people are mobilized through savings. From the outset, members of savings schemes practice self-reliance as they guide and run their own organizations with their own resources. Though it has no political affiliation, the Federation is sometimes referred to as the black consciousness movement of the urban poor. The housing savings scheme affirms the dignity and agency of the homeless poor.

Housing savings schemes are made up of groups who save regularly. Though men are not excluded, the majority of members are women. All members of the Federation must belong to one of these schemes. While members can save only a small part of the total cost of housing construction, the Federation perceives a much more complex relationship between its savings schemes and housing finance. They have no illusions that the savings will be adequate for building houses but emphasize the importance of saving for mobilizing poor people, ensuring high levels of participation, for the creation of space for the participation of women and enabling community organizations to learn to manage finances.

Savings are banked locally and used to provide small-scale finance to members for emergencies and for supporting income-generating activities. All matters relating to the management of these finances are determined locally and are undertaken by treasurers, book-keepers and collectors drawn from the scheme's members.

Housing savings schemes concentrate the resources and the knowledge of the communities. This tends to create tensions because established patriarchal organizations, accustomed to controlling resource flows and dominating development in informal settlements, perceive these groups as threats to their power. Over time, many of these organizations recognize that the housing savings schemes are an enormous asset to their communities. Instead of seeking to undermine them, they give them support, understanding that by supporting the schemes they maximize the development opportunities of their communities.

The number of savers and of housing savings schemes is growing rapidly. Between 1993 and 1998 the numbers of saving schemes increased from 58 to 1 200; the numbers of individual savers increased from 2 178 to more than 55 000. Some are stronger then others but most are the strongest organizations in their communities. They are not strong in terms of access to force or to power but strong in terms of empowering their members and creating the space for them to make their own life decisions and carry them out. Many of them have also initiated small-scale emergency loans and loans to support income-generating activities to ensure that the money that is collected reduces their vulnerability to economic shocks and supports local development activity.

Following the elections in April 1994, the government continued to prepare and enact strategies and policies designed to promote the formal-sector delivery of low-income housing. At that time, the People's Dialogue managed to raise approximately Rand 4 million to initiate a capital fund for loan finance and the Federation started designing houses with the assumption that their members would have to bridge all the costs through loan finance. Later in 1994 the new housing minister committed the government to supporting the People's Dialogue fund with a grant of R10 million. By June 1995, the Federation was ready to start building houses and in the following year, the number of housing construction starts by members increased rapidly. Negotiations with government continued throughout 1995 to 1998 with the aim of obtaining direct access of members to the government's capital subsidy.

Community-based Training and Enumeration

Contrary to the perceptions of the formal sector, poor communities are the major producers of houses and will continue this role in the future. Among the poor, women play the role of designers and often partial builders. Yet the communities rarely acknowledge this role and poor women generally do not feel proud of their creations. It is natural for women to take this role, since it is they who aspire to better living conditions for their families. However their lack of *opportunity* and *recognition* makes it difficult for them to feel confident enough to help create alternative designs for houses and amenities.

The experience of South African squatter leaders when they visited India reinforced an awareness within South Africa that, in order to upgrade informal settlements, communities must get organized, declare to themselves and to the state what they want and be prepared to participate in the redevelopment of their communities. South African members of the Federation *participated directly* in training programmes developed by their Indian partner, Mahila Milan and adapted elements appropriate to the South African context. They subsequently incorporated similar programmes into their other activities in settlements where housing savings schemes were flourishing and were strong enough to begin housing development.

The training programme is appended to the Federations's exchange programmes. As a result, each settlement in need of such community-driven training automatically becomes a training and learning ground for a number of other areas. Collectives of men and women belonging to housing savings schemes from many areas gather together and participate in this process. The strategy is simple. Women who have mastered the training process work with men and women from other settlements who are also eager to learn. This is all done in an atmosphere of excitement, festivity and camaraderie which helps to create a good learning environment. After an initial evening of socializing, the community volunteers plan the exercise. First groups are formed and each is allocated an area in the settlement. During the first day, each team goes over their assigned area at least four times, doing different tasks each time. In this way they become completely familiar with the physical layout and the population profile of their area.

In the first instance the teams count huts and families. It is important to count families as well as dwellings, since there is often more than one family in one hut. This information is given to and collated by someone from the community. A large map of the area is created in the process, noting houses, roads and churches etc. Finally sections are created on the map and houses numbered. Mobilization accompanies training and the number of participants grows rapidly and the work speeds up.

In the afternoon, the household enumeration begins, utilizing a simple standardized format identifying household composition by age, sex, education, occupation and income. In addition the team collects migration histories of the families, their savings and investment histories and their participation in organizational processes. About one quarter of the households are enumerated with the help of outside participants. At the end of the data-gathering process, one set of people begins to compile the information while another set works with sections of the community to begin house and settlement modelling.

These exercises ensure that everyone working together has developed a detailed understanding of their settlement. The last task is for the participants to design new houses and neighbourhoods. Before long, cardboard boxes, tins and other such tools are used to build models. Women do very well in this process; they bring their understanding of the use of space and the needs of their families to the design process.

By sunset on the first day, there are processions coming from all parts of the settlement. People take their models and layouts to the centre and, in the midst of a community gathering, explain the features of their design. Everyone is sheepish about the clumsy models but nevertheless proud of them. The day ends with everyone talking about what they have learnt from this process.

What happens on the first day is that the energy of local residents and residents from other areas creates the conditions for taking entire settlements through an educational process through which they can talk about their own areas, their structures and their layouts in a collective way. Because the process purposely creates conditions to allow women to take a central role in the proceedings, it unlocks the knowledge and skill women have developed in the creation and management of their homes.

Until they go through this process, communities tend to believe that only professionals can perform this task and they abdicate from contributing to the changes that are needed for their settlement's improvement. Once a training process has been launched, the people have a set of ideas and inputs which can guide the formalization of the design. When professionals arrive, they can add value to the people's ideas and actions. When the team disbands on the second day, the outsiders leave and their jobs are taken over by the local people supported by the trainers. These activities are a way of helping communities understand what changes can be guided by their needs, how the process occurs and what to expect at the end of the process. At this point, the Federation provides technical advice and training at their Building Information and Training centres.

The uTshani Funds for Housing Loans

One of the more ambitious element of the Federation's activities has been the establishment of a credit mechanism controlled by the homeless themselves. This is called the uTshani Fund.

From the outset, the network of homeless poor that was to become the Homeless People's Federation realised the importance of access to credit. This need was one of the main motives for starting housing savings schemes. Whilst the homeless poor possess energy, initiative, skill and experience in abundance, they lack the material resources to transform their situation. The Alliance decided in 1993 that the only way around this problem was for People's Dialogue to assist the Federation in establishing its own finance scheme. After a period of capacity-building the uTshani Fund began operations in January 1995. This fund is managed on a day-to-day basis by People's Dialogue staff in Cape Town. The fund's executive decision-making structure is a governing body comprised by representatives from each of the nine regions in the Homeless People's Federation and the Federation's three national convenors.

The uTshani Fund was initiated with European donor support. Obviously for any housing finance scheme to reach a large number of households, more funding had to be found. Late in 1994, the late Housing Minister Joe Slovo offered the Federation a grant of R10 million to enable it to expand the reach of the uTshani Fund. This was done in the hope of demonstrating the effectiveness of this model in order to provide a mechanism to reach very low income households. This offer was maintained by the new Minister, Sankie Mthembi-Mahanyele, although there were considerable delays before the funds were secured. The uTshani Fund has historically been incorporated as a part of People's Dialogue, and has needed no separate legal standing of its own. This is an adequate and appropriate arrangement, since the uTshani Fund only works with the Federation. However as a result of concerns expressed the National Housing Department, a further organization was required.

This separate legal holding body, known as uTshani Trust, now serves as a conduit for the Department's R10 million grant. The agreement was drafted so that the uTshani Trust would be able to channel funds from government or other donors to the uTshani Fund and thence to the Federation in a highly transparent and accountable way. The trustees are drawn in equal proportions from government and the Federation. The Trust is audited and its records are open to inspection by government at any time. Now that the R10 million has been drawn down (and repaid) the trust funds are passed over to the Federation and the only remaining obligation to the government is an annual audit and report on activities.

The Trust has been structured in such a way that any grant, subsidy, government allocation, or other sum can be channelled through it and remain subject to the same procedures governing the R10 million grant. This makes it possible for the Trust to act as a legal conduit for other forms of government assistance to the Federation, whether in the form of housing subsidies, grants to building centres, or further seed capital for loan finance. This conduit is now being used by the Department of Welfare and the Land Bank as well.

The disbursement of funds by the actual Fund, is fairly straightforward. The uTshani Fund makes finance available directly to housing savings schemes. Any scheme is eligible to apply for an uTshani loan. In order to apply, a scheme must provide affordability assessments for the potential borrowers and building plans. Schemes which are new to housing loans normally receive finance for a group of ten members. Second and subsequent groups may be larger. Once the member's monthly repayments have been worked out, uTshani Fund staff determine the amount which can be borrowed over a 15 year period at a simple interest rate of one per cent per month. If necessary, the housing savings scheme then adjusts its house designs to build within this budget.

Once the money has been advanced, the scheme distributes the funds to members and is responsible for all further aspects of local loan management. Loans are disbursed to members in the form of building materials, not cash. Great emphasis is placed on simplicity and transparency. The schemes are encouraged to hold weekly and bi-weekly meetings with open access to information. Book-keeping, the release of funds, the distribution of building materials and the management of the construction process are undertaken by the members. Support is provided by other Federation groups in the course of regular settlement-to-settlement schemes to follow their loan balance and repayments. Thus, the uTshani Fund develops systems which fit with the systems evolved by the savings schemes and not the other way around. By April 1998, the fund made 2 915 loans, disbursing over R23 million with a repayment rate of 95 per cent.

It is clear that improved housing has made a difference to both the physical comfort and self-respect of those with new houses. The maximum size loan of R10 000 (the most popular loan) is sufficient to purchase the materials and employ a skilled builder for a 54-square-metre, two-bedroom house with a living room and kitchen, a corrugated iron roof and re-use of some materials. (Unskilled labour from the household is contributed free of charge.) These houses are considerably cheaper than the private sector alternatives which the people would not be able to afford. A contractor-built house of the same size would cost an estimated R45 000. The average monthly loan repayments are now between R100–120.

A loan of R10 000 is probably only affordable by those with an income of R700 a month (which is currently about the average in the Federation) on uTshani fund terms and conditions of an interest rate of 12 per cent per annum and a 15 year loan. The households that manage to obtain the capital housing subsidy of R7 500 from the government will only have to raise R2 500 through loan finance. The repayments for a loan of this size are affordable by a wider income group.

The Fund is obliged to deal with some contradictions. The major ones are not of its own making nor does the problem lie with the Federation. There has been a lot of thought in recent months within People's Dialogue and the Federation about what function the Fund is really performing in terms of national housing policy and delivery. The Fund is covering up for the failure of the government's housing subsidy programme. By giving large loans to very poor households, the uTshani Fund is helping them to build houses but at the expense of burdening them with a large debt for many years.

This problem has arisen because the government's subsidy system for housing is inaccessible to the very poor, even if they are organized in housing savings schemes. This is because a low-income household can only get the housing subsidy for a housing unit built by a contractor. Thus, it is the contractor who builds 'the low-cost housing unit' for the poor whilst low-income households cannot get the subsidy directly to support their own efforts to build or improve their homes. By borrowing the full cost of their house from the uTshani Fund, the Federation members are providing their own 'bridging finance' for an indefinite period.

The Federation/People's Dialogue Alliance is constantly challenging the discrimination against the poor within the subsidy system and in several provinces has successfully negotiated for direct release of subsidies to housing savings schemes. This has been an effective way to achieve a lasting victory for the people's housing process. It has now enabled the uTshani Fund to make smaller loans, thus reducing the time needed to repay the loans and the interest rate charges, and will enable many more of the tens of thousands of families linked to the Federation to build houses.

Conclusion

The People's Dialogue/Homeless People's Federation Alliance has managed to take advantage of an historic window of opportunity that was opened by the birth of the new South Africa. This created an environment that was extraordinary in the chance it provided for innovation and experiment. The ability of the Alliance to maximize this opportunity came directly from its grassroots practice. By creating a framework which ensured that local community-level initiatives were self-conscious and autonomous and by developing systems which maximized decision-making and control at grassroots level, the Alliance was able to edge government towards the provision of support for a people's housing process. In a very uneven and incomplete way the Alliance has been able to hold government accountable to its professed mandate of supporting the 'marginalized' and the poor. This has not been easy or unproblematical. Tensions and contradictions have increased rather than diminished as the Alliance has made headway. Many of the challenges now come from the fact that the Federation's very successes in developing appropriate mechanisms for a people's housing process has propelled it into a pioneering role in which its formal partners in government still struggle to understand the dynamics of the process.

The poor women and men of the South African Homeless People's Federation can thank their own extraordinary resourcefulness for the progress they have made.

10. Diversity in Practice: An international NGO's experience of micro-finance

HELEN PANKHURST and DEBORAH JOHNSTON

Introduction

This chapter highlights some of the experiences of ACORD in using micro-finance as a strategy for urban poverty alleviation in Africa. ACORD, the Agency for Co-operation and Research in Development is an international development organization working in over 17 countries in Africa, with a secretariat based in London. In its field programmes, staff are, almost exclusively, nationals of the relevant country. Programmes generally focus on long-term development issues rather than short-term emergency responses.

This chapter overviews ACORD's micro-finance experiences in Africa, with particular concentration on the Horn. These are analysed within the context of the wider theoretical debates and the practice in micro-finance schemes. The concluding section highlights the key themes that emerge from ACORD's urban programmes.

A Short History

ACORD, like most other NGOs, has its history in rural development. Urban work was avoided because of a perception that working in towns would exacerbate urban migration and from a sense that urban poverty was less acute and, in absolute terms, less characteristic of Africa's poverty. Urban programmes did, however, start emerging, primarily due to an increased incidence of 'refugee-affected urbanization' and ACORD's conflict-related work. There was also a gradual recognition of the validity of working on urban poverty. By its twentieth anniversary in 1996, ACORD had a network of over 40 programmes. Nine programmes, in five different countries, were urban, and at least two other programmes had a partial urban content. Of the total, eight were situated in the Horn – the area where most of ACORD's refugee- and conflict-related work took place.

Around the same time, ACORD had twenty-two micro-finance programmes and it was estimated that 20 000 poor people had been supported (ACORD 1997:6). Overall, 40 per cent of these clients were women. In early 1998, there were five programmes in the Horn, eight programmes in central Africa, two in southern Africa and seven in West Africa. However, only five programmes involved micro-finance as a central activity: two in Ethiopia, two in Sudan and one in Eritrea. All had a strong focus on women, with proportions of women beneficiaries ranging from 30 to 75 per cent. Other programmes had 'minor' micro-finance components but were primarily oriented towards activities such as water provision, health services and agricultural activities. Some programmes, particularly those in West Africa, involved the provision of credit in-kind, usually in the form of animals. Overall, both ACORD's urban and its major micro-finance programmes have been mainly in the Horn.

From Credit to Micro-finance

ACORD first embarked on a formal finance programme in 1984, as part of its programme in Sudan's north-eastern city of Port Sudan. The work reflected the growing belief that credit could overcome obstacles facing poor people through access to a fund that could remove constraints associated with insufficient liquidity (Hulme and Mosely 1996, Robinson 1994, Yagub 1995). Gradually, ACORD's initial concern with credit widened, first, to an inclusion of savings and then, to a more general focus on micro-finance.[1]

The move away from credit-only schemes reflected ACORD's incorporation of academic findings suggesting the importance of a wider concern with the networks in which poor people operated. There were also practical experiences suggesting that the financial needs of the poor could also be met through savings services and that the incorporation of savings opportunities increased people's 'ownership' of schemes and provided incentives to repay (ACORD 1992: section 2.10).

In the Horn, all the credit programmes came to have a savings component, though the attention given to this varied considerably. In some programmes there was a forced savings or collateral component, i.e., people could only borrow against a proportion of their savings. Also, in some cases the savings could not be accessed, functioning only as a guarantee for as long as the individual remained in the scheme. In other cases, a flexible savings scheme operated, individuals being able to build up or draw down balances as they wished.

Despite the increased sophistication of the savings schemes, primarily outside Sudan where authorizations to collect savings were limited by government legizlation to formally recognized banking institutions, it is clear that the savings component is still very much an add-on in ACORD's programmes, not as carefully developed as the credit delivery mechanisms. If the solution to poverty is thought to lie primarily in additional sources of capital, then clearly development organizations' and people's own prioritization of credit over savings is incontestable. However, it is also about reducing insecurity as well as providing new expanded possibilities. The contribution to be made through a safe savings scheme is often underestimated, despite the importance that women in particular attach to it.

A problem for many of ACORD's programmes, and especially those in Sudan and Angola, is the effect of inflation. This is often not dealt with in textbooks on micro-finance. When it is, the argument is made that inflation creates distortions to the financial market and micro-finance schemes should not be carried out (Yaqub 1996). In particular, these distortions and the eroding effect of inflation on both loan funds and on savings initiatives make it extremely difficult to achieve financial sustainability (Rhyne and Otero 1994:19, Nagarajan 1997:17-20, McGeehan 1998). Some practitioners have argued that, under such circumstances, NGOs should withdraw from financial service provision. However, ACORD has continued operating, despite the difficulties of achieving financial sustainability, believing that microfinance remains a useful development tool, even in such contexts.

In addition to the direct provision of savings and credit opportunities, some of ACORD's programmes also became engaged in 'indirect' microfinance activities. These involved: building relationships between local people and banks or other financial institutions; training groups in the use of credit funds; and acting as a conduit for the micro-finance programmes of other organizations, particularly government schemes. Finally, the Ethiopia programmes operated through existing burial associations, i.e., traditional community insurance and mutual support structures. People belonging to the associations paid regular fees and attended funeral functions. In exchange, the funeral costs of a member of the household or near relative were met by the organization. Members provided logistical and moral support. Thus, a new credit and savings structure was built upon an existing traditional insurance scheme.

Group vs. Individual

Some of ACORD's programmes disbursed credit directly, undertaking all aspects of delivery, from identification and selection to policing the scheme. Others – most of the schemes in the Horn – have found a variety of ways to channel credit through existing or created local groups. The process of administering and enforcing credit recovery was therefore shared between community groups and ACORD staff. Structures have included loan advisory committees (Sudan), and village loan committees (Eritrea) and the executives of existing community-based organizations (Ethiopia).

Most schemes provided micro-finance services to individuals; i.e. credit is borrowed and repaid by an individual for her or his and their household's usage, irrespective of the existence of a community-group structure underpinning the scheme. In a minority of cases, however, a group work could also borrow money for group-based income-generation. For example, among other activities, the Seraye scheme supported groups of female ex-fighters in setting up a general-purpose retail shop. Likewise the Addis Ababa programme included support to a group jointly undertaking urban agriculture. Problems of group disintegration have, however, plagued ACORD's work in joint income-generating initiatives. In contrast, individual borrowing has proved more successful and is therefore predominant.

Financial Sustainability vs. Poverty Alleviation

ACORD schemes attempting poverty reduction in the very short-term have not turned to financial intermediation. Instead, they have relied on relief aid and grants in order to quickly transfer a subsidy to needy groups. Loaning money over a period of time provides a less valuable immediate input but one which can service more people over a greater period. Analysis suggests that the recurrent and embedded nature of poverty requires solutions which people can continue to rely on. A revolving loan allows the money to be circulated and thereby to be used and reused by a greater number of people.

However, once the decision is made to develop a revolving loan fund, the problem for all NGOs arises of how far to pursue future benefits over present subsidies. The 'harder' the terms of the loan, the more sustainable the fund and the more people will benefit over the lifetime of the scheme. However, the 'harder' the terms, the more unfavourable the scheme becomes for its *present* users and the less it is able to meet the objective of rapid poverty reduction. There is an associated gender dimension: more expensive loans disproportionately penalize women given their reduced access to high-yielding investment opportunities.

The balance between poverty alleviation in the face of current poverty versus the creation of a scheme that can provide a service beyond the immediate present has been achieved in different ways by ACORD's programmes. Schemes that originated in a concern with welfare or as an adjunct to other major programme components have tended to have 'softer' terms. For example, in many of its central African programmes, ACORD provides funds on concessionary terms (either no interest rates or low interest rates) to those affected by HIV/AIDS as part of a more general support package. 'Soft' loans were adopted in practice, although there was debate within ACORD about whether, even in such cases, the subsidized system was in danger of being hijacked for the benefit of the more influential and whether or not it was inciting people to invest in suboptimal activities which would collapse as soon as the subsidy ended.

ACORD schemes where micro-finance was a major activity have tended to have market-related ('harder') terms and a greater concern with sustainability. In both the Eritrean and Ethiopian programmes, interest rates were real and costs greater than those charged by the banks – yet still well below the rates charged by moneylenders in the informal economy. In both these countries it was hoped that the programmes would foster the formation of a long-term facility which would be self-sustaining after ACORD's withdrawal. In Sudan, the necessity of addressing the issue of phase-out became increasingly apparent given the choice between closing-down in the face of dwindling funding, or increasing the charges to ensure that the internal revenue covered the administrative costs of continuing to run the scheme.

Loan Conditionality

Some of ACORD's Horn programmes adopted a tied lending approach (i.e. restricting the use to which the loan can be put, usually focusing on investment in production). Others have been more flexible, allowing people greater choice in the use of loans.

The two early Sudan programmes prioritized credit for investment, formal feasibility studies being undertaken before credit provision was accepted. In addition, because of the restrictions of Islamic finance, the credit was in-kind, involving the loan deliverer in the purchase of goods. Some flexibility was introduced, however, through different forms of finance acceptable under Islamic regulations. These included *musharaka* (a system of profit-sharing between lender and borrower based on the analysis of the enterprise to be undertaken), *murabaha* (based on a fixed mark-up on a loan and attached to a particular activity), and, exceptionally, *gard hassan* (an interest-free loan also for a particular purpose).

The Eritrean scheme was also investment-based and loans were likewise disbursed on the basis of feasibility studies. By contrast, in the Ethiopian schemes, loans were not tied. Prioritization criteria for who could borrow money, for what purpose and over what period, were chosen by the community-based organizations (CBOs). Their decisions were pragmatic not formulaic: all members had a right to funds in turn. However, people with particular constraints tended to be given higher priority and there was usually a graduation to larger loans.

While there is no comparative evaluation of impact across the schemes, the practice of tying loans and carrying out standard feasibility studies has clearly been inefficient and ineffective. Furthermore, policing the scheme is expensive in staff time. More fundamentally, poor people need access to capital for a range of different reasons. Sometimes, they need it to meet unexpected needs, such as funeral expenses. At other times, there is a regular, seasonal constraint, for example during hungry periods before the harvest. At all times, there is interconnectedness in poor people's investment and consumption activities, particularly for women. If poor people cannot meet the range of their needs for funds through the credit scheme, they will either sell off precious assets or borrow from alternative, more expensive sources.

In our view, it is advantageous both for the individual and for the scheme to allow credit funds to be used for consumption/social needs. Poverty alleviation is best met by a system that people will protect because they believe that it is of benefit to them, and to be of benefit, it must be flexible enough to respond to their different needs. There is increasing support for this view (Johnson and Rogaly 1997:48, Rhyne and Otero 1994:15). In effect, whether the loans are provided for investment or consumption becomes irrelevant. What is important is that there is an analysis of the ability to repay and that it is in people's interest to borrow, i.e., that the loan provides a solution.

Activity Mix

From the mid-1980s there was a drive in the wider academic literature towards a 'minimalist' approach, which concentrated exclusively on the delivery of an efficient and financially sustainable micro-finance scheme. This was based on the belief that financial liquidity is the crucial constraint for the poor. However, the complexity and interconnectedness of people's constraints was ignored by this approach. Johnson and Rogaly (1997:53) argue that a range of problems, other than financial, is likely to exist for poor people. Dawson and Jeans (1997) similarly suggest that the simplistic focus of minimalist credit schemes results in their failure to upgrade productive technology or productivity, although they do prove generally beneficial. It is our view that, in practice, the goal of sustainability, which is usually at the heart of the minimalist theory, although important, does sometimes obscure the objective of poverty reduction. There is no necessary trade off. However, when conflicts between the two do arise, as they do both in terms of targeting and in terms of the cost of impact assessment, the poverty objective may be sacrificed.

In ACORD's programmes, the way micro-finance fitted in with other activities varied. Furthermore, this 'mix' changed over time. For example, the Port Sudan programme began as an integrated urban development programme and then gradually focused on credit. The Kassala programme, also in Sudan, adopted an approach closer to the minimalist one, but it continued to invest in some gender training and research, although even this was dropped in the context of shrinking funding.

By contrast, the Seraye programme started solely as a credit-and-savings scheme. Over time, it was felt that for the programme to succeed there was an equally important training need to be met. The programme changed its goals to encompass the establishment of a training centre. In contrast, the Dire Dawa programme in Ethiopia had a multi-pronged focus from the beginning, with a parallel emphasis on infrastructural, gender and training components.

The main problems with the multi-pronged, 'credit-plus' approach, which characterizes most of ACORD's programmes, revolve around capacity constraints – people trying to do too much and ending up not doing anything well. Abugre identified a range of reasons why NGOs tend to implement credit programmes badly. He argued that NGOs remain averse to charging positive real interest rates and so undermine existing financial systems (Abugre 1992). They do not submit themselves to the discipline necessary for the provision of financial services, schemes are managed by untrained staff, and are often carelessly designed. Much of this arises from a lack of specialist experience in micro-finance, something particularly common to NGOs when credit became popular in the 1980s. Problems also arise from the attempt to mix different activities in one programme, as the same staff often carries them out. For this reason, writers, like Otero (1994:99), argue that as a first step in moving into micro-finance programmes NGOs should concentrate first on financial services.

In the early nineties, external evaluations of ACORD programmes were interpreted as recommending a minimalist credit and savings scheme. In fact, they were more often arguing for a tightening-up of the financial management of the micro-finance element, and more strategic decision-making about other components. By the late nineties, amongst development practitioners and at ACORD, there was an acceptance of the need for much better financial analysis but there was also widespread disillusionment with the minimalist approach. The overall conclusion we can draw from ACORD's experience is that there are dangers in both of these extremes (the integrated approach favoured by many practitioners and the 'minimalist approach' favoured in much of the financial systems literature). Success is most likely to follow from a well-planned, participatory process, rather than from a particular 'recipe'.

Community Involvement and Structures

ACORD has a range of experiences in terms of the kind, and extent, of community involvement in its urban credit schemes. In the Port Sudan programme, the credit and savings work was built upon a history of community outreach. The extension structures were, however, staffed by ACORD personnel. In contrast, the Kassala programme had a smaller history of community involvement; it likewise had developed a delivery process staffed only by ACORD personnel. As part of a rationalization process, both Sudanese programmes attempted to create community structures that would share the tasks of beneficiary selection, credit delivery and monitoring. The structures proved to be more successful in Port Sudan, arguably because of historical links to the community.

In contrast to both of these, the Seraye programme in Eritrea was conceptualized as a 'people-owned' process. This was because the money initially used to set up the revolving fund was local money belonging to the community. At one level, participation was embedded in the scheme, through group formation, election of voluntary committees at the village level, a sub-provincial and a provincial board. However, strategic changes to scheme design and the practical implementation side was developed and managed by ACORD staff. Ownership by the community through an elected process was not achieved, despite the ideas on paper. This may have been because ACORD's energy was focused on financial sustainability and impact, and not on institutional ownership.

Institutional ownership was not – and is still not – given as much focus in the general literature on micro-finance. However, the practical need to hand over schemes has meant that ACORD has had to tackle ownership issues. With phase-out on the horizon in Eritrea, the establishment of village banks was experimented with. A few pilot villages were given financial and administrative independence from the overall regional scheme. At the same time, links with the local government structure had been strong, and a hand-over of the running of the scheme to regional government looked possible. However, before a clear institutional path had emerged, the national government decided to close down all international NGOs and the country went onto a military footing following tensions with Ethiopia.

In the Dire Dawa programme in Ethiopia the groups set their own rules and regulations about credit delivery from the beginning. The role of ACORD was one of training and guidance in improved financial management and transparency. Funds were only donated once the groups had raised an agreed proportion of money. This procedure increased the sense of local ownership of the fund. Individual savings, voluntary or compulsory, also maintained ownership. Where compulsory, a minimum rate was determined by the groups themselves.

In order to increase the longer-term impact of its work, the Dire Dawa programme initially planned to facilitate the emergence of 'superstructures' above the CBO level, which would act as a platform for advocacy and strategic action. Two paths were planned. A top-down one, based on an advisory board which it was thought might be able to take on an increasing role. This failed to happen, primarily because the constituency of board members was too diverse and too wide. The second path planned in parallel was to look out for an umbrella structure emerging from within CBOs. Should an incipient structure start to form, ACORD planned to encourage it and build its capacity. In the event, CBOs' common interests did start to emerge, but these turned out to be practical rather than strategic and to have a smaller interest group logic. In practice, rather than working together to look at external possibilities as envisaged, the CBOs came together to solve an internal constraint – the bureaucratic problem of the time needed to maintain accurate and transparent accounts. ACORD is now fostering these intermediary, functional linkages between groups of CBOs coming together to share bookkeepers.

Greater linkages to existing banks are one of the obvious solutions to the institutional problem of credit and savings delivery. ACORD's experience is that effective connection between banks and the poor can be forged where groups open bank accounts in their own name. However, ACORD has not succeeded in encouraging banks to loan directly to groups. A number of specific attempts in Ethiopia, Eritrea and Sudan at making banks more accessible to the poor have likewise failed. However, in countries facing high inflation and economic instability, tying community micro-finance schemes too tightly to nationally-controlled, bureaucratic banks is an unattractive option. On the other hand, to set the schemes up as independent networks can run up against national legislation, and this is likely to be increasingly the case as governments seek to bring NGO schemes in line with regulations governing formal-sector financial institutions.

Conclusion

Micro-finance appears particularly suited to urban areas because of the visibility of the informal sector and the proximity to markets. At the same time, the density of habitation means that schemes have a greater chance of success, as groups can be formed and can meet more easily. Furthermore, NGOs often find it easier to design schemes involving women in urban areas because of their greater social and geographic freedom. On the negative side, groups might be weak if there is a high-proportion of in-migrants and shifting residence within the urban area (Vandenberg 1997).

In addition, micro-finance schemes seem more appropriate to urban areas as many other income-generating tools used by NGOs present specific problems. Obviously, interventions aimed at agricultural inputs will be inappropriate (although the importance of urban 'agriculture' is increasingly recognized). Small business support schemes, the main alternative to micro-finance, have a poor record. Dawson and Jeans (1997) have listed the problems experienced, and they argue that these failures contributed to the general excitement about credit in the 1980s.

Micro-finance initiatives are currently a very popular tool for NGOs, particularly in urban contexts. This popularity arises largely from the realization that livelihoods and insecurity need to be targeted and that, otherwise, infrastructural support and improved services in health, education and shelter, etc. are unsustainable.

Micro-finance interventions seem to epitomize the characteristics needed for an effective development intervention. Clients make their own choices about source and means of livelihoods. This can be achieved at the same time as a high degree of both financial and institutional sustainability. Micro-finance therefore appears to combine the current obsessions with participatory development and sustainability/cost-effectiveness. Part of the innovative work by practitioners (ACORD included) within urban micro-finance initiatives has, therefore, been around levels and forms of community involvement in the drive towards more sustainable systems. These have increasingly handed administrative control to different forms of local structures with considerably more flexibility in fund-usage resulting in a more efficient and more valuable resource. The goal is democratic and financial accountability: flexibility and adaptability in the context of financial rigour and transparency.

There is also another reason for the current appeal of micro-finance initiatives among development practitioners, namely the combination of working within a community whilst being able to target support for the individual. The methodology that many of the programmes in ACORD, as elsewhere, seem to have adopted is group security and collateral, with individual usage of funds. This combination of individual liberty within a context of community supervision is attractive and our experience is that, particularly in the urban context, it tends to work. Furthermore, community organizations' capacity and confidence building are seen as a central and valued output of micro-finance delivery, rather than simply being considered as a by-product of the process. The difficulties lie in overseeing the development of a mechanism that local people own and protect and which continues to meet the needs of poor individuals at an affordable price.

Critiques of micro-finance programmes argue that socio-economic and political structures underpin the differentiation separating rich from poor. According to this view, unless underlying causal constraints are addressed, the financial micro-finance tool is more likely to work within existing inequalities, exacerbating the risks to the poor. From ACORD's experience, the danger is real and some poor urban people have suffered. However, the overall assessment from different internal and external evaluations is clearly that poor people have benefited significantly. Furthermore, the way that micro-finance schemes are implemented can start to challenge existing structures by the very provision of an alternative. For example, as with other agencies involved in micro-finance delivery, ACORD's record in terms of the involvement of women centrally within the urban micro-finance schemes and its gender analysis of impact is impressive – much more so than in its non-micro-finance programmes.

However, ACORD's experience suggests that micro-finance activities should be treated with caution and should only be carried out after considerable local research that considers 'up-stream' and 'down-stream' preconditions of success. These would include the quality of training, technology and social networks and the availability of inputs and access to markets. Micro-finance schemes should not be about universally transferable blueprints. Where credit is the main element of the scheme, credit needs to be identified as a key constraint, rather than assumed to be a panacea which can address all manifestations of poverty.

The variation in the design of schemes undertaken by ACORD and the lack of a uniform solution might at first seem surprising. However, it reflects as much the complex contexts within which urban development work takes place, as historical differences in the way programmes were established. Conflict, inflation, the constraints of Government legislation or of Islamic finance, and the prevalence of HIV/AIDS provide but some of the most visible and obvious factors within which many programmes operate. Wider political and economic contexts play a role, as do cultural and social differences in the relationship between individual and community and in attitudes to debt and to savings.

The design of ACORD schemes also needs to be interpreted within the wider debate about the efficacy of micro-finance programmes. Early attempts by NGOs to undertake credit and savings as a form of poverty reduction often suffered because insufficient attention was paid to sustainability issues, thereby undermining the concept of a revolving loan fund. At the other extreme, the eighties and early nineties seem to have seen the heyday of the theory of 'minimalist' credit, which allowed both academic and practitioner focus to shift to an analysis of the financial management of schemes with insufficient attention to impact, empowerment or ownership. Out of past experience a healthy middle ground can emerge, one in which the three objectives of financial sustainability, institutional ownership and social targeting are elaborated jointly. In each separate endeavour, and within the parameters set by national governments, community and NGO will need to work through these three key objectives, developing a process of participatory management. The result is an evolving diversity in practice.

11. Municipal Responses to Urban Poverty: A case study of Gaborone

A.C. MOSHA

Introduction

When Botswana, which occupies an area of 582 000 sq. kms, attained independence in 1966, the economic prospect seemed bleak. It was one of the poorest countries in Africa, but today, the country is financially strong. The government budget is in surplus, the balance of payments is secure, and international reserves are high and rising, currently standing at US$4.41 billion (Bank of Botswana 1996). In 1996, the per capita income was US$4 027 (equivalent to Pula 10 330).

The current population is estimated at 1 800 000 million. There is a declining mortality and relatively high fertility of the population which has resulted in a young population. Almost half (48%) are below the age of 15. The dependency, ratio even though it is expected to fall, will still remain high, about 66% by 2001 (Government of Botswana (GoB) 1991). This has far-reaching implications for the welfare and care of children especially against the background of a relatively high level of poverty prevailing in the country.

Today, in spite of having great wealth and a sound economy, Botswana is faced with problems of rural and urban development which have resulted in poverty. Poverty is endemic in the midst of plenty and incomes are highly skewed. The distribution of incomes is such that the poorest 40% of the people earn 11.6% of the national income; the next 40% earn 29.1% of the national income and the richest 20% earn 59.3% of the total income.

From several poverty assessment studies, including the most recent one of 1993–94, it has emerged that around 38% of Botswana's households were living in poverty; poverty was higher and more severe in rural areas and urban villages and that the proportion of Botswana living in income poverty has fallen sharply. Between 1985–86 and 1993–94 the proportion of poor and very poor households declined from 49% to 38%. Most of the decline in national poverty rates was due to a sharp fall in the proportion of very poor people in rural areas and also in urban villages. The incidence and severity of poverty in urban areas remained roughly unchanged. Female-headed households were poorer than male-headed households and their situation had improved less over the period from 1985/86 to 1993/94. Lastly, Botswana has been relatively successful in addressing capability poverty, but less successful in alleviating income poverty.

Compared to many other developing countries, Botswana has made significant progress in improving the standard of living of the poor, of rural dwellers and of women; but much remains to be done. Programmes introduced include the following: programmes implemented to increase or supplement incomes through employment creation; the giving of financial grants through the Financial Assistance Policy; the general expansion of government services, such as schools and health clinics, which also provided low-paid unskilled work for cleaners, night watchmen, cooks etc.; programmes such as self-help housing through site and services and squatter upgrading and a few others.

All in all, these policies and programmes have helped overcome some of the fundamental constraints to development in both urban and rural areas and have thus reduced the incidence of poverty. However, these programmes have not been enough to make up for the lack of jobs. Without addressing this lack it is impossible to make a dent in urban poverty. This is the backdrop against which we now examine and evaluate the various poverty-reduction initiatives undertaken at a lower level, i.e. by the municipality of Gaborone.

Municipal Responses to Urban Poverty: the City of Gaborone

After establishment of Gaborone as the national capital in 1963, it grew from a population of 3 812 to 6 000 by 1966. Since then, the city has been experiencing the highest population growth in absolute terms. Today it is estimated to have a population of 174 586 and it is projected to grow to a population of 342 029 in 2010 and 490 939 in 2021 (GoB-CSO 1995). Because of its status as the national capital and a major centre of economic activities, it has become a centre for employment opportunities with a magnetic attraction for immigrants seeking employment. This has led to the swelling of its population. Gaborone accounted for 10.1% of the country's total population in 1991 as against 6.3% in 1981.

Extent of poverty in the city
Urban poverty in the city has been due to a number of reasons – the chief one is rural-urban migration, as well as unemployment, a young population which in turn causes heavy dependency, the status of women in society and female-headed households.

The number of poor in the city is difficult to estimate, but official Household and Income Expenditure Studies (HIES) show that the number of those living below the poverty line are in the range of 40–45% (GoB 1996). Several studies (Kgosidintsi 1992:12) have identified the following as vulnerable groups in the city: recipients of direct feeding and supplementary feeding especially during droughts; the chronically destitute, whose numbers are quite small; disabled persons (1 273 in 1991, see CSO 1991); *de facto* female-headed households including teenage mothers; children in difficult circumstances including school drop-outs, street children and AIDS orphans.

The 1991 population census showed that in Gaborone, out of a total of 36 639 households, 24 361 were male-headed and 12 278 were female-headed. In all HIES studies it has been shown that the female-headed households are generally poorer than male-headed households, men having 2.6 times as much earning power as women in urban areas; in rural areas the ratio is 1.8 (GoB 1991). The rise in the numbers of teenage mothers is a most disturbing dimension of the female-headed household phenomenon. Already strained households are taxed further, with the grandmother or great grandmother becoming the main caretaker of the offspring.

The rise in population has also meant an increase in the labour force with little chance of all people getting employment. According to the 1991 population census, the total labour force in the city was 75 161 of which 44 831 were male and 30,330 are female with the bulk of these employed either in the formal or informal sectors. The greatest employer was manufacturing and construction at 32% and government with 31%, followed by sectors like wholesale, retail and communications at 20%; finance, insurance and business services 8% and community and personal services at 7% and agriculture 1% (GoB 1991: vol.1)

On the negative side, the economically inactive population numbered 27 563, the bulk of which were women 18 856, compared to 8 707 men. The majority were housewives (women without formal employment), followed by students. This forms the group that is prone to poverty and thus needs help.

In terms of employment opportunities, the most hard hit was the 15–19 years age group which makes up 12% of the city's population. The high level of unemployment within this group is because most of them do not have marketable skills and only attained low-level education. 42% of females were unemployed and 25% of males. The high youth unemployment rates may be linked to education since many of the Form II leavers are hardly employed (GoB 1996). To address the issue of poverty the municipal council with the help of central government and others have taken various poverty reduction measures and these are discussed below.

Municipal responses
Poverty-reduction initiatives to help the poor in the city have come mainly from the Gaborone City Council (GCC) with some help from NGOs, CBOs and the community at large. The Gaborone City Council has embarked on a number of its own and government-led programmes and projects aimed at poverty alleviation with a remarkable measure of success. The programmes cover various sectors including: social welfare activities, a destitute programme, a street children programme, housing for the poor, supporting the informal sector through the introduction of microenterprises and other more limited action.

Welfare programmes
The bulk of the poverty-alleviation activities are carried out by the Department of Social Welfare and Community Development which is currently facing a problem of shortage of manpower and poor co-ordination of its programmes. The department has been dealing with the problems of street children, the destitute, poor women abandoned by their husbands and now burdened with the task of raising their kids, unmarried teenage mothers etc. They have been assisted with help from donor agencies and NGOs. The department has also helped set up school youth groups and a youth advisory team. It also runs a home economics course and even organizes a Disabled Day to highlight the plight of the handicapped. As with some government departments, funding is not enough to cater for all the needs of the poor.

With the destitute programme, the deserving destitute are given help in the form of food, clothing, blankets and toiletries. Further, destitute families are not required to pay service levies unless they have working children. The council also provides housing for the destitute and there are now ten houses in Naledi and four in Broadhurst low-income areas. In addition to this there is also a temporary shelter in Gaborone West provided by a Roman Catholic church organization.

Help is also given to the children of the destitute and street children through a 'Needy Student Programme'. Children are sent to primary schools or brigade centres where they acquire survival skills. They are given school fees, boarding fees (where necessary), school uniforms, travel fares to and from school etc.

The Department of Social Welfare also provides meals to needy persons on a regular basis – at least two meals a day. If it cannot cope, it seeks supplementary help from other agencies like the Roman Catholic church, who engage in the same line of work. The department also provides burials for paupers where all costs are met by the Council.

Initiatives to provide access to land by the poor
In Gaborone, although land is somewhat restricted due to high prices, a confusing and expensive institutional framework, a costly land registration process, and high standards associated with its development, the poor have adequate access to land due to various initiatives that have been undertaken by government and the municipality.

Low-income people have access to subsidized serviced land in the city through a government-run programme that ensures that land is serviced before allocation. Residential low-income plots under this programme get a servicing subsidy of 32%, and for the middle-income lower group the subsidy is 23%

Again, low-income people in the city of Gaborone receive preferential treatment in acquiring a plot following the government policy on land allocation. The plot allocation system gives everybody an equal chance of owning a plot according to income – the poor go to the Self-Help Housing Agency (SHHA) department at the city hall where conditions for plot acquisition are simpler and the queues are shorter whilst middle-income people and the well-to-do join the queue at the Department of Surveys and Lands, Ministry of Local Government, Lands and Housing, for state land allocation where it can take upwards of ten years to get a plot. To increase affordability, plots are sold to would-be developers in instalments over a four-year period, thus easing the burden for the poor segments of the population.

Low-income people also have security of tenure on the land they occupy in the city under a simplified tenurial system. They occupy land under the Certificate of Rights (COR). The system was introduced in the 1970s as a means of providing a secure tenure for urban squatters and new plot holders in Self-Help Housing Agency schemes. The intention was to provide the urban poor with secure tenure while avoiding the complexities and cost of title registration. The state retains ownership and the plot-holder has the usufruct. It is perpetual, inheritable and transferable. It can be converted into 99 years Fixed Period State Grant (FPSG). In addition to the above, a person staying in a squatter area does get a Temporary Occupancy Permit, while waiting for the area to be upgraded, and once this is done, the permit can be upgraded to a Certificate of Rights. This permit is only for a year but can also be renewed.

Enabling physical planning practices

Poor residents in the city benefit from enabling planning procedures and regulations that the government has adopted in planning their areas. First, in the city there is equitable spatial organization with socially and economically mixed residential neighbourhoods to avoid low-income ghettoes. The policy implies that in the planning of a new district, provision is made for all income groups. This mixing is unique in the region.

Secondly, the country's development code is enabling for low-income people in that it attempts greater land use efficiency, setbacks are reduced, plot coverage is increased and informal economic activities are now allowed on residential plots where low-income people can try to earn a living. Hence we find a lot of small-scale activities in residential areas, including knitting and sewing, hairdressing salons, tailoring, furniture repair etc.

Thirdly, low-income people in Gaborone can develop their plots using watered-down and enabling urban development standards that were introduced for SHHA areas. These have been changed and improved over time, reflecting the government's concern to better the life of low-income people (Mosha 1993). The plot size in these areas is 375m^2, reduced from 450m^2 in 1991, and basic infrastructure is provided including earth roads, drains and stand-pipes. These plot sizes seem appropriate considering the cost of servicing them. Other features include flexible plot coverage percentages, flexible setbacks and flexible height-of-building standards.

Fourthly, there are specific watered-down or relaxed building regulations for low-income housing areas – the Building Control Grade II Dwelling Houses Regulations, 1981 (BCGIIR). Low-income people can use either temporary or permanent materials to build their houses so long as these are durable. The purpose of the regulations is essentially to enable the city council (or SHHA) to take action against structures which are clearly unsafe or unsuitable, rather than to provide a textbook on how houses should be built.

Housing the poor

As expected, the attractiveness of Gaborone to migrants has been part of the reason for a severe housing shortage in the city with the poor facing the greatest brunt. However, several programmes have been established to ensure suitable accommodation. Among these programmes are the following: low-cost housing through the Botswana Housing Corporation, a site and services and squatter upgrading programme administered by the Self-Help Housing Agency, a department of the City Council (under State Land Act – Cap32:01) which currently provides 52% of the housing stock in the city; accepting and legalizing the only informal settlement of Naledi in the city as a way of life; giving financial and material loans for housing and introducing the above-mentioned accelerated land servicing programme to produce residential plots in great numbers.

SHHA was introduced in the city and elsewhere in 1974 to provide an efficient means of allowing access to affordable housing for low-income groups. The approach was based on the concept of 'sites and services'. The programme sought to emphasise self-reliance and the spirit of self-help. Government prepares plots and certain basic physical infrastructure like earth roads, drains and stand-pipes for water and allocates these at subsidized prices to low-income people. Plots are allocated to citizens with low income, who are residents of the area concerned, employed or self-employed, not less than 21 years old, and who do not already own or lease another plot. The yearly income range for an eligible household is US$600–5 000. Plot prices are subsidized under the government policy of cross-subsidy whereby the people in these areas pay subsidized rates whereas those in high-income areas pay market rates. The plot holder is given several free plans to choose from and also has security of tenure.

Credit for building materials is available through a Building Materials Loan (BML) with a ceiling of US$1 200 and repayment at 9% over 15 years. Although it is felt that the loan is too small to make a contribution to the construction of a house, a number of people in the city who have taken such loans have failed to pay back due to poverty.

Access to municipal infrastructure and social services
While poor neighbourhoods in most Third World countries are not the first targets for road upgrading, water supply, sewerage, drainage or municipal solid waste collection, in Gaborone the situation is quite different. At least the basic services are provided and these are accessible to all those with a low income. The city infrastructure has been designed to allow for incremental upgrading as poor communities improve and their incomes and ability to pay for services increases.

Low-income areas are provided with free water stand pipes with each stand pipe servicing 20 plots; pit latrines have been the form of sanitation in SHHA areas but as from 1992, the policy has changed into a full sewerage system and the city is now busy introducing this system; and lastly solid waste is collected once a week.

As far as social services provision is concerned, the situation is also encouraging. Primary health care reaches all the poor. In both the council clinics and the government referral hospital, the service is virtually free to everybody as the cost per visit is less than one US dollar (equivalent to 4 Pula). AIDS victims are taken care of by the GCC's department of Social Welfare which is already spending a lot of energy and time counselling and taking care of HIV/AIDS patients.

Apart from the privately-run schools which charge exorbitant school fees, education in the city for all is free and the students also get free meals up to university level. For poor children, the Council or NGOs even provide school uniforms, so the lack of affordability is not a major cause of school drop outs.

As far as public transport in the city is concerned, the poor, though catered for by privately-run mini-buses, seem to have received a raw deal as most of the investment has gone into encouraging and accommodating the private car. Although in the planning of Gaborone some efforts have been made to reduce walking strain by the creation of local centres where locals can purchase their day to day needs without having to go to the city centre, by and large the transportation network is inefficient and unjust for the poor. It seems to prioritize a roads network for the private motor car, hence favouring the rich. There is no concerted effort towards an enabling mass transportation system, including footpaths and a bicycle network. Those who cannot afford public transport have to go on foot or by bicycle, but even then facilities in the city are unsatisfactory and more needs to be done in the future.

Municipal initiatives in the development of microenterprises
In the quest for low-income jobs in the city the GCC has created the climate for small-scale industries through the FAP. The GCC has zoned specific areas where the poor can carry on their activities; it has ensured that the poor traders are not harassed; licences are given for petty trading

etc. As a result, today in the city, several groups engage in microenterprises which, besides being survival strategies, contribute to economic development in a small way. Among these groups are: craftsmen, hawkers, daily labourers on building sites or in households, street children and food vendors. In 1994, it was estimated that 1 901 persons were employed, 8 out of 10 of whom were women (Toteng 1995).

In general, studies show that informal enterprises are dominated by production, procurement and supply and service types of activities. Most are new and the majority are single-employee firms. Roughly 40% employ between two and five persons and from 6 to 9% employ five persons. The majority (68%) of enterprises are owned by females. A number of these activities take place along the streets, on road reserves, in open spaces, on shop pavements or within the plots creating vast environmental problems (Mosha 1993:12).

The involvement of NGOs, CBOs and the grassroots in poverty alleviation

For a very long time non-governmental organizations (NGOs) have played an important role in alleviating the plight of the urban poor by reinforcing government, municipal and community activities. The only problem is that there is no co-ordination of these activities and so sometimes there is duplication of effort. There are several such organizations operating in the city. The Botswana Christian Council (BCC) is known to have participated in the provision of housing to individuals within the low-income groups. This NGO has helped the poor who have acquired SHHA plots but cannot raise the money to build their houses by providing interest-free loans. They sometimes provide all the necessary materials and labour and allow the owner to let out one room to ensure a return of their money. The Council has always provided bursaries for poor children and raised money for uniforms and even blankets.

A lot of other secular and church organizations run activities to help the poor. For example, the Roman Catholic Centre in Naledi provides school facilities for school drop-outs, runs evening classes for needy children and gives food and blankets to the poor; the St. Bernadette church at Gaborone West runs a community centre and a secondary school geared mainly towards the poor; the Lions Club, too, gives material help to the needy, raises money through charity walks to finance projects for the poor, helps destitute persons and rehabilitates the disabled and lastly the Nurses Association runs a feeding programme in Naledi.

Other NGOs include the Red Cross, which is actively involved in community-based rehabilitation of disabled children, raising money and clothes especially blankets for the poor and other material help at all times. The YWCA runs a commercial and ordinary secondary school for those who have not been able to enter the government schools, a hostel for girls, a day-care centre for working mothers and a number of fundraising programmes to help the needy. Co-operation for Research, Development and Education (CORDE), a service organization formed in 1986, promotes the activities of self-managed producer groups particularly the poor and has recently ventured into research on low-cost housing to provide a solution for the housing needs of the poor.

International organizations have also played some part, either directly or indirectly, in the efforts to alleviate the plight of the poor. The WHO is involved in water supply and sanitation and UNICEF has a three-year programme cycle of assistance and focuses on programmes aimed at the survival of mothers and children both in urban and rural areas. This organization has carried out studies that have touched upon poverty and lately participated in helping the government work out its Human Resources Initiative. The World Bank has been involved in squatter upgrading programmes within the city; USAID in developing appropriate planning standards; SIDA in planning and other organizations like the UNDP, NORAD and others have participated in one way or another by giving financial help in various development programmes in the city.

Apart from the help rendered by both the municipality, government, NGOs and international organizations, households and communities have sought various ways to alleviate the poverty afflicting them so that they can become self-reliant. Such independent activities have gained momentum and have become an acknowledged path towards urban improvement. Some studies have reported the existence of informal associations through which the poor meet some of their needs in the city (Feddema 1990). However, cast against the total background of need for assistance, they are comparatively small with internal limitations. Some of these efforts are as follows:

At the individual level:

- Multi-source income activity, combining part-time jobs in addition to a permanent job; beer brewing, seasonal jobs, full-time low-paid jobs like domestic service, cleaning in local institutions, moonlighting etc.
- Peddling merchandise either from office to office or from home to home.
- Depending on family or relations for income from the formally employed members of the household. Unfortunately, this puts a lot of burden on those employed, especially if the earned salary is low.
- Some individuals have opted for urban agriculture which either supplements their food requirements or provides supplementary cash incomes. The GCC has zoned and allocated land for such activities.

At community level:

There are several community groups in the city that have been formed to run community projects for the uplifting of the poor and the community as a whole. Currently, there are groups running day-care centres in low-income areas like White City, Naledi and Tsholofelo. Other groups help women learn skills like sewing, knitting or basket making.

Village Development Committees also run a number of projects to help the poor. They run day-care centres and five community centres located at Old Naledi, White City, Broadhurst, Bontleng and Lesedi managing recreational facilities, games, dancing, indoor games, cookery classes, knitting, handicraft activities etc.

It can be seen that grassroots associations are certainly involved in helping themselves and the poor and this potential should be exploited more in the future as Council money diminishes. The Gaborone City Council has to recognise the key importance of participation in terms of encouraging communities to be involved in the processes of decision making and influencing how resources are utilized, which also increases the self-esteem of individuals and households, and stimulates community organization. This way more will be achieved.

Conclusion: the Search for Future Poverty Reduction Initiatives

The above has amply demonstrated that with a wealthy economy a lot of enabling policies and programmes have been implemented by the Gaborone City Council to alleviate poverty in the city. However, it is not time for complacency. More concerted efforts should continue to be made to reduce the incidence of poverty in the future. There can be no doubt that for the city the thrust towards urban poverty alleviation should concentrate on a reduction of the people dependent on public and private handouts while broadening and strengthening the productive base of the city through industrialization. This can be done through the development of articulate priority poverty-reduction plans by the city council in collaboration with all stakeholders, NGOs, and the community at large.

The action that is envisaged calls for a three-pronged approach: First, improvement of on-going activities or the implementation of projects that are self-financed by the GCC or local actors (NGOs and CBOs), secondly, the introduction of new projects that will create more jobs and incomes and lastly more personal initiatives from the poor to alleviate their own poverty. Only through this partnership will poverty be reduced in the future.

PART THREE:
COPING WITH URBAN POVERTY: LIVELIHOOD STRATEGIES

12. Decision-making in Poor Households: The case of Kampala, Uganda
GRACE BANTEBYA KYOMUHENDO

Introduction/Background

> For us decision-making is a daily, hourly possibly moment-by-moment process we have to deal with.

Decision-making is a critical element in the status of family members since it involves the allocation of resources and the distribution of roles within the household. A number of clearly identifiable theoretical schools have been developed with the aim of offering insights into power relations in households. The resource theory developed by Blood and Wolfe is based on the hypothesis that the balance of power in decision-making depends on the resources an individual can offer. The greater the resources one has, the greater the decision-making powers within the household (Blood and Wolfe 1960: 12). They identified income, education and occupational status as the key resources in influencing decision-making within households.

Safilios Rothschild (1970) pointed out the limitations of the resource theory in that it does not cover the full range of resources exchanged between spouses. She argued that the overemphasis on income, occupation and education neglected non-material resources like love. Safilios Rothschild further drew attention to the importance of women's status which she distinguished from women's power. Status refers to women's overall position in the society, while power refers to women's ability to influence and control at the interpersonal level (Safilios-Rothschild 1982: 117), a factor which the resource theory does not take into account. She argued that in developing countries, which are predominantly patriarchal with a high degree of sex discrimination, women find it difficult to translate their work and earning into power (ibid.).

Feminist literature, like the resource theory, focuses on resources and the marginalization of women in the larger economy and the loss of control by women over the means of production (Mustafa 1990, Townsend and Momsen 1987, Standing 1991). They argue that inequalities persist within modern marriages and that these inequalities arise out of unequal access to resources between the sexes in favour of males (ibid.).

The normative resource theory, on the other hand, notes that decision-making powers in the household depend both on the comparative resources of husbands or wives and the cultural and sub-cultural expectations about distribution of marital power (Rodman 1972). Rodman's model introduces an element of historical and societal development which brings cultural attributes into decision-making. He argues that decision-making within the household depends on cultural norms which change as the country becomes industrialized. By implication, individuals' socio-economic position improves with industrialization, the end result being egalitarian decision-making principles (ibid.). However, other writers are of the view that although the formal authority structure of a society may declare that women are powerless and irrelevant, close attention to women's strategies and motives, to the sort of choices they make, to the relations they establish and to the ends they achieve indicates that even in situations of overt sex role asymmetry, women have a good deal more power than conventional theorists have assumed (Rosaldo and Lamphere 1974: 9).

The normative resource theory fell into a similar trap to that of the resource theory by assuming that tradition and culture disappear with industrialization, which is not the case (see Constance Hardesty and Janet Bokermier 1989). Rodman also focuses on the family, ignoring other actors who are relevant in the case of developing countries such as extended family members and friends (see Omari 1995). Further, the theory ignores the basis of patriarchal relations which is unequal distribution of resources favouring men. Because men have access to vital resources like land, education and income, they have been able to dominate decision-making in the family for decades and this has become a right in itself. When men can no longer provide for their families, their right as decision-makers is challenged.

Regarding the situation in Africa, there are two main contrasting views about the relative equality of African sex roles. One view holds that African women are dominated by men in all spheres of life. The proponents of this view usually condemn African marriage customs and practices like bride wealth payment and polygamy on the grounds that they debase women.

The other view is that the position of African women is neither superior nor inferior to that of men but simply different and complementary (Little 1973). Little and other scholars argue that the social distance between men and women which is reinforced by the sex division of labour is essentially a form of co-operation (ibid.)

Studies from developing countries seem to support Rothschild's argument. For instance, Omari found that in Tanzania, decision-making was influenced predominantly by labour based on age and sex. He comments that Tanzania, like many African societies, is still dominated by patriarchal relations and male domination is regarded as a prerogative by many people – male and female alike (Omari 1995: 217). Wright (1993), studying unemployment, migration and changing gender relations in Lesotho, also showed that despite the relative economic independence of women, men still enjoyed enormous power and the monopoly of decision-making within their household. In South Africa, money management and continued dominance by men over women, despite the latter's main contributions in the household were found to be central to household conflict, finally leading to divorce (Sibongile 1995). Mustafa (1990), in Iraq, observed that economic activities carried out within the home were made invisible by cultural norms and hence did little to increase women's power, while those women working outside the home in traditional male occupations had more power.

Studies have also indicated that the introduction of the monetary economy has not only altered conjugal economic relations, but also the basis of decision-making. In urban situations for example, most household decisions hinge around money to which the majority of women in the developing world have less access than their male counterparts. Factors like education, employment opportunities which favour men (Brydon and Chant 1989, Hay and Sticher 1995) as well the weakening of the traditional complementary sex division of labour (by elevating the husband's position to that of chief breadwinner) have all combined to make the woman dependent on her husband economically and consequently to weaken her relative power position within the household.

However, this situation is changing in Uganda due to increased access to income by women in both rural and urban areas (Banbebya Kyomuhendo 1992, Obbo 1980, Tadria 1987). Many women are now contributing to household incomes. Some are even the sole contributors while others are household heads solely supporting themselves (ibid.). This changing situation has implications for gender relations in households.

This chapter discusses decision-making in poor urban households in Uganda where resources and ideologies are not merely the main basis of decision-making but rather a question of *survival*. Although decision-making within households was generally examined, the main focus was decisions related to health care (treatment-seeking during illness episodes)[1].

Uganda in Context

Since the attainment of independence from Great Britain in October 1962, Uganda's political history has been characterized by violence and instability (World Bank 1989, Holger and Twaddle 1991, Weibe and Dodge 1987). These instabilities radically reversed the economic and social progress attained since independence.

Although currently, the country has registered economic recovery in some sectors (e.g. increased industrial investment and improvement in physical infrastructure, especially roads), at the micro level there is growing realization that these achievements have been at the expense of equity, growth and economic transformation. In particular, severe cuts in government social spending have dealt a crippling blow to vulnerable social groups like women and children (World Bank 1993, National Council for Children 1994).

Structural adjustment programmes (SAPs) adopted since 1981 and fully embraced in 1986 by the National Resistance Movement have had an effect on people's livelihoods. The retrenchment of public servants and commoditization of traditional social welfare systems have compelled many people to participate in the informal economy. As a result, more women, in both rural and urban settings in Uganda, are in one way or another engaged in income-generating activities to counteract the economic pressure exerted on their families (Tadria 1987, Bantebya Kyomuhendo 1992, Obbo 1991). Mwaka also noted that there has been an influx into the informal sector of both men and women due to SAP (Mwaka et al. 1994).

The Study Area: Kamwokya II Parish

Kamwokya II parish, the study area, is one of the numerous peri-urban slums surrounding Kampala city. It is located 4km from the city centre, on the slopes of Kololo Hill. The population of Kamwokya has recently risen from 7 800 in 1980 to over 12 709 in 1991 (Uganda Census Bureau 1991). Like most poor congested areas, Kamwokya II is a melting pot of various cultures with people from different parts of the country and different ethnic groupings. Over 50 per cent of the residents were born outside Kampala, implying that the bulk of the population are migrants (see Wallman 1996).

Like most slums in Kampala, Kamwokya has undergone various development phases. Twenty-five years ago there were only a few dwellings in Kamwokya. This development, however, has taken place in an unplanned, headlong fashion with the net result that there are virtually no proper public services or facilities (i.e. drainage, sanitation, public health units etc.). Most residents earn a living as market traders, shopkeepers, hawkers, wheelbarrow pushers, food vendors, brewers and sellers of local beer and gin, drivers, factory workers, domestic servants or low paid office workers (ibid.).

Kamwokya as an urban system has been described as

> vibrant, crowded, mixed, 'open'. These features are the bones of it as an urban system and have important implications for identity and the way resources are managed. Its people are mixed by ethnicity and economic status, cluster in different parts of the parish, and associated with different style. Residents value its mixed housing options and therefore the possibility for improving without moving; movement in, out and within is linked to opportunities in the vibrant informal economy (Wallman 1996: 227–8)

This study adopted a retrospective approach based on case histories of women, and analysis of the logic of situations relating to income generation, resource management and treatment of illness among the women themselves and their children under five. The methods included lifelines/reproductive history, treatment-seeking charts and in-depth interviews on topics like time use and household expenditure and an observation checklist of items and events in and around the house.

There were four categories of women reflecting different marital status and socio-economic status. These were:

- Married women earning own income with a husband earning income,
- Women heads of households,
- Married women earning income with resident men not working,
- Married women relying entirely on their husbands' income.

Case 1. Resty: Dynamics in income generation for women
Resty is married with her husband working. However, husband works on and off and has never had stable employment. This compelled her to engage in income-generating activities to support her family. Resty began with making of handicrafts, a venture which failed to raise enough money. Resty then borrowed Shs 10 000 (US$ 10) and started selling small quantities of vegetables and basic consumer items first on her veranda and then at a stall. The business kept the family going for a year, until the stall was destroyed and her stock confiscated. She then joined a women's self-help group making handicrafts for sale but lack of demand and market outlets defeated them. When Resty's husband lost his job and gave her the rest of his money to start up again, she made and sold local pastries for a while then started a business selling cow hooves (*mulokonyi*) at a nearby open air pub.

By late January 1995, Resty had given up the hooves business and had resumed her former one of preparing and selling pastries. In early February she was back to selling fresh vegetables and mats. When asked about the lack of consistency, she pointed out that there are many factors which dictate this, prominent among which is the search for larger profit margins and time convenience and that many businesses face stiff competition as everyone deals in similar commodities. She also noted that the *mulokonyi* business, though a bit more profitable than, say, pastries, requires good health among family members, especially among the children, if it is to be operated at all. Her absence when treatment seeking, for example, will bring it to a halt; it is a laborious business and cannot easily be delegated.
Source: Bantebya Kyomuhendo 1997

'We have to work': Kamwokya Women Accessing Income

In Kamwokya generally the opportunity for women to generate income from a number of sources is enhanced by the concentration of economic activity in or near the homes (Wallman 1996). In an attempt to broaden their incomes the women have become 'occupation pluralists', participating in numerous smaller businesses, or alternatively changing from one activity to another depending on demand, anticipated profit margins or simple convenience.

In Kamwokya, almost all women, whether married or single contributed over 70 per cent towards all household expenditures. Betty, though married with a husband running a private hire car, contributes 90 per cent towards household expenditures which include school fees for nine children, food, clothing, health care etc. Others, like Yatek, cover most of their household expenditures. Some women support their families all alone. Other cases, like Resty, though married were covering all household expenditures as their husbands were unemployed. Most of the women reported spending their money on food, and basic necessities for the family. Half of the women reported that, in addition to food and other basics, they were paying rent and school fees for their children.

Some men, on the other hand, contributed to the rent and school fees for children. Men, when contributing to food or other basic necessities, did not hand over an allowance for food and other basic necessities to their wives but purchased everything themselves. This falls under what Pahl and other scholars described as an 'independent management system' which is characterized by neither partner having access to all household income. This model depends on separate incomes for each member of a couple, which is not pooled and for which different areas of expenditure are designated (Pahl 1982).

The women in Kamwokya never know how much their men earn. This causes rifts in families where men claim to be unemployed, yet are absent from the home all day. The men, likewise, never know how much their women earn and as a consequence there is a lot of laxity on their part in contributing to family needs in the belief that women earn enough to sustain the families without their support. Women reported a decrease in men's financial contributions to the families when women were earning income. This has meant that increasingly women have had to take on expenditure items like rent and school fees which were formerly covered by men.

One strategy men use to avoid providing funds, as reported by women, is deliberate absence from their homes most of the time, forcing the women to spend what ever little they have on the family. Another strategy is aggressiveness and sometimes violence by men towards women when they

> *Case 2. Yatek's Household Expenditure*
> Yatek's family's main expenditures include: fees for three children and Yatek's cousin, food, clothing, health care and rent. No formal agreement exists on who covers what, but Yatek says before her husband lost his job as a store keeper, he used to pay rent, school fees and buy food, especially meat. Yatek would cover school fees for her cousin, food and all the other basic necessities in the family. Now her husband has lost his job, everything has fallen on Yatek's shoulders. Whatever her husband earns is sent to the village where he maintains a second family of a wife and six children. He claims that what he earns cannot meet all the requirements of the two families. This, according to Yatek, causes a lot of rifts between them. Yatek's salary at the university of about Shs 30 000 (US$60) plus income from other activities enables her to maintain her children in school and provide the basic necessities of the family. Yatek says her salary is always reserved for school fees and income from her other activities is used for daily survival.
> *Source*: Bantebya Kyomuhendo 1997

request money. They usually retort, as one woman put it, 'Why didn't you earn enough, maybe you were just talking to other men', or 'Where do you put all the money? do you want to become a man like me?'.

The explanation for this is probably two-fold. Firstly, the men, due to the prevailing economic circumstances in the country lack sufficient monetary resources to spare some for the wife and others are unemployed. The second factor which I believe is at the core of the problem is the non-existence of formal inter-spousal modalities about domestic budgetary allocations. Similar findings have been reported else where in Africa (see Munachonga 1988, Oppong 1981). As a result, a number of the women could only ask for money when they had no other options. In one case, a child aged 10 asked for shoes from his Dad, only to be hit on the head and pushed to his mother while saying to the child, 'Your mother has become the head of the family'. These kinds of conflicts are very common in Kamwokya. As a result women tend to downplay their earnings to the satisfaction of the men who feel threatened by women's economic power.

While it is obvious that women have become key decision-makers in their families, many of them do not feel that it makes them more powerful than men in their homes. Men still wield a lot of power. There are instances where women agreed to have more children against their will, just to please their husbands. Many also reported giving some money to their husbands for them to spend on drink. Some even defended men's right not to participate in household chores.

Similar situations have been reported elsewhere in Africa. For instance, Mwaipopo reports that, in Tanzania, despite women's greater autonomy, men's authority within the household still seems supreme and most women claimed that wealth should not make one disrespectful to one's husband, because men are 'heads of household' (Mwaipopo 1995: 170). She further points out that despite its significance for the household, and for women's own lives, women's wealth in money is not publicly acknowledged (particularly by men) as significant. This is because fixed assets such as houses or boats have more social prestige than cash, whatever its daily purchasing power (Ibid.).

It is apparent that decision-making is an outcome through which the relative power of husbands or wives may or may not be assessed, especially in developing countries. The bases of women's power and authority in the household are absent from theories of decision-making. These theories do not offer much help in explaining decision-making related to gendered responsibilities like household chores, childcare, food and health care done by women. They have tended to be male biased, highlighting resources most accessible to men (income, education and employment).

In relation to health care, particularly treatment-seeking behaviour, decision-making theories do not offer plausible explanations. To fully understand health care decisions within the household, we move beyond decision-making theories and discuss heath care theories to explain the behaviour of people when seeking treatment during illness episodes.

Treatment-seeking Behaviour

Treatment seeking has been subject to numerous investigations world wide, the literature providing insight into the possible factors that impact on the treatment-seeking process. There are differences in the ways people perceive, evaluate and act with respect to health and illness. Further, as Mechanic pointed out, illness behaviour follows from the manner in which persons monitor their bodies, define and interpret their symptoms, take remedial action and utilize the health care system (Mechanic 1962: 1).

There are two main categories of health care models developed by researchers to demonstrate the variations in illness management in different settings. They are (i) pathway models, which have tended to describe different steps in the process of illness management and (ii) determinant models which focus on a set of explanatory variables or determinants which are associated with the choice of different forms of health services (Kroeger 1983: 147–8).

The proponents of pathway models include Suchman (1965), who first described illness behaviour as a logical sequence of steps starting with definition and perception of symptoms up to the use of different health care providers (Kroeger 1983: 148). This was further developed to nine stages by Frabrega (1973) who also stressed the importance of different illness concepts and the medical orientation in developing countries. The model was further developed by Igun (1979) to ten steps. Chrisman (1977) and Geertsen (1975) (cited in Kroeger 1983) further incorporated cultural and social factors, past medical experience and individual orientation in pathways models.

The determinant models on the other hand stress the importance of the 'determinants' and explanatory variables in illness management. The proponents of these models include Ludwig and Gibson (1969) who pointed out that utilization of services depends on recognition of symptoms and their significance and faith in medical care. Shuval (1981) on the other hand identified the perceived seriousness and potential consequences of symptoms and the perceived cause as factors. Further, Unschuld (1975) with reference to developing countries identified economic factors, communication gaps and structural and conceptual differences as important for health-seeking behaviour. Young (1980) in his model of illness treatment decisions in a Tarascan town identified gravity, knowledge of a home remedy, faith, and accessibility (cost and transportation) as key factors in treatment decisions. These explanatory variables now widely used in health care studies are divided into (i) predisposing factors i.e. demographic characteristics, household composition, education, attitudes; (ii) enabling factors e.g. access to a regular source of health care, income, insurance; (iii) health service system factors i.e. structure of the health care system (Kroeger 1983).

Unlike the decision-making theories, health care theories present multiple possible factors that can be used to explain the illness behaviour of people in different settings. A number of factors were found to influence women's illness behaviour, particularly what they chose as 'appropriate' treatment options for specific illness symptoms for themselves and their children. These included; money, interpretations and definitions of symptoms and their severity, networks, time use and spouse influence. However, it was found that women delayed seeking 'outside' treatment even when they defined the symptoms as 'serious enough' to warrant outside treatment. Many children were rushed to Mulago hospital when they were already in a critical condition. When they themselves were ill many women relied on self-treatment, using mainly herbs and over the counter (OTC) drugs. They only visited clinics and hospitals when they were in a critical condition and could no longer work. Illness management was not done in isolation to other things happening in the family. Women had other responsibilities to fulfil and hence treatment seeking was done in a manner that would ensure minimum disruption to other activities and things happening within the household.

Compromise, which was emphasized by Blackburn (1991) in her study of poverty and health in the UK, is a major theme in the lives of Kamwokya women too. A similar situation exists in Kamwokya, where women have competing obligations to provide for their families. Thus, illness management

Case 3 Resty's time use
Resty says her business is quite taxing. She wakes up very early in the morning between five and six a.m. and walks over 8kms to the central abattoir in Industrial Area to buy fresh cow hooves. She arrives by 7.30 a.m., purchases the hooves and then walks back to Kamwokya with her often heavy load. Resty cannot afford public transport and therefore has to walk the round trip of about 16km every morning to buy the hooves. She normally arrives back home before ten a.m. Preparation of the hooves and cooking takes the whole day. Cooking has be continuous for over six hours if the *mulokonyi* is to be tender and palatable. Thus, Resty usually gets through with the preparation just before six p.m. after which she takes the stuff to a popular drinking place near her home. Business proper starts from 6.30 p.m. and on some good days (weekends) she sells everything by nine p.m. On weekdays there are fewer customers and usually she gets home late (between ten and eleven p.m.) having waited, often in vain, to sell off everything.
Source: Bantebya Kyomuhendo 1997

Case 4. Mildred's treatment-seeking process
Mildred admits falling sick several times but considers it not worth mentioning and presumably not worth seeking treatment for. When she suffered a severe bout of pneumonia, which she took to be malaria, she opted for self treatment at home with over-the-counter drugs. Later, when she failed to respond to self treatment, a nurse was called in to treat her at home. All the treatment choices utilized by Mildred are home-based and her reluctance to utilize other options is evident. On several occasions she even denies herself treatment on the pretext of her illness not being serious enough to mention, let alone warrant treatment. One of the explanations for this illness behaviour was time-related constraints. If she utilized options away from home, these would adversely affect not only her business but also her family's survival. Mildred points out that, though bedridden for four days at home while recuperating from illness, she at least had time and opportunity to direct her business from her bed and to ensure its continuity. This was unlike the previous episode when she was away for eight days attending her child at Mulago hospital and the business had collapsed.
Source: Bantebya Kyomuhendo 1997

involves either compromising the needs of the family for the sake of women's or children's health; or compromising the health of the children or the woman herself for the sake of other family needs.

The Kamwokya women made many compromises. Prominent among these, was compromising their own health for the sake of the children and other family needs. The women of Kamwokya found it extremely difficult to be ill and went to great lengths to deny being ill. Even when ill, they carried on as normal until the symptoms became very serious.

> *Case 5. Betty's treatment seeking process*
> For her own illnesses, Betty relies mostly on self treatment and when seriously ill, she visits facilities like Kisenyi valley clinic which is nearby. When she suffered from sharp chest pains, locally referred to as *kinsimbye* she could not take time off to seek care until she collapsed at school. The fact that Betty is reluctant to visit even those care facilities where time costs are low or to take even a recommended short sick leave (2 days) provides further evidence of how highly she values business time. She explained that time spent on treatment seeking is a sacrifice of time that would otherwise be devoted to business.
> *Source*: Bantebya Kyomuhendo 1997

The lack of change in gendered division of labour within the household, to some extent explains why women deny being ill in order to fulfil their responsibilities as 'good' mothers and wives. Women are the 'centre' of family survival and well-being, and thus they strive to make ends meet which may involve denying being ill. These coping strategies and compromises highlight what Graham has referred to as 'a paradox of successful caring: the responsibility of irresponsible behaviour' (Graham 1984: 185). From a professional point of view, Kamwokya women ought to have themselves treated rather than continuing to work while they are sick. As Graham observed in a different context, when conflicting pressures and shortages of resources are a problem, Kamwokya women prioritize the pursuit of family welfare and the survival of family (ibid.). Behaviour considered irresponsible by outsiders is the means by which responsibilities are met by Kamwokya women. In essence, such a paradox can only be understood in the context of the family which shapes the meaning and range of choice available to women.

Conclusion

Decision-making in poor urban households is not only critical but also complex as it relates to the survival of families. Decisions are made that seem irrational to an outsider, but make sense to them as exemplified by this quote from one woman who was very ill but at the same time engaged in business. Asked why she had not sought treatment and yet she had bought material for her business she answered, 'you do not understand'.

Women have to utilize every minute on their hands to make ends meet. Any disruption, like an illness, may mean starvation of the whole family. That is why for poor urban people decisions have to be made almost every minute.

It is evident that the decision-making theories discussed above do not take into account the factors found to be vital in health care decisions in Kamwokya, such as networks, time, women's definitions and interpretations. Further, health care decisions are seen as part of women's reproductive roles and hence, could not be used as an indicator of power relations in the household. In relation to other decisions in the household, women were found to be key decision-makers in ensuring the 'well-being' of the families. While it may sound good for women to be key decision-makers in most poor urban households, many of them experienced stress and exhaustion from having to engage in sexual activities to make ends meet. This, in the long run, has grave health implications. There is also evidence that an increase in women's access to income and control has not only improved their decision-making status but has come with more responsibilities which traditionally were men's and a basis for their authority and power in the family. This, in a number of families, has resulted in domestic violence and an increased burden for women. One woman wondered whether our grandmothers were not better off than we are today!

Further, the secrecy surrounding the source and amount of money husbands earned, made it impossible for women to transform their actions into strong power-bargaining positions. At most, their decisions were seen as part of their bid to fulfil their reproductive and productive roles. The withholding of money earned by men from their families, when their wives begin earning, meant that women spent most of their money, leaving them with few savings if any. Decision-making theories do not take into account situations like this which can be manipulated so as to reduce the power held by the individuals with more resources.

Health care theories, on the other hand, can to some extent explain women's treatment-seeking behaviour in Kamwokya, because their perspective is wider and includes most of the determinant or explanatory variables. Variables such as money, time, perceptions, faith in healers, and networks, were identified in this study as factors that influence women's behaviour. The re-negotiations by women about when to seek treatment and where, indicate that illness management is a process beginning with symptom definition and ending in seeking treatment. However, in contrast to what has been suggested by the path models and determinant or explanatory models, this study has revealed that illness management is a process whose steps are influenced by various factors (determinants). Consequently, illness management cannot be isolated from what is happening in the household.

To address the health situation of women and children in particular, a quick response to illnesses, policy makers, health care providers and professionals need to understand that women's choice of treatment seeking occurs within and is affected by the routines of everyday life.

13. Truck Pushers, Grain Pickers and Grandmothers: 'Street children' and some gender and age aspects of vulnerability in Tamale, Northern Ghana

CAROLYNE DENNIS

Introduction

The starting point for this chapter was hearing a story while researching poverty and community-based organizations in Tamale: a tale about a little girl of eight years old who lived with her disabled grandmother. They lived on the proceeds of the child picking up grain in the market and the grandmother selling cigarettes from the house, paying a neighbour to bring them cooked food. This story had emerged as part of the research which preceded the setting up of the ActionAid Tamale Street Children Project. It seemed to encapsulate the problems created for individuals and households by the long-term and recent intensification of poverty in northern Ghana.

The focus of this chapter is on the kinds of 'street children' found in Tamale, northern Ghana. One's first reaction is how different these categories of street children are from those which have been identified in the literature as predominating in other third world cities including those in Africa[1]. The discussion which follows is concerned both to explain the particularity of the situation of the children in Tamale and also to relate it to the general causes of vulnerability of children and the old in African cities. It depends heavily on background research produced for ActionAid as a preliminary to the setting up of the Tamale Street Children Project and on reports for the ActionAid Street Children Project (Annorbah-Sarpei 1995, Kusters 1995). It uses data that was originally collected for an urgent development intervention for a more reflective purpose.

The Northern Ghana Background

The causes of the increase in the number of street children in Tamale are to be found in the historical background of the region which is explored briefly here. This history has determined the present structure and processes of northern communities and the manner in which vulnerability is created and intensified in families and rural and urban communities.

The colonial authorities and the later independent Ghanaian governments perceived northern Ghana as a 'labour reserve' for cocoa production and unskilled urban labour needs in the south. The lack of investment in infrastructure, social facilities and the economy made this role a self-fulfilling prophecy. It was also a predominantly Moslem region in a country in which the clearest signs of educational and social change were associated with the spread of Christianity.

Northern Ghana, like other parts of the West Africa savannah has suffered periodic drought and famine since the 1970s (Shepherd 1981). This has increased migration flows from the north to the south and intensified the 'distress' element of that migration. This is likely to have meant that the ability of migrants and home communities to maintain contact with each other would have become more difficult in this period. Periodic drought has also led to increasing 'distress' migration to Tamale, the administrative capital and major urban centre of the north. This has led to a rapid increase in the population of the city which is composed of increasingly complex ethnic mix. The ability of migrants to maintain contact with their households of origin is greater from Tamale than from Accra. However, one should not underestimate the difficulty of poor migrants to Tamale maintaining systematic links with their home communities. The continuing migration south and from rural areas into Tamale suggests that there are huge problems of systemic vulnerability in many northern rural communities (Seidu 1997). Anecdotal evidence and the accounts of the children attending the Street Children Project suggest that, in Tamale, the experience has also intensified the instability and fragility of marriages and households.

In 1994 open conflict broke out between the Dagomba and other ethnic groups over land ownership which created physical insecurity in rural communities. The experience of conflict and the expectation of future insecurity has had the effect of increasing migration into Tamale which has become the fastest-growing urban area in Ghana. The population of Tamale has been estimated to be 250 000 of which 45 per cent are children under the age of 15 and the town has an estimated annual growth rate of population of 3.5 per cent (Ghana Living Standards Survey 1995). Much of this migration can be categorized as 'distress' migration which means that those arriving in Tamale have a problem as to how to generate an income in an urban area for which they are often ill-equipped. The conflict has precipitated the emigration of those most able to come to Tamale; 'mobile' young men and adolescent boys. It has thus intensified the existing character of rural migration to Tamale.

'Fostering' and Upbringing Arrangements

In many African societies there are practices of rearing children which are usually defined in English as 'fostering', in which children are brought up by someone other than their own parents. This is an inadequate and even misleading description of African practices which do not denote situations in which parents have been forced to or voluntarily pass over the rearing of their children to strangers, implicitly or explicitly, because of their own inadequacies or lack of resources (Goody 1982: 8). These 'upbringing' agreements are institutional arrangements by which the care of children is shared for defined periods with specific categories of kin or non-kin because of the perception that this is a preferred method of child-rearing. The arrangements often vary for boys and girls, with boys being sent to kin or non-kin as a form of apprenticeship or preparation for becoming an adult male and girls being sent to elder female relatives in order to learn the skills of a woman and to assist the receiving household with their labour. In the anthropological literature on the Dagomba and other peoples in northern Ghana there are many references to the importance of 'fostering' or upbringing agreements in these societies. There was also a practice in Dagomba of sending daughters to their maternal grandmothers or their father's eldest sister. This provided assistance to the female relative concerned while creating an opportunity for the girl to learn the necessary skills to become a woman from a defined relative who is not too close to discipline and train the child.

In relation to the vulnerable position of a minority of small girls and old women in Tamale, it is now clearer than before that in order for these mutual benefits to occur, the situation of the receiving female relative and the child must be such that sustainable resources for the subsistence of the child and the grandmother must be accessible. It is also clear that these practices emerged in rural societies in which there was the possibility of continual contact between the kin groups involved and that the women concerned were unlikely to be isolated and without the support of other adult kin and their wider communities. The transplantation of these practices into the urban context of Tamale has different implications, especially for individuals and households without the necessary resources.

Street Children in Ghana – general Characteristics

In many societies a visible sign of problems in rural communities and households and in urban society itself is the emergence of the phenomenon of 'street children'. Three categories of street children have been distinguished by UNICEF and ActionAid; children 'on' the street, children 'of' the street and abandoned children. Abandoned children and children 'of' the street are children who live on the street, are responsible for their own subsistence and live without evidence of substantial links with their own families, conforming to the conventional definition of street children. Children 'on' the street are a more diffuse category of children who spend most of their time on the streets, often engaging in economic activities of marginal character, and go home at night to their families with whom they have strong links. They are different in degree from child petty traders in societies where this is common. There is evidence of substantial numbers of these children in the cities of Latin America, Asia and Africa (Johnson et al. 1995, Swift 1997) and their conditions vary according to particular social structures and household relationships. It is difficult to estimate the numbers of all these types of 'street children' as the data understandably tends to come from agencies working to help them. This means that a self-selected, visible group of children tends to be counted.

The circumstances which propel children to live on the street in Tamale are a combination of factors common to many economies and societies undergoing rapid change and of characteristics particular to the societies concerned. The category of children who tend to turn up most frequently in all urban areas are adolescent and pre-adolescent boys who have either run away from or been thrown out of their own family households. The factors which precipitate this departure are a combination of the related factors of the intensification of poverty and family instability. This phenomenon has been noted in other Ghanaian cities and research has been undertaken to investigate the cause and extent of the problem (Apt van Ham et al. 1992). There have also been reports which have identified the particular characteristics and problems of adolescent girls who are 'on the streets' of Accra and who originate from the north (Agarwal et al. 1994).

The rapid expansion of the population of Tamale and the series of problems which have given a particular character to that increase have made the numbers of street children in the city much more visible than before. It is difficult to obtain any reliable figures of the numbers of children who can be defined as being 'of' or 'on' the street. The emergence of this as a visible social issue has led to the establishment of a Street Children Project by ActionAid in Tamale with the objectives of providing the children with support and training to enable them to earn their own living when they grow up. One of the most important features of the project is the manner in which it operates as a 'drop-in centre' with health facilities, play space and schooling and training available. The children are therefore not forced to choose between being kept in an institution and living unsupported on the streets.

The project required a preparatory collection of data and identification of the causes of children being 'of or on the street' in Tamale. Each child who uses the facilities of the Street Children Project provides an autobiography and an account of their work experiences. Kuster undertook a survey of 75 boys and 75 girls and carried out detailed interviews with 15 children. This survey provides an invaluable overview of the conditions of street children in Tamale and the hopes for the future of the children concerned. The discussion below is informed by this research and uses the children's accounts supplemented with material from informal discussions with the staff and children at the project.

The initial data collection for the planning of the project identified two main categories of street children in Tamale. The first was that of pre-adolescent and adolescent boys who had usually run away from home as the result of family breakdown or death. Once in Tamale, they live on the street, sleeping in abandoned buildings with other boys and earning money by carrying loads and pushing trucks around the market. Kuster's interviews with the boys clearly show how isolated they feel and how distrusted and abused they are by the public. The situation in Tamale does not bear comparison with the situation of street children in some Latin American cities in which police and vigilantes appear to be able to harass and kill such children with impunity, but they do suffer the punitive response of adults in terms of abuse and random violence. The children are perceived as being in the 'wrong' place. They are not members of identifiable households and in the case of adolescent boys they are feared as potential criminals. In fact the boys usually have some kind of link with their family although it may be tenuous and remote.

The reasons which have led these children to leave home appear to be associated with the long-term problems for the survival of households in northern Ghana as a result of the economic and security problems outlined above. The immediate proximate cause of the individual boys leaving home and coming to Tamale appears in most cases to be the death of a parent or the splitting up and remarriage of parents. The mechanism by which economic problems and marital stress are connected is not clear but one would expect there to be some link. As in many other situations, it is adolescent boys who are most subject to the pressures to leave their homes with a chance of surviving and generating an income in the city.

Such boys tend to perceive their stay in Tamale as a 'transit' station which will enable them to raise the money and obtain the information necessary to travel south to larger, richer cities (ActionAid 1996: 2), presumably to carry on the same type of occupation. The particular characteristic of rural northern Ghana is the long term intensity of the pressures known to create street children. This becomes self-fulfilling, in the sense that at least part of the reason for the growth of the city is the economic problems of the rural hinterland and the increase in the size of the town. The number of street children increases its attraction to other children, often related to street children already in Tamale.

One of the particular features of the situation in relation to street children in Tamale is that there appears to be a significant category of small girls of less than ten years old who fall into the category of children 'on the street'. They live with their grandmothers or elderly aunts rather than on the street. On the other hand, they do spend most of their time in public places such as the market and the lorry park in a manner which is not regarded as appropriate for girls of that age. They pick up the grains which are left on the ground after the lorries have been loaded and unloaded or they trade ice-water, *kenkey* or *poha*[2] on the streets for a small commission for their guardians. They are not at school and are not under the protection of an adult in the market like other children who help older female relatives trading in the market. There is obviously a continuum rather than a complete distinction between these girls and other young children who are acting as petty traders and carrying headloads of fruit and other goods around the market and households. However, these little girls who fall under the remit of the Street Children Project are living with isolated old women who are not themselves capable of generating their own subsistence. Both the child and the grandmother are contributing equally to a household of fragile sustainability. The girls are then an intermediate category but they have some of the most important characteristics of street children; they are isolated, abused in public places and do not have the prospect of changing their lives or of getting access to training to equip them to obtain an income as adults in Tamale today without external intervention.

The explanation of how this category of young girls has been generated and what structural conditions have caused their present condition is related to but distinct from that of how adolescent boys become street children. The importance of fostering arrangements in the upbringing of girls in Dagomba society was discussed briefly above. There have always been elderly women marginal to society because they did not have children or whose children were dead. These women lead hazardous existences on the margins of communities and are consequently feared. But the recent history of northern Ghana outlined above and the long term outward migration of men, usually for poorly paid occupations in southern Ghana has meant that there is an identifiable group of elderly women whose sons are in Accra or Kumasi and who have limited resources to visit or send remittances. In this situation the importance of the 'fostering' or upbringing agreement, becomes even greater as isolated old women have an even greater need for assistance. Recent events have also increased the migration of these unsupported old women to Tamale. However, an isolated old woman in an urban environment cannot provide for two people so the contribution made by the child picking up grain in the market is disproportionately important. The old women often have limited mobility and do not come out of their houses although they may carry on a little 'house trade'. This means that the girls do not have visible identifiable attachments to particular adults with defined positions in Tamale. The only exception might be that they are 'known' by their immediate neighbours.

Two comments might be made on this situation. First, the households of the old women and little girls are not completely isolated. They do receive help and support from neighbours and kin. While this mitigates their position it does not improve their access to resources and prospects for the future. Secondly, the data does not yet make it clear whether this phenomenon is found in other towns and rural communities in northern Ghana. It is certainly evident that street children are a growing phenomenon in other towns such as Bolgatanga, presumably for similar reasons to those which apply in Tamale[3]. Meanwhile, it might be helpful to conceptualize the situation as a continuum of 'fostering' and upbringing arrangements which at one end of the continuum are those households with the necessary resources, access to income and supportive networks to incorporate the girl and benefit both the child and the foster mother while at the other end, there are households without these resources in which both the fosterer and the child are at risk. Even if the number of these latter households is not numerically significant, they are important because they indicate the particular resources or entitlements needed for such arrangements to be viable and the mechanisms of survival for those households which do not possess those entitlements.

Street Children – Personal Experiences

The accounts by children of their personal histories and the conditions of their existence which follow were collected by the workers at the Street Children Project in Tamale as part of the work of the project in tracking the children concerned and in developing initiatives which address their needs. This process requires patience and commitment. It is also clear that these are rare accounts of the lives, desires and feelings of vulnerable children and that even in this exploratory discussion, they indicate the impact of severe long-term poverty, economic crisis and the break-up of households on society's most vulnerable members.

On the other hand, the children are very resourceful and are eager to take advantage of the opportunities for training and education provided by the project. This is perhaps an indication of the way in which these long-term economic crises lead to the neglect of the potential of the most vulnerable members of society with important and disturbing implications for the future of the societies concerned.

Here are seven family histories of three boys and four girls who attend the Street Children Project. They provide detailed accounts of the kind of family circumstances which have led to them being children 'of' or 'on' the street. They were chosen not for their typicality but for the links with the factors outlined above which propel children onto the street.

XB is a boy of 19. He was born in Tenzuck, the capital of Tallensi. His mother is a farmer who had two children, both sons. His father died when he was ten and his mother then married his father's younger brother according to Tallensi custom. XB's mother financed him at junior secondary school where he obtained a 26 aggregate[4] and then dropped out. He joined his senior brother as a truck boy in Tamale three years ago. His elder brother did not attend school. So now both his mother's sons are truck boys in Tamale. They do not send remittances to their mother.

Here are three immediate observations on this history. First, this boy was the first member of his family to have significant experience of the formal education system but it has made very little difference to his prospects. Second, this history demonstrates the impact of bereavement on their prospects. This is a common theme in the stories of the children. The third question is about the future of his mother. Both of her sons are earning a precarious existence as truck boys, send her no remittances and are hoping to go to Accra where they will have the same kind of occupation with even less possibility of sending her money. This may be the kind of woman who later becomes involved in a fostering arrangement with the very young daughter of her brother.

> YB is 18 and Tallensi by ethnic group. His father worked at the Akosombo Dam in the Eastern Region for 20 years until his retirement 16 years ago because of ill health. He was very sick for the last seven years of his life and died six months ago. YB was four years old when his father returned home. He was enrolled in the junior secondary school and completed with a 23 aggregate. As his father was very sick, YB dropped out of school to help his mother on the farm. He moved to Tamale three years ago to live with his sister and her husband and to look for work. He now works as a truck boy and chats and relaxes with the other truck boys when there is no work.
>
> ZB is Dagomba by ethnic origin. His father is ill and an alcoholic. He attended junior secondary school but dropped out when his father became sick. His mother left home to look after her own sick mother. He then ran away to Tamale. He cannot rent a room as truck boys are regarded by the community as bad children.

These descriptions of the boys indicate the long term significance of low-wage emigration from northern Ghana as a factor in family breakdown and the 'ordinariness' of their lives until broken up by ill-health, death and subsequent family break-up. One is struck by the effect on these children of the ill health of their parents. The inability of these boys to take advantage of the expansion of the Junior Secondary School system which appears to merely postpone their decision to travel to the streets of Tamale is striking. It is also clear that they tend to leave behind an unsupported mother which potentially links these accounts to the histories of the young girls who are 'on the streets' to support isolated old female relatives.

> WG is 10 years old, lives with her paternal grandmother and is a grain picker. She does not go to school but after supper she goes to Arabic classes until ten p.m. She was born at Nanti in Brong Ahafo where her mother and father are farmers. They migrated there and have lived in Nanti for 25 years. Her father has two wives, the other wife has four boys and her own mother has eight children of whom WG is the fifth. Four boys and one girl are in Nanti. Three boys have completed junior

secondary school and are in senior secondary school. The sister is married and lives in Techiman with her husband. Her grandmother is 62 years old and has had a stroke so she cannot work. She pays C2 000[5] per month to rent the room they live in. WG's father sends money to pay for his mother's medical expenses and maize regularly from Nanti which WG supplements by grain selling. WG goes to Nanti once a year. She has never been to school but would like to be a teacher or seamstress.

This case illustrates the impact of long-term migration and how a young girl may bear the cost of supporting and retaining links with her father's mother. It is striking in this case how different are the prospects of the sons who have had considerable amounts of money invested in their secondary education and the daughter who has apparently very little chance of obtaining any training or education.

XG is 14 years old and was born in Tlshigu Tamale. She lives with her parents in the family house in Tamale and is a grain picker. Her father used to be a painter with the State Housing Corporation and was retrenched six years ago. He is now a *jinjeli* – a local dance singer. Her mother was married before and had four children. Her first husband left home after two children died. She has four children, three boys and one girl, XG, with the second husband. Her mother's first son is now a farmer near Tamale and XG visits him at harvest time. Her second son is an unemployed driver. Of XG's full brothers, one has dropped out of school. One completed senior secondary school with low passes and her father sold the roofing sheets on their house to finance his resits. He still failed. There are two other wives with six children. XG attended school for three days but her mother begged her father to withdraw her as the only daughter to help her at home and in the market. At the Street Children Project, she is learning hairdressing.

This again illustrates the differential impact on boys and girls in northern Ghana of the expansion of educational facilities, complicated by the problem of paying for access to them. It also illustrates the great pressure on some children, especially girls, to provide household labour. This has been translated under present conditions into the need to contribute money by whatever means possible.

YG is 14 years old and a grain picker. She was born at Sabonjida in Tamale and lives with her maternal grandmother. Her mother is divorced from her second husband. She is unemployed at present and lives in the family home at Yendi. YG's father was her first husband and they had three children. He is currently working as a casual labourer with TAYSEC (a large expatriate road construction company). One child was killed by a lorry in a road accident two years ago. The other child, a boy, lives in the father's family house. YG's mother has two children, a boy and a girl, with her second husband from whom she is now divorced. These two children live with her at Yendi. YG's grandmother's husband was a chief of Gbungbaliga near Yendi who died about ten years ago. The grandmother has one son who works for the State Construction Company but the company has not been able to pay its workers for more than a year. This son provides food for his mother, his own wife and his five children. but he does not have sufficient resources without his salary and his children have to supplement this by working on the street. YG's father sends some money every year for her upkeep. She was enrolled in school by her father but dropped out in Class 5 because the father had no job and could not pay her school fees or buy her school uniform. The project is training YG to be a hairdresser.

Here is a description of YG's daily routine which, while it may not be representative, demonstrates common features for such girls of family responsibilities, combined with the need to negotiate the streets and market to earn money:

5.00 a.m. Wake up and collect water for the household at the waterworks. Three to four trips with a container.
Sweep the grandmother's room and the compound, heat the water for bathing, wash dishes and have bath.
Breakfast of *koko* and leftover *TZ*[6] from the night before.
8.00 a.m. Leave for Aboabu market to pick grain: maize, millet, guinea corn, groundnuts and rice which have fallen from sacks or trucks.
Sometimes drivers allow her to sweep their trucks for grain.
She will carry heavy sacks of grain for the traders and is given some grain as commission.
2.00 p.m. Short break for lunch.
6.00 p.m. Finish picking grain. Return home to help grandmother cook supper.
Take bath.
Supper of *TZ*.
Wash dishes.
9.00 p.m. Go to bed.

At the market as a grain picker, she is insulted, manhandled and beaten by the traders.

ZG is 14 years old, lives with her grandmother and is a grainpicker. Her mother was the daughter of an Ewe father and a Dagomba mother. She now lives at Yendi and is unemployed. Her father was killed in the 1994 Nariumba-Konkomba war with four other family members in a dawn attack by the Konkombas. ZG used to live with her maternal grandmother who died four years ago. Then she was told to live with her grandmother's sister. She has a seventeen-year-old brother. ZG has never been to school because the grandmother could not afford the fees and is now learning hairdressing, sponsored by the Street Children Project.

In some ways what is striking about these accounts is how ordinary they are. These children are like other children in rural northern Ghana and have had a similar range of experiences. The defining aspect of their lives appears to be that in poor rural households with connections in Tamale, they have been affected by the sickness, death or divorce of their parents. The crucial differences between the girls and boys appears to be that the boys are older and run away from home as a prelude to moving to larger cities and they have often had some contact with the educational system. By contrast, the girls have had little contact with education and are supporting their elderly female relatives in a situation of great vulnerability but have had more contact with their family networks. They move between the expectations of the household and the marketplace in which they occupy a problematic and marginal place. It cannot be predicted in these cases whether they will move on to other cities like other northern girls (Agarwal et al. 1994) or make an acceptable transition to female adulthood in Tamale. The craving of these girls for training suggests that they know this is an extremely hazardous process if they do not have the necessary resources. There is a sense in which all these children appear to bear the burden of the long-term poverty and recent intensification of the problems of generating a living and maintaining a household in northern Ghana along with the isolated old women whom the sons leave and the granddaughters support.

Conclusion

This is an indicative and exploratory discussion using data which was collected for an agency's practical purpose and trying to place it in a historical and socio-economic perspective. On the level of the particular characteristics of street children, it suggests that there are common factors in all situations of rapid social change which have their greatest negative impact on the poorest members of society and propel certain children onto urban streets. It is likely that these children will be adolescent or pre-adolescent boys although as these groups become established on the street it is likely that they will be joined by ever younger boys. In Tamale there is a particular group of much younger girls who have some of the most relevant characteristics of street children and whose position appears to have a risen out of the manner in which a 'traditional' method of arranging for the upbringing of girls is experienced in particularly poor and vulnerable urban households. The key dimension of vulnerability which is important here is the isolation of the older female relative concerned. This situation is particular to Tamale but it does suggest that possible equivalent groups of girls or very young boys may be living in other urban situations in which the composition of vulnerability is changing as a result of recent history, the relationship between the urban centre and its rural hinterland and arrangements for bringing up children. It also suggests that there may often be a connection between the situation of street children who are apparently isolated from contact with their own family and other supportive adults and other vulnerable adults, in this case elderly unsupported women. In other situations it might be unsupported mothers or sick and disabled adults. There needs to be further investigation of the impact of poverty and economic crises on patterns of parenting and bringing up children and the range of negotiations between children and their family.

This chapter has been primarily concerned to explore the issues around the phenomenon street children, to stand back from the particular concerns of the Street Children Project and to place them in an historical context which goes beyond the focus on the present which is almost inevitable in research which is part of the project of addressing the immediate situation of distressed children. However, this data also shows the resilience and hopefulness of the children and the possibility of developing initiatives which may help them to realize their hopes for the future.

Acknowledgements

I wish to thank the staff and children at the Street Children Project in Tamale for their assistance. It is invidious to name anyone but I wish to particularly acknowledge the help given to me by Husain Suleman Jaafar, field worker and social worker at ActionAid, Tamale who was responsible for collecting much of the information referred to above. The data on the children at the Street Children's Project were collected in July 1997. The Development and Project Planning Centre, University of Bradford provided a research grant partly for this purpose which is gratefully acknowledged.

14. Street Children and their Families in Nairobi

PRISCILLA W. KARIUKI

Introduction

In recent years, several studies on street children in Kenya have been carried out. In spite of the abundance of information obtained from these studies, there are still some crucial questions about the life and nature of street children that remain unanswered. Are street children poor, dishonest persons who survive on begging and scavenging or can they engage in productive work given the opportunity? Do the families of street children abuse and neglect them because they are irresponsible or because of the poverty which prevents the parents from providing the basic necessities of life? Do the children look unkempt and dirty because they are poor and on their own or are they psychopathological drug abusers?

This article is based on a larger study undertaken to address these and other questions and to examine the difficulties for authorities dealing with these children. The discussion will concentrate on the first two questions to explore the extent to which poverty has been responsible for the increase in street children in Kenya.

Origins of the Phenomenon of Street Children

Researchers have advanced several hypotheses concerning the origins of the phenomenon of street children in Kenya. One attributes a breakdown of families and moral values to urban poverty (Agnelli 1986, Dallape 1987, Aptekar et al. 1995). Children in this situation take to the streets in search of an opportunity to earn some money to support themselves and their families. Some are seeking open space where they can have some 'peace', while others are in search of supportive new 'families'. Others wish for better lives or full responsibility for their own lives. Family breakdown also leads to increased poverty, especially in female-headed families, due to women's inferior access to property rights. Such poor families live in the unsanitary slums of Kibera and Mathare, which are said to be the main source of street children in Nairobi.

A second hypothesis claims that the phenomenon of street children is caused by aberrant families who abandon, abuse or neglect their children (Onyango and Kariuki 1992, Aptekar 1992, Dallape 1987). This abuse is occasioned by such things as teenage pregnancies, extramarital relationships, pregnancies arising from rape, sexual abuse in a domestic setting or domestic violence. Many young women and girls are unprepared to be single parents with the attendant responsibilities. Many in this situation set off for the urban centres, in search of a livelihood. Sadly, a certain number of these women or their children end up on the streets.

A third hypothesis blames the adverse effects of modernization which lead to the breakdown of extended family values (Agnelli 1986, Dallape 1987, Kariuki 1989, Kilbride and Kilbride 1990, Nowrojee 1990, Onyango and Kariuki 1991). The traditional ethos of the African family was to be a form of social security for members of a broken family, absorbing children who needed care and preventing the phenomenon of street children. The existence of these children is seen as an indicator that such traditions are being eroded by the modern culture of individualism. As a result, a non-caring society has emerged which has given rise to such hopeless, homeless street children. Other contributing factors to this 'modernization' of values include rapid population growth, rural-urban migration, hospitalization and the imprisonment or death of a partner. These social changes have led to imbalances in the deployment of resources for social welfare. Such imbalances have particularly affected the urban areas, creating great disparities between the rich and the poor. Consequently, the poorest of the poor often have highly limited access to essential services such as reasonable housing, educational opportunities, health care and leisure. Children living in such conditions have drifted onto the streets of towns.

These hypotheses about the origins of street children point to the dysfunction of the family as the major causative factor. Studies have shown, however, that families which produce street children are not necessarily deviant. It is possible that such children are taught by their impoverished mothers to survive in poverty by becoming independent at a much earlier age than the society deems appropriate (Aptekar 1993, Aptekar et al. 1994). Among the urban poor, children, especially boys become much more resilient than their home-based counterparts, since they have to cope with the vagaries of poverty and a myriad of other problems on the streets. To be able to cope, the children need a high degree of cognitive and entrepreneurial skill.

Categories of Street Children

Observations indicate that there is a great diversity among street children in Kenya and it is therefore difficult and incorrect to make blanket statements about them. Their ages range from five to sixteen years plus. This means that their cognitive and psychological processes are as divergent as their personalities. With respect to gender, both boys and girls are represented on the streets. While on the streets, the children engage in different 'occupations'. Some beg, others scavenge, and still others are involved in petty theft and other antisocial activities. Certain children do honest casual work for hawkers, shoppers, traders, motorists and others for small sums of money. Calling these young people 'street children' tends to minimize the considerable differences between them.

A number of studies (Onyango and Kariuki 1992, Njeru 1994, Suda 1994, Onyango et al. 1991a) have indicated that street children have differential status on the street. 'Children *in* the street' have parents who have encouraged them to go onto the streets to secure additional financial support for the family. 'Children *of* the streets' do not have parents who can afford to keep them in school. So these children, of their own volition, wander through the streets looking for ways to support themselves. There is also a growing number of orphans and abandoned children, whose only 'homes' are the streets. These distinctions become important because many poor children work on the streets as a normal part of their duties in the family's division of labour, but return regularly. They are therefore not 'children of the streets'. Wainaina (1981), for example, found that 85 per cent of street children in her sample lived with their families and contributed to their families' incomes.

It should be noted that the distinction between '*in* the streets' and '*of* the streets' can be inaccurate and arbitrary as the children frequently move between the streets and their homes. This depends on many factors including the weather, changing family dynamics, availability of friends on the streets, degree of harassment by the police or the economic conditions of the home and the streets.

Study Methods

Previous studies of the problem of street children have been based on questionnaires, interviews or participant observation. In this study, we used a combination of different methods to obtain the children's own life experiences, aspirations and self-evaluations. The rationale for variety of methods was that being evasive and dishonest about their family background, age and reasons for being on the streets are all part of the children's survival skills (Aptekar 1994, Muraya 1993).

This article is based on data that were collected between 1992 and 1995 in Nairobi and environs. We concentrated on four contrasting areas: the slums of Kibera, Kenyatta market, Westlands and the city centre. The research team was multidisciplinary, comprising anthropologists, psychologists, sociologists and social workers. The research assistants were university students and they were paired in order to countercheck information and record as much detail as possible about the context of street childhood. Some of the street children were themselves research assistants.

During the data collection process, various ethnographic methods, including direct observation, guided interviews, casual observation and focus-group discussions were utilized. Suitable written documentation and press reports were also examined. In addition, several in-depth psychological case studies were conducted on selected streets. The critical issue was to listen to the voices of the children themselves.

From street boys in the Westlands area and Kenyatta Market a wealth of data was obtained on coping strategies for functioning in the midst of poverty. In their own 'voices' they narrated personal experiences and views making use of the methods of 'humanistic ethnography' (Child 1973, Kilbride and Njeru 1995).

An anthropologist established residence for three months in the peri-urban area of Westlands where he was visited by other members of the team who visited this study site periodically to compare experiences gathered in other locations. This locality was chosen because between 30 and 40 boys regularly slept in one of four shared sleeping areas and more children came because of a free food distribution programme. Over time, a rapport was established with the boys and discussions deepened. In addition, the current writer, a psychologist, maintained contact with 25 boys at Kenyatta Market who were visited regularly once a week until 1996. The boys came from the surrounding slums of Kibera and Laini Saba. During these visits, small group discussions were held in Kikuyu and Kiswahili on their plight. For variety the boys were also provided with paper, colouring pencils and crayons and asked to draw self-portraits and then pictures of school children. They were also encouraged to tell stories about *watoto wa barabarani* (children of the street).

Coping Strategies

In response to the situation of poverty that they find themselves in, street children in Westlands have developed coping strategies for life in an affluent, socially diverse community. This growing shopping centre produces a great deal of waste, particularly food, paper, and metal products. The availability of this waste and other garbage has become the basis of the economic livelihood of the street children who collect the used products for sale.

On a daily basis, the street boys are occupied with the collection of waste paper, tin products, and scrap metal, which they later sell at specific buying places in the locality. Some of the older and more energetic boys also assist in carrying, packing and preparing the products for transportation to recycling plants and for this they are paid small amounts of money by middlemen. The boys prefer collecting and selling waste products to begging, for which they get between 30 and 50 shillings a day. As they say, 'We are old and strong enough to do some useful work and earn an honest living'. Most of these boys said they visited their home areas in other city locations or in the rural areas when they had something to give to their mothers. In addition, the boys were happy to demonstrate that they could be creative and better their lives economically by participating in *jua kali* (informal) business. Since they lack the skills needed to compete for the scarce resources, they have become realistic about their situations and wish to make the best of what is available.

Similarly, the street boys at Kenyatta Market are a determined group of young men who get a steady income from washing people's cars. They come to the parking lot at the market on a daily basis, equipped with old buckets, brushes, dusters and other paraphernalia, to target lunchtime customers, traders and shoppers who might wish to have their cars cleaned and polished. The boys have become quite adept at their work which has earned them a good name in the market and regular customers who sometimes travel long distances to have their cars washed there. The youngest boys (9 and over) fetch water in smaller containers for use by the older boys (16 and over) who are 'training' them to do useful work, to shun idleness and to kick the glue-sniffing habit. An ordinary saloon car brings the fee of 40 shillings and each boy cleans at least three cars in a day. On weekends and at the end of the month, this figure rises to between 6 and 10 cars. The cost of cleaning depends on the size of the vehicle (buses and vans cost more), the amount of dirt, time spent on it and whether the inside is to be washed and dusted as well.

In order to exist in an orderly fashion and to continue using the water there, this group has developed its own organization and rules for those who wish to operate at the parking lot. They have to be reliable and hardworking, avoid stealing or otherwise interfering with customers cars and shun fighting or making a disturbance at the market among other things. Customers pay for the services rendered and sometimes give tips which encourages the boys to behave well. For boys who have known nothing but poverty since they learnt to walk and whose lives are beset by so many socio-economic problems, including hunger, beating, neglect, abandonment and other forms of abuse, these coping strategies are laudable. From their earnings the boys can afford cheap, decent meals at the market as well as a shared sleeping space and even save something for their mothers.

Voices of Street Children

When we spoke to the streetchildren about their lives, they talked from the wisdom of their personal experiences of suffering. The conversations were tape-recorded as they narrated their painful experiences with the police and the general public. The children made moving confessions about being misunderstood, harassed, victimized and stigmatized by a society that claims to care for its children. Many interviews and discussions recounted depressing tales of police harassment and brutality which seemed aimed mainly at preventing the street children from hassling the foreign tourists. More concern was shown that the foreign visitors should go away with a positive image of Kenya than with the welfare of her children.

It is apparent that street children have to survive in a precarious situation full of dangers inflicted not only by the physical environment but also brought about by the skirmishes they have with the custodians of the law. While some of them admit to having been involved in many forms of socially undesirable activities such as begging, pickpocketing or outright stealing, they expressed a desire to find alternatives and forget this part of their lives. One of the boys, Hassan, had this to say:

> Two years ago, I was snatching necklaces and watches from tourists in the city centre until a police bullet missed me. I had to think seriously about my life. I abandoned stealing and started a purposeful life. I do menial jobs for shoppers including guarding and washing their cars, helping to carry their shopping bags to the car and chasing away boys identified as thieves at the market. What I hate most is being idle, so I would do any work to earn a meal.

The suffering of so many children on the streets is compounded by poverty, hunger and the sheer misery engulfing their daily lives. Poverty results in inadequate food supply and malnutrition; while poor sanitation and poor housing are risks to health. The children's capacity to acquire skills for survival through gainful employment is also undermined by their lack of education (Njeru et al. 1996).

In the many conversations held with the street children, they also voiced concerns about the hostility directed toward them by the public. They say they steal because they have no food to eat. When Kobo was caught stealing bread in a shop, he said:

> I just sat there with my bread and ate it until it was finished. I had no strength to run away. As I started to move away the shopkeeper kicked my back and I fell on the pavement, badly injuring my knee.

This reaction towards the street child may be viewed as a manifestation of anger against the poor, in which the poor are blamed for their impoverishment. To the public, stealing illustrates lack of respect for another person's property and they may not stop to examine the circumstances surrounding the act. This further shows the collapse of family and traditional values which have come through the process of social change and modernization. In the 'good old days' if a person stole something to eat such as fruit and consumed it on the spot, no one really minded as long as the person did not take any of it home. The community never allowed anyone to die of hunger and was not morally judgemental about this type of act. This is not to say that stealing should be condoned but rather to say that the perception that street children are not children should be altered.

In her studies of the ways street children have been treated by their communities, Boyden (1990), describes a related source of moral judgement towards street children. She says street children become the 'objects of moral judgement' because they violate the norms society has given to children by not being under the same roof as their parents, by working instead of going to school, and by assuming the right to enjoy the fruits of their work as they choose. Similar studies in Brazil (Aptekar 1988) have indicated that street children have been killed for nothing more than petty crimes and haughty behaviour. A generally negative perception of children attempting to live like adults seems to be usual when the society is moving from traditional codes of conduct to urban lifestyles, and the children then represent the transitional tensions experienced by the society as a whole.

Focus-group Discussions

In order to further understand the attitudes towards street children, we conducted a series of focus-group discussions with street children themselves and with working adults. For the purposes of guiding the discussion, three main questions were presented to groups of at least six discussants, namely:

- Who are street children?
- Why are there streetchildren in Kenya?
- What should be done about the problem of street children?

Since the boys had firsthand knowledge of street life, they had no problem responding to these questions. In defining a street child they gave the following definitions: a child who eats from a dustbin; a child who feeds on waste food that is spoiled and rotten; one who comes from a poor family; one who sleeps out anywhere because he has no parents; a child with a glue-sniffing addiction; one who begs on the streets but goes home; a child who does not wash and dresses badly.

When asked why there are street children in Kenya they answered: because there are many problems at home; poverty in families with insufficient food and clothing; no parental love at home; parents with no jobs; unplanned teenage pregnancies; parents sending children to beg in the streets; children who run away from domestic violence.

Finally, when asked what should be done about the problem of street children the children said that: they should be provided with food, clothing and shelter; they should receive schooling and training; self-employment should be facilitated; they should be listened to and loved; they should be reunited with their families; adult supervision should be provided where parents are unable to do it; identity cards should be issued to the children so they can obtain employment.

The above responses are indicative of the fact that street children are clearly aware of the adverse living conditions surrounding their livelihoods. Poverty and family breakdown were cited as major causal factors explaining the street child phenomenon. Generally speaking, poverty has an extremely negative effect on the child's welfare in the family, food availability and access to schooling. Solutions addressed their immediate concerns such as the provision of food, clothing and shelter. It is also apparent that these children are starved for love. They would like to be listened to and reunited with their families.

Discounting the common perception that street children are an idle and lazy lot, they said that they would like to work to improve their lifestyles, even though they are quite well aware of their lack of education and skills (Njeru et al. 1996). Space does not permit a detailed analysis of adults' responses to the same questions. However, in comparison with the children, adults defined the issues in a more abstract and understandably more widely-informed manner, devoid of the real feeling expressed by the children. Both groups agreed that poverty and parental problems were significant. The adults' suggested solutions placing emphasis on institutional and material strategies, recognizing like the children, the importance of education and skills training. However, the children also emphasized the need for love and nurturing.

Street Children's Self-perceptions

From the above discussions, it is clear that through the harsh experiences that street children have endured, they have obtained practical knowledge and their survival instincts have been exceptionally well developed. For their own psychological well-being, they have refused to be condemned to a meaningless existence by the general public. Thus they see themselves differently from the way in which the authorities and the public see them. This adds to their coping strategies (Njeru et al. 1996). They have developed a 'subculture' with a clear social structure, leadership, recreation and work patterns, revolving around their day to day experiences which gives them a sense of purpose. This has been skilfully done through the use of nicknames. Such nicknames indicate that street children should be seen as fellow human beings searching like the rest of us for a sense of belonging, identity and self-worth.

The general public generally refers to street children by negative stereotypes such as *chokora pipas* (eaters from garbage bins) which implies that the children are delinquent, dirty and unhealthy. In contrast to this perception from others the children use their own names which are more relevant to their lifestyle and enhance communication between them.

A few of these names collected from Westlands by Kilbride, are presented below:

- 'Landlord'   A long time area resident and leader of the group.
- *Mrefu*   A tall person who can see ahead physically and warn of imminent danger.
- *Jothee*   A slow boy in everything he does.

- *Wamzee*   A polite, gentle boy with the characteristics of a good old man.
- *Buda*   A fat boy, looking like a wealthy man. Being fat is associated with wealth.
- 'Papa'   A tough boy who fights when he gets drunk and a long time resident.

The street children clearly attached great significance to these names and were able to pass secret messages amongst themselves which an outsider would not understand. The meanings attached to these names boosted the children's ego and gave them the confidence they needed to face another day. Similarly, a close look at the self-portraits made by the children showed that they perceived themselves differently from school-going children who produce essentially simple drawings, much less detailed and using fewer colours than those used by the street children. School children produced more outlines of persons without any details. The explanation given was that the street children wore tattered clothes with patches of different colours because they were poor, while the school children wore clean uniforms because they had parents who provided for them.

From the foregoing, it becomes clear that in terms of perception, the problem is not the children but the grown-ups. The vast majority of Kenyans are still turning the other way when they meet one of their own children on the streets. Evidently, 'their' poverty has not become 'our' poverty until a change in attitude has taken root.

Outcomes of Changing Family Dynamics

In the ideal situation, the family is defined as the union of a married couple which may or may not result in the bearing and bringing up of children. This unit is normally referred to as the nuclear family and when there are children, it is responsible for creating an appropriate environment for them to grow up in. There are also extended families, a common phenomenon in African cultures. The family today includes single-parent families, which are said to be the main cause of the phenomenon street children today. It is true that the majority of the street children in our larger study, as well as those discussed in this article, have grown up in a family headed by a woman, indicating that their fathers were neither present nor available to them. Studies in Nairobi have shown that nearly 85 per cent of the mothers of street children were unmarried (Onyango and Kariuki 1992, Wainaina 1981, Onyango et al. 1991b). According to Suda (1994), nearly two-thirds of the households in her sample taken in the slums of Nairobi were headed by unmarried women.

In addition to the fact that the homes of street children were headed by women, these women also lived in impoverished situations. The boys discussed here reported many times how their mothers often cried because the children slept without having eaten anything. Those who had started school had to drop out since they could hardly concentrate on empty stomachs. Many of them had also lived in one crowded room without water, electricity, privacy and other basic amenities.

While hypotheses that describe the origins of the phenomenon of street children blame aberrant families who allegedly neglect or abuse their children, the findings discussed here largely indicate that the phenomenon of street children is the result of poverty. Parents have been blamed in some studies which tend to overlook the fact that parents are forced to adapt to poverty and the lack of social equality in society (Aptekar et al. 1995). The view that parents were to blame for their children escaping to the streets has also been expressed in the media and other fora. Keraro (1994) pointed out that the causes of the increase in numbers of street children included broken families, single-parenthood and irresponsibility among parents. Thus, because the parents of street children had not fulfilled their responsibility as parents, society should intervene. Often, however, strategies for intervention have not been clearly thought out.

As we have seen, it is easy to condemn the mothers if their poverty is not taken into account. In this regard, an example of a working intervention is provided by the African Housing Fund who, with other donor organizations, have been funding several projects aimed at improving the financial position of mothers of street children (Katumba 1990). Prior to 1990, many of these mothers were in the streets begging with their children. Discussions with several of the women in our study indicated that they were on the streets because they were too poor and had no alternatives but not because they were irresponsible. Indeed, after the African Housing Fund trains them in a skill, for example, making cement blocks used for home construction, many of them have been able to earn enough money to support their children, send them back to school and build their own homes.

Thus, as indicated by Aptekar et al. (1995), the notion that single poor mothers are, by virtue of being single and poor, irresponsible and incapable of raising moral and productive children, ignores their considerable coping skills. Since the traditional extended family structure which took care of all members is declining, many Kenyan women have made a decision to cope with the low status of women in marriage by opting to have children outside of marriage. Studies have shown that marriage tends to 'spoil' a relationship by giving the man too much power and control over the woman (Kariuki 1989, Suda 1993).

While many people, including the custodians of the law, consider families headed by single women to be 'broken', this is hardly the perception of the street children themselves. Many of them grew up in situations where the women were extramarital partners and where fathers were never expected to be permanently around the home. Other street children were accustomed to living in a family where a series of men stayed for short periods of time. Thus the mothers have also had to develop different criteria for supervision and protection of their children by teaching them to make their own way outside the home.

Conclusion

It has been argued in this article that the problem of street children is complex and cannot be tackled without addressing the obstacles faced by the families and communities these children come from. Many people have been led to believe that the origins of the phenomenon street children have something to do with parental irresponsibility, ignoring the fact that these children were born and brought up in poor environments, where they were poorly fed and poorly sheltered and have never known anything but poverty. This attitude results in hostilities towards street children, perhaps because it is an easier response than having to confront the impact of poverty in the society.

In spite of the fact that street children are constantly exposed to many dangers, health hazards and other difficult circumstances, their 'voices' indicate that they have developed effective coping strategies. Having made conscious decisions to be on the streets due to lack of alternatives, they have had to endure stigmatization, overt discrimination, beatings, harassment from the police and the general public. They are able to survive because their background forces them to adopt survival mechanisms that enable them to compete for scarce resources on the streets.

The implications that can be drawn from the foregoing discussion include the need to find ways of addressing the street children's educational and vocational needs and aspirations as well as their desires for personal growth and their mental health problems. It is imperative to address and change public attitudes towards street children which result in hostility towards them. The more vulnerable families should be empowered economically, to enable them to provide adequate care and protection for their children. As the majority of street children come from a home, assistance in the form of income-generating projects should be given to their mothers to enable them to create conditions that are conducive to children staying at home rather than straying into the streets of the city.

15. Gender and Urban Poverty in the Days of AIDS in Uganda

CHRISTINE OBBO

I sat reading a postcard of Edvard Munch's 'The Scream (1895)', in a hair salon in Uganda. It bore the news of an African student's suicide at an American University and led me to a new understanding of how urban Ugandans define and understand their situations and then adopt what they consider are appropriate survival strategies in the days of AIDS.

AIDS has accentuated the tendency to create, join and maintain networks that are based on diverse interests such as work, religious inclinations, residential proximity and compatibility: these are *ad hoc* caring communities. Even people who may have distanced themselves from family, friends and colleagues often end up in some form of caring community network. These networks serve the purpose of caring for the living and ensuring decent burials for the dead. The moral that is often repeated is that, 'since AIDS is an equal opportunities disease, one should care for others if one hopes to get a decent funeral, which everyone deserves'. Yet another proverb is often invoked to remind the survivors that in the days of AIDS none will be spared either suffering the pain of the disease or the tears of mourning a loved one.

The postcard I was reading invoked two distinct reactions that were revealing about deep-seated attitudes to AIDS and suicide as states of loneliness with potential for social isolation. Reactions to 'The Scream' produced the following exchanges between four clients, two workers and the hair salon owner.

> 'It is a woman!'
> 'It could be a man or woman.'
> 'No, it is a woman. Can't you tell?'
> 'You tell us. What is it?'
> 'This is a picture made long ago in 1895 by an artist from Norway and he called it "The Scream"' the anthropologist replied.
> 'I knew it! It is only a woman who could scream and look so crazy while other people are peacefully strolling by!'
> 'I am convinced that it was a woman afflicted by a disease similar to "ours" (AIDS) and she was screaming herself to death.'
> 'You may be right! But I have also seen women looking like that as a result of the fatigue due to caring for relatives suffering from our disease. Women nursing husbands seem particularly to have that haunted look.'

'It looks like a woman who has nursed her husband for a long time and while mourning his death, the relatives have dispossessed her and her children.'

'It could be a woman whose husband, upon learning that she has AIDS, has thrown her out of a home she helped build.'

'I felt like that when my husband told me to send for my sister to nurse me. I had suddenly become untouchable because I was infected with HIV. Never mind that I had helped nurse two of his siblings who died of AIDS.'

'It reminds me of a poor woman who was brought to hospital for delivery and the nurse asked her if she had brought a sister to help her as they were not going to contaminate themselves with HIV.'

'My mentor, who is not a poor woman, screamed audibly in hospital and still screams silently for her baby who died as a result of carelessness in the delivery room.'

'In relationship to AIDS all women in this country are only a step away from poverty but the poor woman's companion is grinding poverty.'

'AIDS has worsened women's vulnerability to poverty. A friend of mine dropped out of school to be with a man whose foreign wife was allegedly bossy and did not understand him! She is pretty and he enjoyed showing her off to his colleagues and during his foreign travels. The saddest thing is that she is lying in hospital dying of AIDS, he does not visit her but goes around town saying to his friends: "I hear Joy has AIDS! Look at me I am healthy!" What a misery men are. She became really ill after a miscarriage of his child, now he has abandoned her. I and four other friends have become her family. We visit her and because she so strong and cheers us up we have all come to share our secrets of being HIV positive: this was not easy even among friends but we drifted into being truthful with each other. When my husband died of AIDS I was in despair but my friend was there for me. She used her boyfriend's influence to set me up in this salon and brought me duty-free hair products whenever she travelled with him.'

The salon owner thus vividly illustrated the gist of the conversation to the clicking of tongues and tearful expressions of those present. At this point the conversation turned to the subject of my letter. I related how an African student had become depressed and committed suicide at an American university. Other African students, together with their friends, had raised money to repatriate the body back to eastern Africa. The efforts of a professor who had accompanied the body, failed to get the relatives to claim the body which in the end was interned near the airport. The story made many tongues click – a non-verbal Ugandan way to express anger, sympathy or exasperation. There followed an outburst of people speaking at once.

'In the villages bodies of those who commit suicide are not accorded proper funerals, the body is unceremoniously dropped into a hastily dug hole which is quickly covered up. No weeping is allowed.'
'That is how robbers who had been apprehended and beaten to death were buried when I was young in the 1950s.'
'What a lonely death!'
'Why did he do it? I can't imagine studies being so difficult.'
'Americans look so happy on television!'
'Yah! but this was an African – he simply did not fit into America. One occasionally hears such stories.'
'Suicide over studies is stupid. For all we know he may have had AIDS.'

These last remarks caused a brief pause before the conversation resumed.

'The thought of suicide passes through the minds of most AIDS patients.'
'But people rarely do it because they know they would condemn themselves to shame twice: they would die slowly of AIDS, they would have no proper funeral. They would for ever remain the restless dead who would inevitably be blamed for being troublesome shades forever disturbing the fortunes of the living.'
'AIDS patients are humiliated by the incurable disease and the prospect of being dropped unceremoniously in an unmarked hole should they commit suicide is a frightful thought.'
'But sometimes loneliness can lead to disappear are and suicide.'
'All I know is that I have never heard of an AIDS patient who committed suicide but I have heard of speculation from the experts.'
'The cure for suicide is to reduce loneliness and the cure for loneliness is friends. AIDS patients have adopted the sayings of our forebears as a guiding principle: One who befriends is better than one who quarrels.'

These two conversations capture the concerns of Ugandans as they contemplate an acceptable way of surviving and dying in the days of AIDS. Throughout the research period people continued to claim knowledge of what AIDS meant to them in their various capacities as people with AIDS or as survivors and care givers. The women tended from their lived experience to identify AIDS as a gender-related, poverty-fuelled disease.

Cultivating Friendship is Better than Quarrelling

The saying 'cultivating friendship is better than quarrelsomeness' represents a deeply ingrained value among Ugandans which has not only inspired songs in the past but has become a design-for-living strategy in the days of AIDS. People from all socio-economic classes benefit from the personal networks they cultivate and maintain. People express the fear of dying without being mourned if they are not friendly to their neighbours, generous with close and distant relatives, or if they are unco-operative at the work place. AIDS has heightened the fear of dying alone in isolation and one way of ensuring that this does not happen is to ensure that people will want to visit and take care of you when you get afflicted with the disease. However, poverty sometimes breaks the connections between people and they die in isolation. In 1992, during my investigation of resources and health needs in six Kampala suburbs in a period of six weeks, I interviewed over 2000 people among whom 34 were quietly dying of AIDS in dark, damp and stinking rooms. I was familiar with a dozen Kampala-based Non-Governmental Organizations (NGOs) associated with assisting people afflicted with the disease. I had attended half a dozen high profile funerals of people who had benefited from adequate hospital and family attention. In fact, it was common to find two neighbours with opposing experiences: one dying in loneliness and poverty and another receiving medical help and counselling as well practical and emotional support. These support systems are provided by NGOs, churches, workplace schemes and networks as well as neighbourly actions. Whether or not people have access to such services depends upon their neighbourhood, their socio-economic status and their personal connections. Place of residence is not a critical factor for people with high incomes who can afford to buy medicines or travel to seek free services available in other parts of the city. The access of afflicted poor people to medicines and services is circumscribed by where they reside in the city. For example, poor people living at Wandegeya, Kamyokya and Mulago could attend the AIDS clinics at Mulago hospital because it was adjacent to the national and teaching hospital, whereas those living at Kabalagala, Gaba and Kibuli were often restrained by the lack of money to cover transport fees (Obbo 1992). Nevertheless, proximity to the hospital and available services did mean that people would always access them. Because people sought affordable rental rooms, recent migrants often found themselves residing adjacent to strangers and thus isolated from information by language barriers. People who worked in public places such as the market, were more likely to be exposed to information about services than those who operated commercial activities from their rooms. Those who sold beer or operated hair salons came into contact with people in a 'relaxed' atmosphere which promoted talking and the exchange of information. Men always had more access to information and the services available because they went out to socialize more than the women. Furthermore, men in areas not adjacent to the hospital or services always managed to find money to travel to the place where paid or free help was available. To summarize, the fortunes of poor urbanites afflicted with HIV depend upon such factors as the proximity of people one is able to converse with, whether as neighbours or customers, the opportunities and capacity go to out to socialize, and access to money to travel to the place where services are available or to pay for services. In the following section are case studies that illustrate the strategies that some urbanites have adopted to survive in the days of AIDS.

Concerned Neighbours

In the days of AIDS, a popular saying stresses, a man without a mother, sister or wife is doomed (to a lonely death because he has no one to care for him). John was a twenty-two year old dying of AIDS in a slum near the university and near Mulago hospital. He became a slum dweller because he was ashamed to let anyone know that he had AIDS and he had spent all his money on cures that did not work.

> I gave up work when my clothes could no longer hide my blisters and sores, when I could no longer eat normally with my colleagues and when I started spending too much time on sick leave. I moved here from the nice neighbourhood I used to live in because I could no longer afford the rent. Everything here is ironic. The radio says that condom use is the best protection until a cure is found and yet here I am feeling cheated of life as I watch condoms from the University dorms float down the open sewer in front of my door. I never thought I would end up like this when I graduated. I am not religious but my patron, for whom I am a reluctant but grateful client, is a Muslim and he brings the Qur'an and Islamic literature. I met him the day I quit my job. I had nowhere to go so I was walking aimlessly but very slowly. He fell in pace with me and soon broached the subject of AIDS. I was angry about his assumptions about my condition which I did not want anyone to know about but eventually I came to admire his candour and he became my confidant. He organized his friends to help pay my rent. He may be motivated by the desire to save my soul! My neighbours are women who are generally despised as poor, prostitutes and promoters of drunkenness. They have shown me the depth of humanness. When I came here I knew no one but after they watched me for a month sitting out to warm myself in the sun, they started bringing me food. These days I cannot eat but they continue to bring me juices. I would have died long ago but for my neighbours on whose kindness and generosity I am surviving.

John had his wishes in death for he had insisted that his family and former colleagues not know that, 'I have become poor, unemployed and I am dying of AIDS'. Potentially, by cutting himself off from the people who knew him he was condemning himself to a lonely death without the care of his two sisters and mother. He providentially became a member of an *ad hoc* community of carers in which his female neighbours took on his nursing care and a casual acquaintance, perhaps prompted by religious fervour, adopted him to the extent of paying his rent. However, his burial was felt by neighbours and former colleagues (who had guessed his condition) to be tragic. Not only was the environment of his grave actually stinking, but the hour of his burial was felt to be too late. Ideally, a funeral that does not take place before four p.m. is postponed until the next day. This last issue is at the centre of this paper: everyone should have a respectful funeral in which the rituals of time and place are honoured. This largely explains the practice of taking sick people and repatriating bodies to their natal homes.

Friendship Transcends Kinship

Although Proscovia was only twenty years old, she had nursed and buried a boyfriend of four years, and was bedridden with AIDS. She lived with a former schoolmate and regularly sent home assuring her parents that her life as an urban working woman was a success. She had had a job as a tea maker in one of the government departmental offices in which half the workforce had been affected by AIDS: five employees had already died, three were bedridden and two were 'hanging on' appearing only irregularly at work. It was an understanding and supportive atmosphere.

> When the burden became too much for me, I confided in my boss that I was pregnant and I was nursing a boyfriend dying of AIDS. He was very understanding. Bless his soul. My boyfriend died of AIDS six months later. My son was born a few days after his father's death. His parents came and took the body back to the village, and his mother told me that if the baby became too burdensome for me she would assume responsibility. She probably suspected rightly that I was infected too.
>
> One day while I was waiting for transport home, I ran into an old classmate, Judith. We had never been close friends but we updated each other about our fortunes since leaving school. She was in the process of leaving her 'husband' and was looking for new lodgings. Although Judith had for the last two years lived with Joseph, had borne him a child and cared for several of his sisters who attended city schools, he had recently suggested that she send for a sister to look after her because of her recent frequent illnesses. This is what men tell wives and girlfriends they suspect of having AIDS.
>
> As I have been unable to work for the last five months, my job has been looking after our children but that is becoming increasingly difficult. Judith continues to work at the bank as a cashier but we barely survive on her salary. Every Sunday we visit her cousin who works as a house girl for an elite family. In this way we get to eat our weekly decent meal and the children even drink milk. The leftovers we bring back usually last us for two days. We worry about what will happen to our children.
>
> Four months ago I joined a prayer group consisting of four men and six women who, although they live in different parts of the city, meet after work and at weekends to make prayer visits to people who are ill and lonely. One day three of them appeared at the door and asked if I was well. I went around with them twice to pray for sick people in their homes but since then I have become too weak so they come here and help with the children, cooking and laundry. I have instructed them that

when I die they should take my son to his paternal grandparents and not to contact my parents.

When Proscovia died, her former colleagues contributed a coffin and a van to repatriate her body. Members of her prayer group and Judith accompanied the body and did everything possible to comfort her aged mother who had became paralysed by shock. Judith took the children to be raised by her mother because she sees her future as precarious.

This case study underscores urban women's perception of AIDS as a gender-related disease in which men get proper care and the women have to bear the burden of being wives, mothers and caregivers even when they themselves are ill. This has been referred to as the 'triple jeopardy of women and AIDS' (SWAA 1989, Panos 1990). This problem is not exclusively urban but urban women, most of them unmarried and doing low-income-generating jobs, feel the brunt of the burden of being poor and affected and infected with AIDS.

The case study illustrates common survival strategies of young people in the city. School dropouts drift to towns where they hope to get good jobs in offices. Once in a while, they reassure worried parents that all is well: they are staying with relatives or friends and will soon be employed or have found jobs. Common rural origins and school background are easily translated into friendships which are indispensable for obtaining accommodation and jobs. When they find jobs, the salaries are usually not adequate for urban survival so they often seek accommodation on the floors of the already cramped rooms of former schoolmates, village mates, friends or even acquaintances of parents and newly-met friends. Another common survival strategy is that of Sunday visits to friends, acquaintances and relatives who have good jobs and live in respectable places because Sunday lunches are substantial.

The last survival strategy is a direct result of the AIDS epidemic: prayer groups that constitute *ad hoc* communities for the AIDS afflicted. Sick people who are isolated voluntarily or involuntarily seek emotional or spiritual solace from strangers. These ad hoc groups provide an invaluable life-support system for those not easily reached by formal religious, counselling and charitable NGOs.

No one wants City Women, they all have AIDS

Mika had operated a store with his mother at Nakasero Market for ten years. They specialized in selling yams, potatoes, onions, passion fruits, grass hoppers and ground nuts. The mother served as a vendor while Mika went around different places in search of produce. His father was blind and did not do much except attract customers with his bewitching tales and his retelling of the current news stories. Mika was also a typical 1970s and 1980s city person: he played hard to make up for the hard life and sufferings resulting from dictatorship and wars. He was a fast-talking and self-promoting twenty-five year old. Through an old friend, he had landed a job as a driver for one of the foreign development agencies. He liked his job because he was assigned many trips out of town which afforded him opportunities to shop for produce. He derived prestige from the four-wheel drive van and soon he was giving lifts to women, some of whom became his girlfriends. After five years, constant sick leaves cost him his job. He used up most of his money trying to cure a cough that would keep him in bed for weeks. His stall at the market became shabby as his mother only sold occasional grasshoppers caught at street lights. The four-walled brick house he was building and in which he lived remained incomplete. Medicines purchased by his girlfriends kept him well for brief periods. Time came when the market stall was closed down and his mother nursed him full time. His father, who was no longer talkative, wept when seven children were 'brought home to their father as custom demanded' by four irate and scared former girlfriends. The children could not be turned away because Mika was an only child. At the funeral his friends expressed great surprise at the number of children he had fathered in the days of AIDS because of his frequently expressed opinion that all men, including him, were afraid of city women because they all had AIDS.

All the four women have since been in different stages of the AIDS disease. As one mourner poignantly put it:

> In Uganda now women have three major problems. Young women have children in the hope of the father marrying them, but a woman's chances of being married are reduced if she has a child. Meanwhile, women are getting infected and dying of AIDS.

Two of the women were employed but struggled to make ends meet, and the other two were unemployed and saw marriage as a rescue option. Fast talking Mika was hypocritical to his friends and was survived by four women who have since been in different stages of the AIDS disease and two elderly parents who are handicapped and have been reduced to poverty by caring for his progeny. The survivors are the real story of poverty and AIDS.

'Hey dead one . . .!' – The Challenge of Humour

> Hey! You dead one, why do you want to blame the car? It will finish you off!

These remarks produced smiles as a group of men watched Misusera slowly dodge his way through the traffic. He was on his way to join his buddies at the bicycle repair shop under a tree. He was warmly greeted and sympathetically listened to as he updated them on his latest 'adventures with

AIDS'. Several people had AIDS stories to share before the conversation shifted to other subjects.

This incident made such an impression on me that I could not resist sharing it with others. One day, my four informants from the salon and I were discussing this incident while waiting to see a doctor at the TASO clinic at Mulago, when we received a severe lesson on insensitivity and stigma from one of the volunteers who had overheard us. The reaction of my HIV-infected acquaintances was: 'We need to laugh or life will become unbearable.' After we left the clinic, one of them said, 'I am tired of the humourless people who try to help us. They should stop speaking for us because one does not cease to have foibles worth laughing at simply because one has AIDS.' When I asked Misusera, at another meeting, why he puts up with the rudeness of his friends, he laughed and said, 'Life would be lonely indeed if we did not laugh at ourselves and allow other people to laugh with us. Those guys are my friends and I never felt that they were abusing our friendship.'

Misusera's group were all bus park 'boys' notorious for their merciless direct and rude language which they developed as touts and hawkers. Addressing a Person Living with AIDS (PLWA) is not something most people would do, but like all humour it was funny in the context of the group dynamics of shared life. In other words, people who exchange AIDS jokes with PLWAs are aware of the difference between stigma (laughing at so as to exclude) and humour (laughing with to make the circumstances bearable). But there was also humour at a distance which was provoked by PLWAs who were not being funny in the days of AIDS. A recently pencil-thin man who is covered with sores but continues to assert that he does not know anyone with AIDS. A PLWA who interprets the Bible literally about cutting off any part of your body that makes you sin and seriously threatens to sever his penis because it caused him to womanize and get AIDS! Jokes are like puddings, their proof is in the presentation and reaction of the audience.

I found that exchanging AIDS jokes helped both patients and caretakers laugh and keep things in perspective, and to survive the daily stress of dealing with AIDS. There were *ad hoc* networks of people who met regularly in the hope of laughing off the burden of depression. I occasionally joined them to relieve the depression of doing AIDS research. Some caregivers became quite skilled comedians at defusing tension with jokes that were based on real incidents and which grabbed the listeners.

My First Act as a Married Woman

Twenty-nine year old Maria had dropped out of school to live with her policeman boyfriend because she wanted to live in the city and to escape her authoritarian father. After she became pregnant, she discovered that he was already a married father of four children.

> He persuaded me to move 'temporarily' to his rural home but I was to spend five years living as a peasant. [She said 'peasant' with words and in a tone that made it sound derogatory – *mukopi* and *mwanjalananda luganda*: uncultured and winnower of weeds respectively.] During this time his wife had died. When he became very ill he sent for me to nurse him. I never knew what killed him but I told everyone that he had died of cancer because I had heard a doctor say 'something something and cancer'. I only learned two years later from his nephew and confidant that he had had AIDS. (The word cancer is no longer translated into the vernacular because it has been naturalized and it is assumed to be an understood medical condition.) My first act as a married woman who was now widowed was to move to the city with my four children and the five children of my deceased co-wife. I knew that this was better than starving in the village. We worked hard selling roast cassava on the streets and at the night market at Namuwongo but when that was closed by the authorities, life became hard. We were reduced to begging from motorists at one of the busy traffic junctures. One day I heard a man say 'that woman should not be here with all those children'. It was a policeman threatening to arrest us. I decided to send my stepchildren back to their rural maternal uncles. I returned to the neighbourhood where I used to live and my acquaintances were still there. 'Mother' gave me a month's free rooming and I helped sell bananas at another night market. 'Mother's white employer has 'adopted' my two elder children: they are enrolled in a good school and she gives them rides back and forth. Through my 'sister's' efforts I now have a job at the Pepsi cola bottling plant.
>
> Recently, I became a born again Christian [*mulokole* or saved one] and so now I have three families: where I was born, where I live and my Church. I know I have AIDS and when I die I think my Balokole family will take care of my children. By meeting educated and rich people I have learned many things. There is an organisation called TASO which helps AIDS victims. One woman has attended meetings of 'people with our disease' and says that once a week she 'talks' to others (PLWAs) in a typing machine (E-mail) at a friend's office at the university. I am no longer as frightened and angry as I was two years ago.

Maria's story illustrates the importance of friendships and fictive kinship for the personal survival of the urban poor. There are also new elements of globalization; the expatriates who are offering support to relieve the orphan burden faced by poor women; knowledge about international PLWAs when the privileged few are sponsored to attend AIDS meetings or read about them, and in rare cases use electronic mail.

Poor Men have no Woman . . . Women are a Step Away from Poverty

These are frequently stated as experiential truisms about men and women in the days of AIDS in Uganda. At the beginning of this chapter women who were apparently infected with HIV reacted in ways that situated their experiences within the cultural and national discourses on AIDS. Thus, although both poor men and women live precarious lives prone to isolation and loneliness, women seem to bear the brunt of the epidemic.

It is taken for granted that women as wives, mothers, sisters and girlfriends (or even acquaintances as in the case of John) will look after the men, yet women are either neglected or encouraged by men to seek female relatives to care for them. Yet in Africa there are already six women with HIV for every five men, and globally close to four-fifths of all infected women are African (UNAIDS 1997 and 1998). Women with poor levels of education and low-paying jobs are vulnerable to relationships with men which put them at risk for HIV infection.

The well-known urban survival strategies of fictive kinship, joining organizations such as churches and ethnic associations (see Williams and Tamale 1991, Parkin 1969) and friendship continue to be cultivated and maintained. However, because the burden of AIDS is seen as the responsibility of everyone because it is 'an equal opportunity disease', *ad hoc* caring groups in the form of helpful neighbours, prayer groups and acquaintances are formed to provide practical, emotional and spiritual support for the afflicted. The urban poor, especially in the days of AIDS with the associated problems faced by widows and elderly grandparents in caring for orphans; and PLWAs, have developed new strategies for tapping the global connections of expatriates, NGOs and friends in modern offices.

16. African Urban Livelihoods: Straddling the rural-urban divide
JO BEALL, NAZNEEN KANJI and CECILIA TACOLI

Introduction

The interactions and linkages between city and countryside are increasingly recognized as central factors in processes of social and economic change in Africa. Despite this, much development theory and practice pertaining to Africa is implicitly based on a dichotomous view of an urban-rural divide. This is reflected in the prevailing division of policies and programmes along spatial and sectoral lines. However, this does not reflect the reality of African household livelihoods, which often include both rural and urban elements. In both cities and countryside, a significant proportion of African households rely on the combination of agricultural and non-agricultural income sources, often involving the migration of one or several members over varying periods of time, or commuting between built-up and peri-urban areas. In addition, many urban enterprises rely on demand from rural consumers, while access to urban markets and services is crucial for many agricultural producers.

This chapter focuses on the importance of rural-urban linkages in the livelihoods of African *urban* dwellers and the impact of macro-level policy changes on rural and urban households. It also points up the need for further policy-oriented research in order to limit the constraints imposed by policy and to enhance the opportunities for poverty reduction provided by rural-urban interactions. A focus on the livelihood initiatives of African urban households and communities serves to highlight the importance of human capabilities and agency. This focus is not meant to obscure the vulnerabilities of people in poverty, or to over-emphasize the options available to them in their efforts to earn incomes, create liveable environments and develop positive social relationships. They frequently pursue these ends in the context of severe structural constraints. Rather, the aim is to point up the significance of the activities of households and communities for policy and planning and to analyse the linkages between the workings of these smaller units and the larger-scale economic, social and political processes operating in, on and beyond African cities.

A Conceptual Framework to Straddle the Rural-urban Divide

A livelihoods approach takes the view that the problem of defining urban boundaries is not simply a matter of official definitions of cities and towns, according to, say, size of population or administrative structures and functions. It impinges on the way people live their lives, consume and make a living and the resource implications of this. For example, urban residents and enterprises depend on an area significantly larger than the built environment for basic resources and ecological functions. Nevertheless, a division between 'urban' and 'rural' policies is common and based on the assumption that the distinction between the two is self-explanatory and uncontroversial. From the vantage point of urban research and planning, the focus is on urban centres, with rural areas constituting a 'residual' category. However, as Rees (1992) has made clear, a city's 'ecological footprint', i.e. the dependence of an urban centre on the countryside, blurs the boundaries between urban and rural areas. Relatedly, in much of sub-Saharan Africa, agriculture still prevails in peri-urban areas, although here as elsewhere significant shifts in land ownership and employment patterns are taking place, often at the expense of both the rural and urban poor.

Households, networks and rural-urban linkages
The term 'household' covers a wide range of residential forms, groupings of people and functions, making a universal definition of 'household' impossible. African urban households may involve close family, wider kin networks and can include unrelated co-residents such as lodgers. It is also vital to acknowledge the role of members who are not directly part of the immediate household. Non-resident family members often make contributions to urban households, for example, workers living away from home in mining compounds, road construction gangs or live-in domestic service. They can also contribute to rural households through remittances and in-kind contributions. Moreover, rural family members might support urban households through production of subsistence foodstuffs, the supply of traditional medicines or through looking after the children or older family members so that the middle generations can take up employment.

Households are usually defined as spatial units characterised by shared residence and daily reproduction, primarily cooking and eating (Robertson 1984). However, the strong ties and reciprocal support between urban-based and rural-based individuals and units suggest that in many instances households are better defined as 'multi-spatial'. Membership can then be defined on the basis of the commitments and obligations individuals maintain towards units in which they may not reside, either temporarily or even on a semi-permanent basis (Caces et al. 1985). This two-way flow of resources and reciprocal relationships highlights the importance of recognizing rural-urban linkages for understanding household-level strategies and livelihood systems in Africa. Nevertheless, in understanding urban households it should be pointed out that while the arms-length contributions of temporarily or permanently absent family members are important, they are qualitatively different from those involving day-to-day resource distribution decisions, accessing services, negotiating social relationships or participating in community-level activities.

It is also important to conceive of urban households rather than 'the urban household' and to avoid getting caught up in conceptualizing households as either nuclear or extended. Despite the conventional wisdom that urban households are more likely to be nucleated, Colin Murray (1981) writing on southern Africa, cautions against what he calls the fallacies of essentialism, because this view of households ignores the developmental cycle of the domestic unit. The developmental cycle manifests itself in a diversity of household types, with any one household changing its shape and form over time. He further warns against the danger of lamenting the growth of nuclear households and glorifying the extended family. To do so, he argues, falls into the trap of seeing the latter in a residual sense as 'something that allegedly accommodates everyone (the sick, the unemployed, older people) in default of decent wages or social security arrangements'.

Social networks of reciprocity, exchange and information-sharing extend beyond family and kinship ties and can also span rural urban areas. Anthropologists such Cohen (1969) on West Africa, have shown how rural patterns of engagement were translated to an urban context. Vulnerable groups increase their security within urban systems by entering into dependency relations with social superiors or by creating neighbourhoods and social groups paralleling rural collectivities. At the same time, access to non-farm production in rural areas is also mediated by culturally-specific formal and informal networks, which may be based on income as well as political and/or religious affiliation, ethnicity, household type, gender and generation. In Tanzania, for example, rural women heading their households and widows living alone are often socially marginalized, and may be forced to find employment in unprofitable occupations (such as harvesting of natural resources) or even in prostitution, while patronage is in many cases a crucial element of access to activities such as intra-regional trade (Seppala 1996).

Livelihoods and rural-urban interactions

Livelihood systems are most conventionally seen in terms of people's productive lives and indeed this is an important dimension, if not the only one. However, the organization of production feeds off and into a complex web of domestic and social relations and is closely linked to how people gain access to resources and the relations they have with the wider economy. For example, in rural areas, access to land and labour can be crucial factors in ensuring agricultural production for consumption and the market. In urban areas where economies are even more monetized and where there is almost exclusive dependence on cash income, livelihoods crucially depend on access to employment and income-earning opportunities. Nevertheless, the crossover between production and reproduction evident in rural economies is not absent from urban contexts either. For example, the growth of urban agriculture since the late 1970s has been largely understood as a response to escalating urban poverty and to rising food prices or shortages, which in turn were exacerbated by the implementation of structural adjustment policies in the 1980s (Drakakis-Smith 1992, Lee-Smith et al. 1987). However, some studies have shown that high and middle-income households constitute a significant and growing proportion of urban farmers, who often engage in this activity for commercial purposes. Consequently, in several cases the poorest groups (often including newly-arrived migrants) are excluded from access to land as a result of both formal and informal gate-keeping processes in the city (Mbiba 1995, Mlozi et al 1992).

Grown and Sebstad (1989: 941) talk about 'livelihood systems' to refer to 'the mix of individual and household survival strategies, developed over a given period of time, that seeks to mobilize available resources and opportunities'. Responses might include labour market involvement, savings accumulation and investment, changing patterns of consumption and income earning, labour and asset-pooling arrangements, or social networking. Thus livelihoods are understood not only in terms of income earning but a much wider range of activities, such as gaining and retaining access to resources and opportunities, dealing with risk, negotiating social relationships within the household and managing social networks and institutions within the city and beyond it. From this perspective, livelihood systems are also seen to embrace the arrangement of reproductive tasks and responsibilities, including domestic work and child-rearing, that accompany and make possible participation in paid work and the public sphere.

There are a number of advantages to a livelihoods perspective, not least that it allows for the disaggregation of low-income households according to the different goals they pursue, namely, survival, security or growth (Grown and Sebstad 1989). Second, it fosters a wider perspective on employment. 'Resources' are seen not only as physical assets such as property, but as human assets such as time and skills, social assets such as networks and collective assets such as public sector services. 'Opportunities' might include kin and friendship networks, institutional mechanisms, or organizational and group membership. Third, a livelihood approach provides the opportunity for integrating a gender and generational perspective into mainstream analysis of development as it is recognized that the responses and contributions of men and women differ from each other and at different stages of their life cycles (Beall 1997).

However, while a livelihood systems approach expands the framework of analysis beyond simply the work place, a too narrow focus on livelihoods risks over-emphasizing micro-level activities, at the expense of analysing wider structures of economic power and social change. In the hands of policymakers and planners not committed to linking livelihood systems with wider economic and political processes, the result can be that poverty is only tackled through micro-level interventions, ignoring the impact of policy at the meso- and macro-levels.

Migration

Any attempt to understand livelihood systems in African and the way they straddle the rural-urban divide needs to include a consideration of migration. Traditional approaches to migration rely on the notion of push-pull factors as the main explanatory elements for population movement. In the neo-classical perspective, decisions to move are made by individuals in response to hardships in source areas (the 'push' factors) and to perceived comparative advantages in destination areas (the 'pull' factors). In other words, individuals rationally decide to migrate because they are attracted by the 'bright lights' of cities, which promise in the long term to offer better economic opportunities than the countryside. The structuralist approach to migration, on the other hand, tends to portray migrants as victims rather than rational decision-makers, since movement is understood as determined by macro-social and historical processes such as the socio-spatial restructuring of production at the national and global levels. 'Push-pull' factors are here seen as a process of polarization with regard to access to resources and migration is seen as one of the few options available to the groups with least assets.

Although relatively little is known about the scale and nature of internal migration in Africa, it is usually seen as an existing or potential contributory factor to the uncontrolled growth and the related management problems of the continent's cities. This has often resulted in policies aiming to control or discourage movement; with apartheid South Africa's draconian 'pass laws' being the most infamous and well-known example. In general, however, legislative restrictions on migration are comparatively infrequent in Africa. Nevertheless, many countries have sought to make cities relatively inhospitable, for example by bulldozing informal low-income settlements or making it difficult for new migrants to secure property rights to land or access to public services. These measures have generally had little impact aside from lowering welfare, especially for the poor. In many cases, policymakers are totally unaware of the impact of macro-economic policies on migration and urban development (Becker and Morrison 1996) and more information is needed on the patterns and processes of population movement.

In particular, two aspects need to be better understood: first the direction (rural-to-urban, urban-to-rural, urban-to-urban and rural-to-rural) and the type of migration (permanent, seasonal, temporary) need to be more accurately described in their specific contexts and with particular attention to the impact of out-migration in source areas. Second, selectivity along gender and age lines requires increased attention since it often overlaps with socio-cultural change and is likely to affect the linkages between urban-based individuals and their relatives in rural areas.

Changes in migration types and direction

'Push-pull' models of migration inherently assume that migration's direction is essentially from rural to urban areas, with the income gap between the two as an important explanatory factor. However, the move to cities or towns is not always permanent. In many cases, urban-to-rural migration is an on-going movement involving the urban population with fewest assets on a temporary or seasonal basis. In Africa, with its long history of the oscillating migration of men, there have been many instances of men's long-term separation from their rural households and their being housed in temporary, single-sex accommodation and tied to fixed term contracts. However, there is sufficient evidence to suggest that this trend has continued well beyond colonial recruitment practices and for South Africa, Mabin (1990) has argued that circular migration will long outlive apartheid labour and urbanization strategies.

Moreover, research in sub-Saharan Africa has pointed out that, since the mid-1970s, economic decline has greatly reduced the gap between real urban incomes and real rural incomes in the region (Jamal and Weeks 1988). In a fascinating article on the medium-sized town of Newcastle in South Africa, Alison Todes (1998) shows that people do not automatically move out of declining areas. She describes how, following growth on the basis of industrial decentralization policies and coinciding with the abolition of influx controls, in recent years Newcastle has entered a period of economic stagnation and employment losses. Despite this, there was net in-migration of population from nearby rural and peri-urban areas, contradicting the neo-liberal view of migration, premised on the assumption that people often move long distances to major urban centres for employment.

It also appears that the rate of urban growth in some African cities has slowed significantly and that new forms of 'return' migration, from the urban to the rural areas are occurring (Potts 1995). Following the implementation of structural adjustment programmes and economic reform, it is thought that a number of retrenched formal-sector urban workers may engage in urban-rural migration and return to 'home' areas where the cost of living is lower. Although little research has been conducted on return migration, it is likely to have a significant impact on destination areas as returnees may compete with the local population for scarce resources while at the same time they may possibly facilitate the introduction of innovations, both technological and socio-cultural.

Linkages between urban-based and rural-based household members
Since the 1980s, a growing body of empirical research has pointed out that migration involves more than just the individual who moves. The migrants are enmeshed in a web of social and economic relationships that influence decisions to move. The domestic unit is one fundamental structure, which embodies such relationships. A livelihood systems approach to migration attempts to link the micro (individual) level with the macro (structural) level by focusing on the household as the unit of analysis, recognizing that

migration, either of some members or of the whole unit, is an important element of household strategies (Wood 1982). Research has shown that generational as well as gender dimensions characterize family migration patterns and the mobility of individual household members varies at different stages of their life cycle.

Todes demonstrates how the dynamics of mobility and immobility are gendered and how in turn, gender relations are mediated by place and space. Although individual employment and migration histories showed tremendous flux and movement in people's lives, this was not the case for households as a whole. What was occurring was a selective out-migration of young people and men from Newcastle, with a 'home' base being maintained largely by women. As Todes (1998: 327) argues, the 'story' of Newcastle provides evidence that 'women (but increasingly men too) are not free agents to move. The establishment of "home bases" in a context of insecurity and constraint and investment in them has provided a significant barrier to wholesale movement'.

Thus, like gender, generation is a key variable in understanding the way livelihood systems straddle the rural-urban divide. Kate Crehan (1992: 114) observes that, for rural contexts, the household as a site for raising children might not coincide with the household as a unit of residence. In some peasant societies, she says, 'children may not live in the same residential unit as their biological parents. They may live with grandparents or other kin and in the course of their childhood they may move freely between different kin'. This often holds for urban areas also as illustrated by the work of Jones (1994) on the worker hostels of Cape Town, South Africa. Here he demonstrates how children move among various family members living in the city, in towns and in rural villages, in response to the fortunes of different household members over the domestic cycle.

Despite their pivotal role in the livelihood strategies of many urban households, older people can sometimes be considered a burden. Gorman (1996) argues that there is a link between the social status and care of older people and their economic power and if the latter diminishes, there is a parallel loss of status within their households and social networks. In Africa this sometimes heralds a return to rural areas. Belinda Bozzoli (1991) points to the trend of older women returning alone to rural areas after years of working in the city because their children are unable or unwilling to support them in their old age. Interviews with women 'retiring' from a working life in Johannesburg to their village of origin in the South African countryside, reveal their diminishing choices as elderly urban dwellers. To the question 'Why didn't you become a township granny?' one woman replied:

> No ways. When you're old your children don't have time to look after you. They have their lives to live. . . . Just because they are staying in an urban area they see me as an interfering old lady. I guess it could have

been better if I were to stay with my children, sharing with them the little that they can get, because groceries are very expensive nowadays (Bozzoli 1991).

In a study of low-income settlements in Harare, Zimbabwe, Kanji (1995: 53) found that older women, usually widows and main householders, had the fewest resources and opportunities and were heavily dependent on adult offspring. 'Much therefore depended upon their relationships especially with sons, who tended to have more available resources than daughters to support the family. When sons did not meet their obligations and where daughters were not able to help, the effect on the household was particularly severe'. Sandra Burman (1994) provides a moving account of elderly family members living in their children's households in a low-income township in Cape Town. Her study reports that when older people were asked where they turned to for social or economic support, they listed in decreasing order, neighbours, friends, sons, daughters and other relatives, underscoring the importance of social networks beyond family and kinship ties.

Conclusions

For some individual households and groups of people, straddling the rural-urban divide is an important part of their livelihood strategies and yet policies have often neglected these linkages. Macro-level policies and economic reform, have often intensified poverty and vulnerability for some groups. For example, in many African countries job insecurity and general increases in prices in the urban areas make it increasingly difficult for urban dwellers to support their relatives in rural areas (Potts with Mutambirwa 1998). By the same token, Kanji's (1993) research in Harare showed that women's seasonal migration from town to rural areas to secure food resources and to maintain kinship relations and social networks, was adversely affected by increasing transport costs under the impact of the Economic Structural Adjustment Policy (ESAP) in the early 1990s. In rural areas, changes in agricultural production systems have often resulted in the marginalization of small farmers, who must turn to non-agricultural rural employment or migrate to the towns. However, although understanding the strong ties between rural-based and urban-based household members can increase understanding of the impact of policy and responses to it on the part of low-income households and groups this is a relatively neglected area of policy research in Africa.

In assessing the links between households, livelihoods and policy, a useful place to start is with the debates on the impact of structural adjustment programmes. Urban populations were seen to more affected by structural adjustment because, in general, they were more integrated into cash and wage economies and more dependent on food and other social-sector subsidies which were lifted. Retrenchment packages, specifically, were largely directed to urban workers who had lost jobs, sometimes defined as the 'new poor'. Rural populations were meant to benefit from the lifting of producer price controls in agriculture and by trade liberalization. City-focused studies revealed that the social response to economic crisis and austerity has produced other changes at the household level. These include increased labour force participation by women and income earning on the part of children, reduced overall consumption often differentiated by gender and in some contexts, increased domestic tensions (Kanji 1995, Moser 1996). There has also been increasing emphasis on the importance of social networks and social capital or social assets as a resource for poor people in their efforts to survive and prosper (Moser 1996 and 1998, Rakodi 1991).

However, in countries with structural adjustment programmes, research which has interrogated this general assumption that urban populations have been worse affected, has found the situation is variable. For example, in countries in Africa small rural farmers have been adversely affected by the rise in the cost of inputs, the lifting of agricultural subsidies and the withdrawal of the state in marketing (Evans 1997, McKay et al. 1997). For example, in Zimbabwe it has been argued that the outcomes of ESAP have been felt more acutely in the city than in the countryside. However recent research suggests that rural populations have also suffered from increases in the prices of basic commodities and in public service fees. Retrenchment and increasing poverty in the cities affects rural households as well, as remittances decline and migrants return to their rural homes, increasing the burden there. Due to the economic interdependence between city and countryside, and to the strength of the ties between members of multi-spatial households, the impact of structural adjustment is not clearly geographically defined, but increases hardship in both locations (Potts with Mutambirwa 1998).

Clearly, urban-rural linkages are complex. Negative effects of policies have often been felt by both urban and rural households, for example, through the reduction of remittances from urban to rural household members or a reduction in demand for rurally produced food. The assumption of a sectoral divide, with rural populations seen as primarily as agricultural producers while urban dwellers are thought to engage in industry and services is increasingly misleading (Tacoli 1998). Although poverty in urban areas may have different characteristics from that in rural areas, Wratten (1995) challenges the usefulness of treating urban poverty as a separate conceptual category. She argues that, from a policy perspective, a narrow focus on the urban context can obscure the underlying causes of poverty and the opportunity of addressing it at a national or regional level. The determinants of urban and rural poverty are interlinked and have to be addressed in tandem. While we have an increasing quantity of research that shows the impact of policy on livelihoods within urban areas and across the rural-urban divide, the challenge remains to draw out the implications for policy of the responses of poor households and groups to policy change.

Notes

Introduction
1. Recognising this, the present author feels uncomfortable using the term 'the urban poor' throughout this article. Where appropriate the different categories of the poor will be indicated. Otherwise, for convenience sake, the undifferentiated term of 'urban poor' will be used.

Chapter 2
1. IIED (International Institute for Environment and Development) publications provide a useful overview, with a wide ranging selection of commentaries.
2. As Amis (1995: 146) – 'Within Africa . . . urban wages have been declining since 1970 . . . these changes predate structural adjustment . . .'.
3. See Thomas (1994) for a useful summary about this programme.
4. Providing profiles of informal sectors, which provide a very different picture to formal sector assessments alone has increasingly been an area where social anthropologists have been playing a role. See for example Wright's consideration of organisation issues (1994).
5. See ODI (Overseas Development Institute) Workshop Papers 1997 for discussion points.
6. See Satterthwaite (1997) and Rakodi (1994) for a detailed discussion of this.
7. See Thomas (1994) for discussion of this programme.
8. As an example of indicators provided (in this case by UNICEF) see Jones, Francis et al. (1996).
9. All credit must go to a Danish consultant (Andreasson) who, in a brief conversation, years ago, first brought this to my attention. He had been doing extensive research in Kenya and identified shoes as a key indicator of levels of poverty. Due to him I have always looked to see if there is something people obtain as soon as they have some cash; something that they see as marking an improvement in their conditions.
10. See Thomas (1994) for a succinct discussion of this.
11. See Part three of this book for particular examples.
12. These are increasingly local people working as international consultants.

Chapter 4
1. An earlier and very much longer version of this paper was tabled at the conference on 'Enterprise in Africa' at the Centre of African Studies, May 1998.
2. 'not all small-scale economic activity is necessarily informal, nor is all informal activity necessarily small-scale' (Swedish Ministry for Foreign Affairs 1997a:119).
3. The author's *African Artisan* (King 1977) was unusual at the time in being as much about the rural as the urban sites of the informal sector in Kenya.
4. The previous UK white paper on development (*More help for the poorest*, Ministry of Overseas Development 1975) was typical of the newer approach in arguing the need for raising agricultural productivity and incomes in agriculture in such a way as to benefit the standard of life of the broad mass of the rural population.

5. Although a good deal is said about the importance of business linkages between microenterprises and larger firms, it remains the case in cities like Nairobi that there are only a handful of African-run firms in the formal industrial area.

Chapter 5
1. The choice of rural-urban migrants was also partly because we wanted a sample which could reasonably be expected to have good links with rural areas, so that we could judge the impact of ESAP on rural livelihoods as well as urban (see Potts and Mutambirwa 1998).
2. It is recognised that this is a very broad generalization, and that many exceptions could be found.
3. Equivalent at the time of the survey (1994) to US$121.
4. Food cost issues in general were the single most frequently mentioned price problem by our sample when discussing their perceptions of the impact of ESAP on Harare (rather than themselves) (see Potts and Mutambirwa 1998).
5. Since the surveys controls on these imports were tightened up but these apparently had relatively little effect on the trade ('Zimbabwe Report', *Economist Intelligence Unit*, January 1995, April 1995, September 1995). However in July 1997, without warning, the government suddenly imposed customs restrictions on the importation of bales of second-hand clothes from Mozambique (where they were originally brought in as charity clothes) at the border – a move which would undoubtedly undermine this informal-sector niche.

Chapter 6
1. That is not to say, of course, that knowledge about poverty is the main factor shaping policy or that it guarantees good policies.

Chapter 7
1. There are, of course, various urban initiatives being undertaken, such as the UN LIFE approach. Donor agencies, especially Scandinavian agencies such as DANIDA and SIDA (Swedish International Development Authority), have targeted action at community level to address poverty. Also, agencies have targeted action at specific countries, such as DFID's work in the slums in India. The concern of this paper is to consider the possibility for larger scale, multi-deprivation frameworks for urban poverty action promoted by donor agencies that could be in a range of countries.
2. Figures quoted in Thomas (1994). Further figures are provided in Chapters 1 and 2.
3. See, for example the recently published UK Government White Paper on International Development – *Eliminating World Poverty: A Challenge for the 21st Century* produced by the Department for International Development (DFID) – the UK donor agency – in November 1997.
4. See Satterthwaite (1997) and Wratten (1995) for discussions about integrated development and multiple deprivation action.
5. See Chapter 1 – Dr Nici Nelson, for a discussion of 'urban bias'.
6. See Chapter 2 for a discussion of the different qualitative definitions of urban poverty.
7. This assessment is based on the publicly available study commissioned by the (then) British Development Division in Eastern Africa, ODA, published in April 1995.
8. The team included Sue Jones (Team Leader), Graham Alder, Bosire Ogero, Dr Joyce Malombe, Muindi Mulili and Gabriel Wambua.

9. This information is not necessarily readily available to local people. I have personally seen local employees try to obtain copies of national studies without success until a donor agency made the request on their behalf.
10. It is an irony that in the 1980s I found myself, as a social scientist, arguing for qualitative assessments to be undertaken alongside quantitative studies and now I find I face fierce opposition suggesting that some quantitative assessments could help to complement the qualitative assessments being undertaken.
11. See Jones (1998: Section 3).
12. See N. Nelson (this volume) for one of the earlier assessments of their conditions.
13. See Satterthwaite (1997) for a discussion of the need for a multi-deprivation approach.
14. As examples, see Jones (1990), Jones (1995).
15. See Ngau (1994). See also Rakodi (1994) for a discussion of household strategies.
16. See, for example Jones (1996).

Chapter 8

1. This chapter contains material which has been shared with audiences in Oslo and Haifa under the title 'Employment in Housing: An overview of shelter as a generator of work'.
2. This assumes also that all existing households have a dwelling, but many, of course, do not.
3. However, these figures are almost certainly underestimates because they make no allowance for the following:
   o shortfalls on current supply;
   o dwellings which are or will become unfit for occupation and must be replaced;
   o any desired improvements in current occupancy rates.
   On the other hand they make no allowance for the fact that many households only occupy rooms in a house rather than a whole dwelling.
4. It can be argued that any increase in low-paid work, or reliance on low-paid workers, is exploitative. I would argue that, as long as there are opportunities for advancement through skills development, low-paid work is an acceptable part of any economy where there are thousands of workers willing to do the work. The general level of wages and extreme differentials between high and low pay may be a cause for concern to us all, and be the subject of complaints about exploitation. But, where there are differentials in any pay system, unskilled builders' labourers are likely to remain at the bottom.
5. This is undoubtedly an underestimate (as official data seldom records informal sector or casual employment) but the figures serve to illustrate the present gap between the rich and poor countries in employment in construction.
6. In Egypt, for example, contracts were signed in 1975 linking Egyptian companies with ten foreign industrialized building companies. The new cities in the desert and many residential areas in the existing cities are now uniformly constructed using the high technology, prefabricated panel systems which have such a poor record in industrialized countries. Similar reliance on high technology systems has been a feature in countries as far apart as Brazil and Indonesia (Hardoy and Satterthwaite 1981).
7. At that time, Mr Sarpong Mensah was the Managing Director of the Kumasi office of SHC.
8. Where a factory is built and commissioned so that all the local operator has to do (in theory) is turn the key to start it up and watch the products roll off the production line. Such technology transfer rarely happens as smoothly as this indicates.

Chapter 9
1. This chapter is based on a more extensive paper published with the International Institute for Environment and Development London in 1996 as 'uTshani buyakhulum (the grass speaks): People's Dialogue and the South African Homeless People's Federation'. The editors thank IIED for permission to reprint part of this report.

Chapter 10
1. Micro-finance is a wider concept than credit. It includes savings, insurance, hire-purchase, etc.

Chapter 12
1. This paper presents part of the data from a larger study (Bantebya Kyomuhendo 1997) which sought to examine the effects of women's access to money and time use on their health care decisions for themselves and their children under five. The study predominantly used qualitative techniques of data collection such as case histories, in-depth interviews and observations.

Chapter 13
1. These categories are discussed further below but they are predominantly concerned with pre-adolescent and adolescent boys who are living separately from their families.
2. *Kenkey* and *poha* are local foods often traded on the street.
3. Personal communication, Dr Joseph Tanga, Chief Executive, Bolgatanga District.
4. A 26 aggregate is not high enough to provide access to the senior secondary school which might provide relevant qualifications for the salaried labour market.
5. The Ghanaian currency is the *cedi*. it has been depreciating rapidly against 'hard' currencies and at present (1999) C2 000 is equivalent to around UK £0.70.
6. TZ is the local starch in northern Ghana made of maize or millet.

References

Chapter 1

Bahemuka, J., Nganda, B. and Nzioka, C. (eds) (1998) *Poverty Revisited: Analysis and strategies towards poverty eradication in Kenya*, Ruraka Printing Press, Nairobi.

Becker, C., Hamer, A. and Morrison, A. (1994) *Beyond Urban Bias in Africa: Urbanization in an era of structural adjustment*, Heineman/James Currey, London.

Bromley, R. and Gerry, C. (eds) *Casual Work and Poverty in Third World Cities*, John Wiley, Chichester.

Brydon, L. and Chant, C. (1989) *Women in the Third World: Gender issues in rural and urban areas*, Elgar Publishing Co., Aldershot.

Chambers, R. (1983) *Rural Development: Putting the last first*, Longman, Harlow.

Gilbert, A. and Gugler, J. (1981) *Cities, Poverty and Development: Urbanization in the Third World*, Oxford University Press, Oxford.

Gugler, J. (ed.) (1997) *Cities in the Developing World: Issues, theory and policy*, Oxford University Press, Oxford.

Gugler, J. and Flanagan, W. (1978) *Urbanisation and Social Change in West Africa*, Cambridge University Press, Cambridge.

Gutkind, P., Wallerstein, I. (eds.) (1976) *The Political Economy of Contemporary Africa*, Sage, London.

Guyer, J. (1987) *Feeding African Cities: Studies in regional social history*, Manchester University Press, Manchester.

Hart, K. (1982) *The Political Economy of West Africa*, Cambridge University Press, Cambridge.

IIED (1995a) *Environment and Urbanization: Urban Poverty Journal I*, vol. 7.1, pp. 3–10.

IIED (1995b) *Environment and Urbanization: Urban Poverty Journal II*, vol. 7.2, pp. 4–12.

Illiffe, J. (1987) *The African Poor: A history*, Cambridge University Press, Cambridge.

Jamal, V. and Weeks, J. (1988) 'The Vanishing Rural-Urban Gap in Sub-Saharan Africa', *International Labour Review*, vol.127 (3), pp.271–291.

Lewis, O. (1966) 'The Culture of Poverty', *Scientific American*, vol. 215 (Oct), pp. 19–25.

Lipton, M. (1977) *Why Poor People Stay Poor: A study of urban bias in world development*, Temple Smith/Harvard University Press, Boston.

Lofchie, M. (1997) 'The Rise and Demise of Urban-Biased Development Policies in Africa' in J. Gugler (ed.) *Cities in the Developing World*, Oxford University Press, Oxford.

Mandaville, E. (1979) 'Poverty, Work and the Financing of Single Women in Kampala', *Africa*, vol. 49, pp. 43–52.

Ministry of Foreign Affairs, The Netherlands (1994) *Urban Poverty Alleviation*, Sectoral Policy Document of Development Co-operation.
Nelson, N. (1981) *African Women in the Development Process*, Frank Cass, London.
Nelson, N. (1997a) 'Urbanism and Urbanization: Housing Issues', *Encyclopaedia of Africa South of the Sahara*, vol. 4, pp 335–346.
Nelson, N. (1997b) 'How Men and Women Got By and Still Get By, Only Not So Well' in Gugler, J. (ed.) *Cities in the Developing World*, Oxford University Press, Oxford.
Nelson, N. and Wright, S. (eds.) (1997) *Power and Participatory Development*, Intermediate Technology Publications, London.
O'Conner, A. (1991) *Poverty in Africa: A geographical approach*, Belhaven Press, London.
Pearlman, J. (1976) *The Myth of Marginality: Urban poverty and politics in Rio de Janeiro*, University of California Press, Berkeley.
Simon, D. (1992) *Cities, Capital and Development: African cities in the world economy*, Belhaven Press, London.
Southall, A. (1967) *Social Change in Modern Africa*, IAI/OUP, London.
Stichter, S. (1982) *Migrant Labour in Kenya: Capitalism and African response 1895–1975*, Longmans, Essex.
Stren, R. (1978) *Housing the Urban Poor in Africa: Policy, Politics and Bureaucracy in Mombasa*, University of California, Berkeley.
Valentine, C. (1968) *Culture of Poverty: Critique and counter-proposals*, University of Chicago Press, Chicago.
Wratten, E. (1995) 'Conceptualising Urban Poverty', *Environment and Urbanisation*, vol. 7.1, pp. 11–35.
White, L. (1990) *The Comforts of Home: Prostitution in colonial Nairobi*, University of Chicago Press, Chicago.
van Zwanenberg, R. (1975) *Colonial Capitalism and Labour in Kenya 1919–1939*, East African Literature Bureau, Nairobi.

Chapter 2

Amis, P. (1995) 'Making Sense of Urban Poverty', *Environment and Urbanisation*, vol. 7 (1).
Chambers, R. (1983) *Rural Development: Putting the last first*, Longman, Harlow.
Chambers, R. (1997) *Whose Reality Counts? Putting the first last*, Intermediate Technology Publications, London.
De Haan, A. with Yaqub, Y. (1996) *Urban Poverty and its Alleviation*, Poverty Research Unit at Sussex (PRUS) Working Papers No. 1, Institute of Development Studies, Sussex.
Jones, S. (1996) 'Cochin Urban Poverty Reduction Project – Design Phase – Poverty Strategy' prepared for ODA in consultation with design phase consultancy team, Corporation of Cochin, Urban Poverty Office and Development, Co-operation Office, New Delhi.
Jones, S. and Francis, S. (1996) 'Cochin Urban Poverty Reduction Project – Design Phase – Urban Poverty Profile Study', prepared for ODA with

the Urban Poverty Profile Study Team, led by Aji Kumaran, Project Officer, the Urban Poverty Alleviation Unit, Community Organisers, Engineers and Health staff from Corporation of Cochin and the urban poor of Cochin.

Jones, S. and Matrix Consultants (1995) 'Urban Poverty in Kenya: Situation analysis and options for ODA assistance' prepared for the British Development Division in Eastern Africa, Overseas Development Administration.

Moser, C. (1998) 'The Asset Vulnerability Framework: Reassessing urban poverty reduction strategies', *World Development*, Vol.26 (1).

Moser, C., Herbert, A. J. and Makonnen, R.E. (1993) 'Urban Poverty in the Context of Structural Adjustment: Recent evidence and policy responses' TWU Discussion Paper 4, Urban Development Division, World Bank, Washington DC.

Overseas Development Institute (1997) 'Indications of Poverty', papers presented at workshop held 8 October, Portland House, Stag Place, London.

Pryer, J., Dowler, E., Clay, E. and Pillai, N. (1997) 'Urban Poverty – Scale, Manifestation and Measurement: Fertile ground for north-south, south-south collaboration?' paper presented at Indicators of Poverty Workshop at ODI, London on 8 October 1997.

Rakodi, C. (1994) *Poverty Lines or Household Strategies? A Review of Conceptual and Methodological Issues in the Study of Urban Poverty*, University of Wales, Cardiff.

Satterthwaite, D. (ed.) (1995a) 'The Under-estimation and Misrepresentation of Urban Poverty', *Environment and Urbanization*, vol. 7 (1).

Satterthwaite, D. (ed.) (1995b) 'The Under-estimation and Misrepresentation of Urban Poverty', *Environment and Urbanization*, vol. 7 (2).

Satterthwaite, D. (1997) 'Urban Poverty: Reconsidering its scale and nature', background paper for the series of workshops on poverty reduction in urban areas organized by the International Institute for Environment and Development (IIED), UK.

Sen, A. (1997) 'Development Thinking at the Beginning of the 21st Century' The Development Economics Research Programme No.2, DERP, London.

Thomas, L. (1994) 'Urban Poverty and Development Interventions', INTRAC Occasional Papers Series No. 4, Intrac, Oxford.

Townshend, P. (1993) *The International Analysis of Poverty*, Harvester Wheatsheaf, New York and London.

Wratten, E. (1995) 'Conceptualizing Urban Poverty' in *Environment and Urbanization* vol. 7 (1).

Wright, S. (ed.) (1994) *Anthropology of Organisations* Routledge, London.

Chapter 3

Abiodun, J. (1997) 'The Challenges of Growth and Development in Metropolitan Lagos' in Rakodi, C. (ed.) *The Urban Challenge in Africa*, United Nations University Press, Tokyo.

Agbola, T. (1987) 'Institutional Constraints on Housing Development: The urban areas of Nigeria: The land-use decree and the building plan approval process', *Third World Planning Review*, vol. 11 (2), p.116.

Aron, J. (1997) 'Africa in the 1990s: The institutional foundations of growth', Working Paper Series 97–15, Centre for the Study of African Economics, Oxford.

Bolade, T. (ed.) (1989) *Urban Mass Transit System in Nigeria*, Ibadan University Press, Ibadan.

Bubba, N. and Lamba, D. (1991) 'Local Government in Kenya', *Environment and Urbanization*, vol. 3 (1), IIED, London.

Collier, P. and Lal, D. (1980) 'Poverty and Growth in Kenya', World Bank Staff Working Paper No. 389, World Bank, Washington DC.

Dubresson, A. (1997) 'Abidjan: From the public making of a modern city to urban management of a metropolis', in Rakodi, C. (ed.) *The Urban Challenge in Africa*, United Nations University Press, Tokyo.

The Economist (1990) 'Africa's Cities', September 15.

Government of Kenya (1986) 'Urban Housing Survey 1983; Basic Report', Nairobi Department of Housing, Ministry of Works, Housing and Physical Planning and Central Bureau of Statistics, Ministry of Planning and National Development, Nairobi.

Government of Zimbabwe (n.d.) 'Midland Provincial Development Plan', Ministry of Local Government, Rural and Urban Development.

Harris, N. (1992) 'Productivity and Poverty in the Cities of the Developing Countries', in Harris, N. (ed.) *Cities in the 1990s: The challenge for developing countries*, UCL Press Ltd, London.

Halfani, M. (1996) 'Marginality and Dynamism: Prospects for the sub-Saharan African city', in Cohen, M., Ruble, B., Tulchin, J. and Garland, A. (eds.) *Preparing for the Urban Future: Global pressures and local forces*, Woodrow Wilson Center Press, Washington DC.

ISTED (1998) 'The Dynamics of Urbanization in Sub-Saharan Africa', Secretariat d'Etat à la Coopération et à la Francophone, Paris.

Jones, S. and Matrix Consultants (1995) 'Urban Poverty in Kenya', prepared for the British Development Division in Eastern Africa, Overseas Development Administration.

Kombe, W. J. (1996) 'Regularizing Urban Land Development During the Transition to Market-Led Land Supply in Tanzania', in Kombe, W. J. and Kreibich, V. (eds.) *Urban Land Management and the Transition to a Market Economy in Tanzania*, Spring Research Series 19, SPRING-Center, University of Dortmund.

Kulaba, S. (1989) 'Local Government and the Management of Urban Services' in Stren, R. and White, R. (eds.) *African Cities in Crisis*, Westview Press, Boulder.

Kumasi Metropolitan Assembly (1996) 'Development Plan for Kumasi Metropolitan Area, Volume II, Profile: Current status', Kumasi Metropolitan Assembly, Kumasi.

Lee, K. S. and Anas, A. (1989) 'Manufacturers' Responses to Infrastructure Deficiencies in Nigeria: Private alternatives and policy options', INU Discussion Paper 50, World Bank, Washington, DC.

Lee-Smith, D. and Stren, R. (1991) 'New Perspectives on African Urban Management', *Environment and Urbanization*, vol. 3 (1), IIED, London.

Lee-Smith, D. and Syagga, P. (1989) 'Access by the Urban Poor to Basic Infrastructure Services', Africa Regional Paper for the Economic Development Unit, Mazingira Institute, Nairobi.

Mabogunje, A. (1993) 'Perspectives on Urban Land and Urban Management Policies in Sub-Saharan Africa', World Bank Technical Paper 196, Washington DC.

McNeill, D. (1983) 'The Changing Practice of Urban Planning', *Habitat International*, Vol 7, (5&6), Pergamon, London.

Mehta, H. and Macharia, E. (1997) 'The Decay of Nairobi Urban Open Space', *The Horizon – DAT*, Vol 1 (1), ICIPE Science Press, Nairobi.

Mghweno, J. (1984) 'Tanzania's Surveyed Plots Programme' in Payne, G., *Low-Income Housing in the Developing World: The role of sites and services and settlement upgrading*, Wiley, New York.

Nelson, N. (1997) 'How Women and Men Got By and Still Do (Only Not So Well): The gender division of labour in a Nairobi shanty town', in Gugler, J. (ed.), *Cities in the Developing World*, Oxford University Press, Oxford.

Njoh, A. (1992) 'Institutional Impediments to Private Residential Development in Cameroon', *Third World Planning Review*, vol. 14 (11), Liverpool.

Nwaka, G. (n.d. circa 1990) 'Urban Planning and Environmental Protection in Nigeria', unpublished paper.

Okpala, D. (1997) 'Urban Planning and the African Urban Landscape', *Interplan*, No 56 March, American Planning Association, Chicago.

Olson, M. (1996) 'Big Bills Left on the Sidewalk: Why some nations are rich and others poor', *Journal of Economic Perspective*, (Spring).

Onokerhoraye, A. G. (1982) *Public Services in Nigerian Urban Areas*, Nigerian Institute of Social and Economic Research, Ibadan.

Reynolds, G. (1985) *Economic Growth in the Third World: 1850–1980*, Yale University Press, New Haven.

Rogerson, C. M. (1996) 'Urban Poverty and the Informal Economy in South Africa's Economic Heartland', *Environment And Urbanization*, vol. 8 (1).

Schmetzer, H. (1990) 'Municipal Planning and Management in Lusaka', unpublished paper, Swedish International Development Authority, Stockholm.

Stren, R. and White, R. (eds.) (1989) *African Cities in Crisis*, Westview Press, Boulder.

Taiwo, Olukayode (1991) 'Social Dimensions of Infrastructural Development in Nigeria' unpublished paper presented to the Infrastructure Development Fund Project Technical Training Seminar, Ota, Lagos, 4–13 August.

Tanner, A. (1990) 'Roads and Stormwater in Low Income Townships: Letting the solutions determine the standards', unpublished paper prepared for a South African Housing Advisory Council/Urban Foundation workshop, Ninham Shand Inc, Pretoria.

United Nations (1973) *Urban Land Policies and Land-Use Control Measures (Volume 1. Africa)*, UN Department of Economic and Social Affairs, New York.
UNCHS (United Nations Centre for Human Settlements) (1987) *Case Study of Sites and Services Schemes in Kenya: Lessons from Dandora and Thika*, UNCHS, Nairobi.
UNCHS (1992a) 'Institutional Innovation in the Management of Secondary Cities in Sub-Saharan Africa: A case study: Mbuji-Mayi, Zaire', unpublished document, UNCHS, Nairobi.
UNCHS (1992b) *Metropolitan Planning and Management in the Developing World: Abidjan and Quito*, UNCHS, Nairobi.
UNCHS (1996) *An Urbanizing World: Global report on human settlements 1996*, Oxford University Press, Oxford.
Wolf, M. (1996) 'The Poverty of Nations', *Financial Times*, 20 August.
World Bank (1991) *Urban Policy and Economic Development: An agenda for the 1990s*, World Bank, Washington DC.

Chapter 4

Danish Association of Development Researchers (1987) *The Informal Sector as an Integral Part of the National Economy: Research needs and aid requirements*, Roskilde University Centre, Roskilde.
Denmark, Ministry of Foreign Affairs – Danida (1998) *Guidelines for Sector Programme Support: Final draft*, Copenhagen.
Department for International Development (DFID) (1997) *Eliminating World Poverty: A challenge for the 21st century*, HMSO, London.
Department of Labour (1997) *Green Paper: Skills development strategy for economic and employment growth in South Africa*, Department of Labour, Pretoria.
Holman, M. (1997) 'Cultivating the Seeds of Recovery in Africa', Paper presented at Japan's Overseas Development Assistance Seminar, sponsored by *Financial Times* and JICA, 27.11 97, London.
International Labour Office (1995) *World Employment Report 1995*. ILO, Geneva.
Jeans, A. (1998) 'Technology, NGOs and Small Enterprise: Securing livelihoods through technical change', paper presented at the conference Enterprise in Africa: Between poverty and growth, Edinburgh, May.
Killick, A. (1998) 'Have Africa's Economies Turned the Corner?', paper presented at the conference Enterprise in Africa: Between poverty and growth, Edinburgh, May.
King, K. (1977) *The African Artisan*, Heinemann Education Books, London.
King, K. (1996) *Jua Kali Kenya*, James Currey, London.
King, K. and Buchert, L. (eds.) (1998) *International Aid to Education: Global patterns and national contexts*, UNESCO/Northern Policy Research and Advisory Network on Education and Training (NORRAG), Paris.
King, K. and Caddell, M. (eds.) (1998) *Partnership and Poverty in Britain and Sweden's New Aid Policies*, Occasional Paper No 75, Centre of African Studies, University of Edinburgh.

McGrath, S. (1998) 'Education, Development and Assistance: The challenge of the new millennium', in King, K. and Buchert, L. (eds.) *International Aid to Education: Global patterns and national contexts*, UNESCO/NORRAG, Paris.

Mead, D. (1998) 'MSEs Tackle Both Poverty and Growth (But in Differing Proportions)', paper presented at the conference Enterprise in Africa: Between poverty and growth, Edinburgh, May.

Mead, D. and Morrison, C. (1996) 'The informal sector elephant', *World Development*, vol. 24 (10), pp. 1611–19.

Ministry of Overseas Development (1975) *Overseas Development: The changing emphasis in British aid policies: More help for the poorest*, cmd. 6270 HMSO, London.

Mkandawire, T. (1998) 'Developmental States and Small Enterprises', paper presented at the conference Enterprise in Africa: Between poverty and growth, Edinburgh, May.

Overseas Development Administration (ODA) (1995) 'Strategy for ODA Support for Small Enterprise Development' ODA, London.

Riddell, R. (1997) 'The Changing Concepts of Aid and Development', in Cummings, W. and McGinn, N. (eds.) *International Handbook on Education and Development*, Pergamon, Oxford.

Rogerson, C. M. (1998a) 'The Gauteng Manufacturing SME Economy: Present status and future prospects' Papers in Education, Training and Enterprise No. 12, Centre of African Studies, University of Edinburgh.

Rogerson, C.M. (1998b) 'Small Enterprise Development in Post-apartheid South Africa: Gearing up for growth and poverty alleviation?', paper presented at the conference Enterprise in Africa: between poverty and growth, Edinburgh, May.

Sweden, Ministry for Foreign Affairs (1997a) *Partnership With Africa: Proposals for a new Swedish policy towards sub-Saharan Africa*, Stockholm.

Sweden, Ministry for Foreign Affairs (1997b) *The Rights of the Poor: Our common responsibility: Combating poverty in Sweden's development cooperation*, Stockholm.

Visser, K. (1998) 'The Export and Growth Potential of Small And Medium-sized Enterprises in the Clothing Industry', Papers in Education, Training and Enterprise No. 13, Centre of African Studies, University of Edinburgh.

Working Group for International Cooperation in Vocational and Technical Skills Development (1997) 'Donor Policies in Skills Development' (London May 1997 meeting), Bern.

Chapter 5

Auret, D. (1995) *Urban Housing: A national crisis?: Overcrowded and inadequate housing and the social and economic effects*, Mambo Press, Gweru, Zimbabwe.

Bijlmakers, L., Bassett, M. and Sanders, D. (1996) *Health and Structural Adjustment in Rural and Urban Zimbabwe*, Nordiska Afrikainstitutet, Uppsala.

Blunt, C. (1997) 'A Critical Analysis of the Nature and role of the informal market sector in Lusaka', unpublished BA dissertation, School of Oriental and African Studies, University of London.

Brand, V., Mupedziswa, R. and Gumbo, P. (1995) 'Structural Adjustment, Women and Informal Sector Trade in Harare', in P. Gibbon (ed.), *Structural Adjustment and the Working Poor in Zimbabwe*, Nordiska Afrikainstitutet, Uppsala.

Chilowa, W. and Roe, G. (1990) 'Expenditure Patterns and Nutritional Status of Low Income Urban Households in Malawi', in G. Roe (ed.) *Workshop on the Effects of the Structural Adjustment Programme in Malawi. Volume 2: Papers presented*, University of Malawi, Centre for Social Research, Zomba.

Guardian (1998) 'Troops Deployed to Quell Harare Riots', by Alex Dural Smith and Andrew Meldrum, Jan 21.

Jeffries, R. (1992) 'Urban Popular Attitudes Towards the Economic Recovery Programme and the PDNC Government in Ghana'. *African Affairs*, 91: pp. 207–226.

Kanji, N. and Kajdowska, N. (1993) 'Structural Adjustment and the Implications for Low-income Urban Women in Zimbabwe', *Review of African Political Economy*, 56, pp. 11–26.

Kasete, Tendai (Harare resident) (1997) Interview by author, July.

King, K. (1996) *Jua Kali Kenya: The African artisan and the informal sector revisited*, James Currey, London.

Potts, D. (1997a) 'Urban Lives: Adopting new strategies and adapting rural links', in Rakodi, C. (ed.), *The Urban Challenge in Africa: Growth and management of its large cities*, United Nations University Press, Tokyo, pp. 447–494.

Potts, D. (1997b) 'Structural Adjustment and Poverty: Perceptions from Zimbabwe', *Indicator South Africa*, vol. 14 (3), pp. 82–88.

Potts, D. (1998) 'Housing policies in Southern Africa', in Jaglin, S., Gervais-Lambony, P. and Mabin, A. (eds.) *Urban Issues in Southern Africa*, Cape Town: David Philip, Paris: Karthala, forthcoming.

Potts, D. and Mutambirwa, C.C. (1998) ' "Basics Are Now a Luxury": Perceptions of ESAP's impact on rural and urban areas in Zimbabwe', *Environment and Urbanization: Special Issue on Rural-Urban Divide*, April.

Rakodi, C. (1994) 'Recession, Drought and Urban Poverty in Zimbabwe: Household coping strategies in Gweru', paper presented at Institute of British Geographers' conference, panel on Coping With Poverty: Urbanisation during an economic crisis, January.

Rakodi, C. (1995) *Harare : Inheriting a settler-colonial city: Change or continuity?*, John Wiley, Chichester.

Rogerson, C. (1997) 'Globalization or Informalization? African urban economies in the 1990s', in Rakodi, C. (ed) *The Urban Challenge in Africa: Growth and management of its large cities*. United Nations University Press, Tokyo, pp. 337–370.

Stoneman, C. (1996) 'Prospects for the Development of Regional Economic and Political Relations in Post-apartheid Southern Africa: Can the

new South Africa dynamise the new Southern African Development Community?', *Ritsumeikan Studies in Language and Culture*, vol. 7 (5-6), pp. 297-319.
Tripp, A.M. (1990) 'The Informal Economy, Labour and the State in Tanzania', *Comparative Politics*, vol. 22 (3), 253-64.

Chapter 6

Blackburn, J. and Holland, J. (eds.) (1997) *Whose Voice? Participatory research and policy change*, Intermediate Technology Publications, London.
Blackden, C.M. and Morris-Hughes, E. (1993) 'Paradigm Postponed: Gender and economic adjustment in sub-Saharan Africa', World Bank, Africa Region, Technical Department, Human Resources and Poverty Division, Technical Note 13, Washington DC.
Booth, D., Holland, J., Hentschel, J., Lanjouw, P. and Herbert, A. (1998) *Participation and Combined Methods in African Poverty Assessment: Renewing the agenda*, DFID, Social Development Division/Africa Division, London.
Carvalho, S. and White, H. (1997) 'Combining the Quantitative and Qualitative Approaches to Poverty Measurement and Analysis: The practice and the potential', World Bank, Technical Paper 366, Washington DC.
Chambers, R. (1982) *Rural Development: Putting the last first*, Longman, London.
Chambers, R. (ed.) (1989) 'Vulnerability: How the Poor Cope', *IDS Bulletin*, Vol. 20 (2).
Chambers, R. (1995) 'Poverty and Livelihoods: Whose reality counts?', IDS Discussion Paper 347, Brighton.
Chambers, R. (1997) *Whose Reality Counts? Putting the last first*, Intermediate Technology Publications, London.
Elson, D., Evers, B. and Gideon, J. (1996) 'Gender Aware Country Economic Report, Working Paper No. 1: Concepts and sources', Graduate School of Social Sciences, University of Manchester.
Hanmer, L., Pyatt, G. and White, H. (1997) *Poverty in Sub-Saharan Africa: What can we learn from the World Bank's poverty assessments?*, Institute of Social Studies, The Hague.
Institute of Development Studies (IDS) (1994) 'Poverty Assessment and Public Expenditure: A Study for the SPA Working Group on Poverty and Social Policy – summary report', IDS, Brighton.
Jodha, N.S. (1988) 'Poverty Debate in India: A minority view', *Economic and Political Weekly*, Special Number, November.
Lipton, M. (1997) 'Editorial: Poverty – are there holes in the consensus?' *World Development*, Vol. 25 (7).
Moser, C.O.N. (1996) *Confronting Crisis: A comparative study of household responses to poverty and vulnerability in four poor urban communities*, World Bank, Environmentally Sustainable Development Studies Monograph 8, Washington DC.

Moser, C.O.N. (1998) 'The Asset Vulnerability Framework: Reassessing urban poverty reduction strategies', *World Development*, Vol. 26 (1).
Narayan, D. (1997) *Voices of the Poor: Poverty and social capital in Tanzania*, World Bank, Environmentally Sustainable Development Studies and Monographs 20, Washington DC.
Narayan, D. and Pritchett, L. (1997) 'Cents and Sociability: Household income and social capital in rural Tanzania', The World Bank, paper presented at Investment, Growth and Risk in Africa conference, April.
Norton, A. (1997) 'Some Reflections on the PPA Process and Lessons Learned', in Blackburn, J. and Holland, J. (eds.) *Whose Voice? Participatory research and policy change*, Intermediate Technology Publications, London.
Norton, A. and Stephens, T. (1995) 'Participation in Poverty Assessments', World Bank, Environment Department Papers 20, Washington DC.
Putnam, R. (1993) *Making Democracy Work: Civic traditions in modern Italy*, Princeton University Press, Princeton.
Robb, C.M. (1998) *Can the Poor Influence Policy? Participatory poverty assessments in the developing world*, World Bank, Washington DC.
Salmen, L.F. (1995) 'Participatory Poverty Assessments: Incorporating poor people's perspectives into poverty assessment work', World Bank, Environment Department Papers 24, Washington DC.
Sen, A. (1981) *Poverty and Famines: An essay on entitlement and deprivation*, Oxford University Press, London.
Sen, A. (1985) *Commodities and Capabilities*, North-Holland, Amsterdam.
Swift, J. (1989) 'Why Are Rural People Vulnerable to Famine', *IDS Bulletin*, Vol. 20 (2).
World Bank (1990) *World Development Report 1990: Poverty*, Oxford University Press, New York.
World Bank (1994) *The Many Faces of Poverty: Status report on poverty in sub-Saharan Africa 1994*, Human Resources and Poverty Division, Africa Technical Department, Washington DC.
World Bank (1996) *Taking Action for Poverty Reduction in Sub-Saharan Africa: Report of an Africa region task force*, Human Resources and Poverty Division, Africa Technical Department, Washington DC.

Chapter 7

Jones, S. (1990) 'The Beni Hamida Weaving Project, Jordan: Its community development impact – An initial assessment' prepared for Save the Children, Jordan.
Jones, S. (1996) 'Cochin Urban Poverty Reduction Project – Design Phase – Poverty Strategy' prepared for ODA in consultation with Design phase consultancy team, Corporation of Cochin, UPO and DCO, New Delhi.
Jones, S. (1998) 'Caribbean Social Development Retreat: Poverty elimination and partnerships' Report of Proceedings prepared for DFID in the Caribbean in collaboration with Wratten,E., Barrow, C., Duncan, N, Retreat Participants and DFID Caribbean staff.

Jones, S. and Matrix Consultants (1995) 'Urban Poverty in Kenya: A situation analysis and options for ODA assistance', prepared for the British Development Division in Eastern Africa, ODA.
Ngau, M. (1994) 'Study of Households in Mathare Valley' prepared for Deutsche Gesellschaft für Technische zu Sammerarbeit, Kenya.
Rakodi, C. (1994) *Poverty Lines or Household Strategies? A review of conceptual and methodological issues in the study of urban poverty*, University of Wales, Cardiff.
Satterthwaite, D. (1997) 'Urban Poverty: Reconsidering its scale and nature' Background Paper for the workshops on Poverty Reduction in Urban Areas organized by IIED, London.
Thomas, L. (1994) 'Urban Poverty and Development Interventions' INTRAC Occasional Papers Series No. 4, INTRAC, Oxford.
Wratten, E. (1995) 'Conceptualising Urban Poverty' in *Environment and Urbanisation*, vol. 7 (1).

Chapter 8

Afrane, S.K. (1990) 'Job Creation in Residential Areas: A comparative study of public and private residential communities in Kumasi, Ghana', in Raj, M. and Nientied, P., (eds.), *Housing and Income in Third World Urban Development*, Aspect Publishing, London.
Arimah, B.C. (1994) 'Self Help Housing Modification for Income Generating Activities: A study of two housing projects in Nigeria', paper presented at 2nd ENHR Symposium on Housing for the Urban Poor, Birmingham, April 11–14.
CNC, (Centro Nacional de la Construcción) (1976) 'Diagnosis of the Economic and Technological State of the Colombian Brickmaking Industry', Doc. No. CEN 10–76, Bogotá.
Gilbert, A.G. (1988) 'Home Enterprises in Poor Urban Settlements: Constraints, potentials, and policy options', *Regional Development Dialogue* vol. 9 (4), pp. 21–37.
Hansen, E. and Williams, J. (1987) 'Economic Issues and the Progressive Housing Development Model', in Patton, C.V. (ed.), *Spontaneous Shelter*, Temple University Press, Philadelphia.
Hansenne, M. (1991) 'The Dilemma of the Informal Sector, Report of the Director-General', International Labour Organisation, Geneva.
Hardoy, J.E. and Satterthwaite, D. (1981) *Shelter: Need and response*, John Wiley, Chichester.
Hays-Mitchell, M. (1993) 'The Ties That Bind. Informal and formal sector linkages in streetvending: The case of Peru's *ambulantes*', *Environment and Planning A* vol. 25 pp. 1085–1102.
Hughes, G. (1976) 'Low-Income Housing: A Kenyan case study', in Little, I.M.F. and Scott, M.F.G. (eds.), *Using Shadow Prices*, Heinemann, London.
ILO (International Labour Office) (1984) 'Small-scale Brickmaking', ILO, Geneva.
ILO (1987) 'Employment Policy and Job Creation in and through the Construction Industry', ILO, Geneva.

Keddie, J. and Cleghorn, W. (1978) 'Least-cost Brickmaking', *Appropriate Technology* vol. 5(3).
Klaassen, L.H., Hoogland, J.G.D. and van Pelt, M.J. (1987) 'Economic Impact and Implications of Shelter Investments', in Rodwin, L. (ed.), *Shelter, Settlement and Development*, Allen and Unwin, Boston.
Laquian, A.A. (1983) 'Sites, Services and Shelter – An evaluation', *Habitat International* vol. 7(5/6).
Lyby, E. (1992) 'Background Paper', UNDP/ILO INT/89/021 Interregional Project Employment Generation in Urban Works Programmes through the Effective Use of Local Resources, Nairobi, Kenya, 6–10 April.
Mensah, A.S. (1997) 'State Housing Company and Housing Delivery in Ghana', Unpublished MA dissertation, University of Newcastle upon Tyne.
Moavenzadeh, F. (1987) 'The Construction Industry', in Rodwin, L. (ed.), *Shelter, Settlement and Development*, Allen & Unwin, Boston.
Moavenzadeh, F. and Hagopian, F. (1983) 'The Construction and Building Materials Industries in Developing Countries', Cambridge, Mass.
Raj, M. and Mitra, B. (1990) 'Households, Housing and Home Based Economic Activities in Low Income Settlements', in Raj, M. and Nientied, P. (eds.), *Housing and Income in Third World Urban Development*, Aspect Publishing, London.
Rondinelli, D.A. and Cheema, G.S. (1985) 'Urban Service Policies in Metropolitan Areas: Meeting the needs of the urban poor in Asia', *Regional Development Dialogue*, 170–90.
Schlyter, A. (1987) 'Commercialisation of Housing in Upgraded Squatter Areas: The case of George, Lusaka, Zambia', *African Urban Quarterly*, 287–97.
Sethuraman, S.V. (1985) 'Basic Needs and the Informal Sector: The case of low-income housing in developing countries', *Habitat International* vol. 9(3/4).
Sinai, I. (forthcoming) 'Using the Home for Income Generation: The case of Kumasi, Ghana', *Cities*.
Spence, R., Wells, J. and Dudley, E. (1993) *Jobs From Housing: Employment, building materials, and enabling strategies for urban development*, Intermediate Technology Publications, London.
Strassmann, W.P. (1986) 'Types of Neighbourhood and Home-Based Enterprises: Evidence from Lima, Peru', *Urban Studies* vol. 23 pp. 485–500.
Strassmann, W.P. (1987) 'Home-based Enterprises in Cities of Developing Countries', *Economic Development and Cultural Change* vol. 36(1) pp. 121–44 (1987).
Syagga, P.M., Kamau, R.G. and Ondiege, P. (1989) 'Access by Women and Urban Poor to Urban Land and Credit: A socio-economic evaluation of the third urban project in Kenya', HRDU, University of Nairobi.
Tipple, A.G. (1993a) 'The Pise Building Method in Low-cost Housing Provision', paper presented at the 21st IAHS World Housing Congress, Cape Town, South Africa, May.
Tipple, A.G. (1993b) 'Shelter as Workplace: A review of home-based enterprises in developing countries', *International Labour Review* vol. 132(4) pp. 521–539.

Tipple, A.G. (1994a) 'A Matter of Interface: The need for a shift in targeting housing interventions', *Habitat International* vol. 18(4) pp. 1–15.
Tipple, A.G. (1994b) 'The Need for New Urban Housing in Sub-Saharan Africa: Problem or opportunity', *African Affairs* 93 pp. 587–608.
Tipple, A.G. and Willis, K.G. (1991) 'Tenure Choice in a West African City', *Third World Planning Review* vol. 13(1) pp. 27–45.
UNCHS (United Nations Centre for Human Settlements) (1987) 'Global Report on Human Settlements 1986', Oxford University Press for UNCHS (Habitat), Oxford.
UNCHS (1990) 'The Global Strategy for Shelter to the Year 2000', UNCHS (Habitat), Nairobi.
UNCHS (1991) 'Human Settlements Development Through Community Participation', UNCHS (Habitat), Nairobi.
UNCHS/ILO (1995) 'Shelter Provision and Employment Generation', United Nations Centre for Human Settlements (Habitat), Nairobi; International Labour Office, Geneva.
Watermeyer, R.B. (1993) 'Community-based Construction: Mobilising communities to construct their own infrastructure', paper presented at the 21st IAHS World Housing Congress, Cape Town, South Africa, May.

Chapter 10

Abugre, C. (1992) 'Thinking of starting a Credit Scheme?', unpublished document, ACORD Research and Policy Programme, London.
ACORD (1997) 'Annual Report', ACORD, London.
ACORD (Agency for Co-operation and Research in Development) (1992) *A Practical Guide to Credit*, ACORD Research and Policy Programme, London.
Dawson, J. and Jeans, A. (1997) *Looking Beyond Credit: Business development services and the promotion of innovation among small producers*, Intermediate Technology Publications, London.
Hulme, D. and Mosely, P. (1996) *Finance Against Poverty*, Routledge, London.
Johnson, S. and Rogaly, B. (1997) *Microfinance and Poverty Reduction*, Oxfam, Oxford.
Mayoux, L. (1998) 'Women's Empowerment and Micro-finance Programmes: Approaches, evidence and ways forward', discussion paper, The Open University, Milton Keynes.
McGeehan, S. (1998) 'Credit and Savings Schemes in High Inflationary Contexts', unpublished document, ACORD Research and Policy Programme, London.
Nagarajan, G. (1997) 'Developing Financial Institutions in Conflict Affected Countries: Emerging issues, first lessons learnt and challenges ahead', paper produced for International Labour Office, Geneva.
Otero, M. (1994) 'The Evolution of Nongovernmental Organizations Toward Financial Intermediation', in Otero, M. and Rhyne, E. (eds.) *The New World of Micro-enterprise Finance: Building healthy financial institutions for the poor*, Intermediate Technology Publications, London.

Rhyne, E. and Otero, M. (1994) 'Financial Services for Micro-enterprises: Principles and institutions', in Otero, M. and Rhyne, E. (eds.) *The New World of Micro-enterprise Finance: Building healthy financial institutions for the poor*, Intermediate Technology Publications, London.

Robinson, M.S. (1994) 'Savings Mobilization and Micro-enterprise Finance: The Indonesian experience', in Otero, M. and Rhyne, E. (eds.), *The New World of Micro-enterprise Finance: Building healthy financial institutions for the poor*, Intermediate Technology Publications, London.

Vandenberg, P. (1997) 'Urban Migration and the Breakdown of Credit Relations', *SOAS (School of Oriental and African Studies) Economic Digest*, vol. 1 (3), pp. 43–6

Yaqub, S. (1995) 'Empowered to Default? Evidence from BRAC's microcredit programmes', *Journal of Small Enterprise Development*, vol. 6 (4).

Yaqub, S. (1996) 'Macroeconomic Conditions for Successful Financial Services for Poor People', paper commissioned by the Policy Department, Oxfam, Oxford, and ActionAid, London.

Chapter 11

Bank of Botswana (1996) 'State of the Economy', Government Printer, Gaborone.

Feddema, H. (1990) *Survival Through Cooperation in Naledi*, Botswana Society, Gaborone.

Government of Botswana (1991) 'Population and Housing Census 1991', Government Printer, Gaborone.

Gaborone City Council/GoB (1995) 'City Traffic Planning and Management Study', Government Printer, Gaborone.

Government of Botswana (1996) 'Household Income and Expenditure Survey: 1993/94', Government Printer, Gaborone.

Kgosidintsi, B.N. (1992) 'Poverty in Botswana. A consultancy report for the Botswana Christian Council', Gaborone.

Mosha, A.C. (1993) *An Evaluation of the Effectiveness of National Land Policies and Instruments in Improving Supply and Access to Land for Human Settlement Development in Botswana*, UNCHS (Habitat), Nairobi.

Mosha, A.C. (1996) 'The City of Gaborone, Botswana: Planning and management', *AMBIO, A Journal of the Human Environment*, vol. 25 (2).

Toteng, E.N. (1994) 'The role of land use planning policies in the development of the informal sector in the Gaborone economy, Botswana', unpublished M.A. thesis, University of Sheffield.

Chapter 12

Bantebya Kyomuhendo, G. (1992) 'The Role of Women in Petty Commodity Production and Commerce in Uganda' in *Gender and Development in Africa: Ethiopia*, Organisation for Social Science Research in Eastern Africa (OSSREA).

Bantebya Kyomuhendo, G. (1994) *The Health Care Providers – Women Client Relationships: Health workers perspectives*, WHO/TDR, Geneva.

Bantebya Kyomuhendo, G. (1997) 'Treatment Seeking Behaviour among Poor Urban Women in Kampala, Uganda', PhD Thesis, Hull University.

Bantebya Kyomuhendo, G. (1996) 'Six Women: Individual accounts of treatment seeking' in Wallman, S. (ed.) *Kampala Women Getting By: Well-being in the time of AIDs*, James Currey, London; Fountain Publishers, Kampala and Ohio University Press, Athens.

Blackburn, C. (1991) *Poverty and Health: Working with families*, Open University Press, Milton Keynes.

Blood, R.O. and Wolfe, D.M. (1960) *Husbands and Wives: The dynamics of married living*, Collier Macmillan, London and The Free Press, New York.

Brydon, L. and Chant, S. (1989) *Women in the Third World: Gender issues in rural and urban areas*, Elgar Publishing Company, Aldershot.

Chrisman, N. (1977) 'The Health Seekers Process', *Culture, Medicine and Psychology*, Vol. 1, pp. 351–378.

Frabrega, H. (1973) 'Towards a Model of Illness Behaviour' *Med. Care*, vol. 9(6) pp. 470–84.

Geertsen, K. (1975) 'A Re-examination of Suchman's View on Social Factors in Healthcare Utilisation', *Journal of Health and Social Behaviour*, Vol. 16, pp. 226–237.

Graham, H. (1984) *Women, Health and the Family*, Wheat Sheaf Books, Brighton.

Hardesty, C. and Bokermier, J. (1989) 'Finding Time and Making Do: Distribution of household labour in non metropolitan marriages' *Journal of Marriage and the Family*, vol. 51 pp. 253–267.

Hay, M. and Stricher, S. (eds.) (1995) *African Women South of the Sahara*, 2nd Edition, Longman, New York.

Holger, H. and Twaddle, M. (1991) *Changing Uganda*, Kampala Fountain Press.

Igun, U.A. (1979) 'Stages in Health Seeking a Descriptive Model' *Soc. Sci. Med.* vol. 13A pp. 445–456.

Kroeger, A. (1983) 'Anthropological and Socio-Medical Health Care Research in Developing Countries' Social Science and Medicine vol. 12 (3) pp. 147–161.

Little, K. (1973) *African Women in Towns*, London, Cambridge University Press.

Ludwig, E.G. and Gibson, G. (1969) 'Self Perception of Sickness and the Seeking of Medical Care' *Journal of Health and Social Behaviour*, vol. 10, pp. 125–133.

Mechanic, D. (1962) 'The Concept of Illness Behaviour' *Journal of Chronic Diseases* vol. 15, pp. 189–94.

Munachonga, M.L. (1988) 'Income Allocations and Marriage Options in Urban Zambia', in Dwyer, D. and Bruce, J. (eds.) *A Home Divided: Women and income in the Third World*, Stanford University Press, Stanford, California.

Mustafa, A.Y. (1990) 'Women and Development in an Urban Context: A study of women migrants in Mosul City (Iraq)', unpublished Ph.D. thesis, Hull University.

Mwaipopo, R.A. (1995) 'Household Resource Management and Patriarchal Relationships: The impact of seaweed farming in Paje Village, Zanzibar', in Creighton, C. and Omari, C.K. (eds.) *Gender Family and Household in Tanzania*, Avebury, Aldershot.

Mwaka, V., Mugyenyi, M. and Banya, . (1994) *Women in Uganda: A profile*, Kampala Makerere University.

National Council for Children (1994) 'Equity and Vulnerability: A situation analysis of women, adolescents and children in Uganda', UNICEF, Kampala.

Obbo, C. (1991) 'Women, Children and a Living Wage' in Holger, H.B. and Twaddle, M. (eds.) *Changing Uganda*, Kampala Fountain Press.

Omari, C.K. (1995) 'Decision Making and the Household: Case studies from Tanzania' in Creighton, C. and Omari, C.K. (eds.) *Gender, Family and Household in Tanzania*, Avebury, Aldershot.

Oppong, C. (1981) *Middle Class African Marriage, A family study of Ghanaian senior civil servants*, Allen Unwin, London.

Ostergaard, L. (1983) 'The Allocation of Money and the Structuring of Inequalities within Marriage', *The Sociological Review*, vol. 31 (2), pp. 237–263.

Pahl, J. (1982) 'Patterns of Money Management Within Marriage', *Journal of Social Policy* vol. 9, pp. 313–315.

Rodman, H. (1972) 'Marital Power and the Theory of Resources in Cultural Context', *Journal of Comparative Family Studies* vol. 3 (Spring), pp. 50–70.

Rosaldo, M.Z. and Lamphere, L. (1974) *Women, Culture and Society*, Stanford, California.

Safilos-Rothschild, C. (1970) 'The Study of Family Power Structure. A review 1960–1969', *Journal of Marriage and the Family*, November, pp. 539–551.

Safilos-Rothschild, C. (1982) 'Female Power, Autonomy and Demographic Change in the Third World' in Anker, A., Buvinic, M. and Youssef, N.H. (eds.) *Women's Roles and Population Trends in the Third World*, Crom Helm, London.

Standing, H. (1991) *Independence and Autonomy, Women's employment and the family in Calcutta, India*, Routledge, London.

Shuval, J.T. (1981) 'The Contribution of Psychological and Social Phenomena to an Understanding of the Aetiology of Disease and Illness' *Social Science and Medicine*, vol. 15A, pp. 337–342.

Sibongile, W.M. (1995) 'Economic Survival Strategies of Female Headed Households. The case of Soweto, South Africa', unpublished Ph.D. thesis, University of London.

Suchman, E. (1965) 'Social Patterns of Illness and Medical Care', *Journal of Health and Human Behaviour*, vol. 6, pp. 2–16.

Tadria, H.M. (1987) 'Changes and Continuities in the Position of Women in Uganda' in Weibe, P. and Dodge, C. (eds.) *Beyond Crisis*, Kampala Makerere Institute of Social Research.

Townsend, J. and Momsen, J. (1987) 'Towards a Geography of Gender in the Third World', in Momsen, J. and Townsend, J. (eds.) *Geography of Gender in the Third World*, Hutchinson, London, pp. 27–81.

Unschuld, U. (1975) 'Medical Cultural Conflicts in Asian Setting: An explanatory theory', *Social Science and Medicine*, vol. 9, pp. 303–312.
Wallman, S. (1996) *Kampala Women Getting by: Well-being in the time of AIDS*, James Currey, London; Kampala Fountain Press and Ohio University Press.
Weibe, P. and Dodge, E. (eds.) (1987) *Beyond Crisis*, Kampala Makerere Institute of Social Research.
Wright, C. (1993) 'Unemployment, Migration and Changing Gender Relations in Lesotho', unpublished Ph.D. thesis, University of Leeds.
World Bank (1993) 'Uganda: Social indicators. A World Bank Country Study', Washington DC.
World Bank (1989) 'Uganda Country Report. A World Bank country study', Washington DC.
Young, J.C. (1980) *Medical Choice in a Mexican Village*, Rutgers University Press, New Brunswick.

Chapter 13

ActionAid (1996) 'Tamale Street Children Project: Annual plan and budget 1996', Tamale.
Agarwal, S., Attah, S.M., Apt, N., Grieco, M.S., Kwakye, E.A. and Turner, J. (1994) *Bearing the Weight: The kayayoo, Ghana's girl working child*, UNICEF Conference on the Girl Child, Accra.
Annorbah-Sarpei, A.J. (1995) *Street Children in Tamale: Addressing an urban problem*, Centre for Community Studies, Action and Development, Accra.
Apt van Ham, N., Blavo, E.Q. and Opoku, S.S. (1992) 'Street Children in Accra: A survey report', Report by the Department of Sociology, University of Ghana (Legon) for the Department of Social Welfare and Save the Children Fund (UK), Accra.
Apt, N.A. and Greico, M. (1995) *Listening to Girls on the Street Tell Their Own Story: What will help them most*, Social Administration Unit, University of Ghana (Legon).
Benneh, G. (1970) 'The Impact of Cocoa Cultivation on the Traditional Land Tenure System of the Akan of Ghana', *Ghana Journal of Sociology*, vol. 6 (1), pp.42–60.
Dei, G. and Sefa, J. (1992) *Hardships and Survival in Rural West Africa: A case study of a Ghanaian community*, CODESRIA (Conseil pour le Développement de la Recheiche Economique et Sociale en Afrique) Monograph Series 3/92, Dakar.
Goody, E. (1982) *Parenthood and Social Reproduction: Fostering and occupational roles in West Africa*, Cambridge University Press.
Ghana Living Standards Survey (1995) Ghana Statistical Service, Accra.
Goody, J. (1967) *The Social Organisation of the LoWiili*, Oxford University.
Johnson, V., Hill J. and Ivan-Smith, E. (1995) *Listening to Smaller Voices: Children in an environment of change*, ActionAid, Chard.
Kusters, C. (1995) 'Listening to Street Children in Tamale: A survey report', ActionAid, Accra.

Nsiah-Gyabaah, K. (1994) 'Land Degradation and Society in Northern Ghana', in Redclift, M. and Sage, C. (eds.), *Strategies for Sustainable Development: Local agendas for the southern hemisphere*, Wiley, Chichester.
Oppong, C. (1973) *Growing Up in Dagbon*, Ghana Publishing Corporation, Accra.
Okali, C. (1983) *Cocoa and Kinship: The matrilineal Akan*, Routledge and Kegan Paul, London.
Seidu Mohamadu (1997) 'Integrating Indigenous Knowledge with Geographical Information Systems: A study of land degradation and rural livelihood sustainability in the northern region of Ghana', unpublished Ph.D. thesis, University of London.
Shepherd, A. (1981) 'Agrarian Change in Northern Ghana: Public investment, capitalist farming and famine', in Heyer, J., Roberts, P. and Williams, G. (eds.), *Rural Development in Tropical Africa*, Macmillan, London.
Staniland, M. (1975) *The Lions of Dagbon*, Cambridge University Press.
Swift, A. (1997) *Children for Social Change: The education for citizenship of street and working children in Brazil*, Educational Heretics, Nottingham.
Tait, D. (1961) *The Konkomba of Northern Ghana*, Oxford University Press.
Whitehead, A. (1984) *Gender and Famine in West Africa*. Ghana, DSA (Development Studies Association) Annual Conference, University of Bradford.
Whitehead, A. (1988) 'Distributional Effects of Cash Crop Innovation: Peripheral commercialised farmers in North East Ghana', *IDS Bulletin*, vol. 19, Part 2.

Chapter 14

Agnelli, S. (1986) *Street Children: A growing urban tragedy*, Weidenfeld & Nicholson, London.
Aptekar, L. (1988) *Street Children of Cali*, Duke University Press, Durham N.C.
Aptekar, L. (1993) 'A Cross-cultural Comparison of Street Children', paper presented at the annual meeting of the Society for Cross-cultural Research, Washington, DC.
Aptekar, L., Kilbrid, P., Kariuki, P. and Njeru, E. (1994) *The Street Children of Kenya: Consequences of modernization and changing family structure*, National Science Foundation Grant, Washington DC.
Aptekar, L. et al. (1995) 'Street Children in Nairobi, Kenya', *African Urban Quarterly*, Nairobi, Kenya.
Boyden, J. (1990) 'A Comparative Perspective of the Globalization of Childhood', in James, A. and Prout, A. (eds.) *Construction and Destruction of Childhood: Issues in the social study of childhood*, Falmer Press, London.
Child, J.L. (1973) *Humanistic Psychology and the Research Tradition*, J. Wiley & Sons, Inc., New York.
Dallape, F. (1987) 'An Experience with Street Children', *Man Graphics*, Nairobi, Kenya.
Erny, G. (1981) *The Child and his Environment in Black Africa. An essay on traditional education*, Oxford University Press, Nairobi.

Kariuki, P.W. (1987) 'Some Educationally Valuable Aspects of African Traditional Approaches to Child Rearing', *Comparative Education*, vol. 23 (2), pp.225–235.

Kariuki, P.W. (1989) 'In Search of a Sense of Identity: Coping with single-parenthood in Kenya.' *Early Child Development and Care*, vol. 50, pp.25–30.

Kariuki, P.W. (1998) 'Methodological Challenges in the Study of Street Children in Nairobi', paper presented at the fourth Africa Region International Society for the Study of Behaviourial Development (ISSBD) Conference, Windhoek, Namibia.

Katambo, R. (1990) 'A New Life for the Squatters of Soweto', African Housing Fund, Nairobi, Kenya.

Keraro, J. (1994) 'Brief Report for the Chairman on Street Children in Nairobi', Provincial Task Force, Nairobi, Kenya.

Kilbride, P. and Kilbride, J. (1990) *Changes in Family Life in East Africa: Women and children at risk*, Penn State University Press, Universit Park.

Kilbride, P. and Njeru, E. (1995) 'An Anthropological Perspective on Social Understanding of Street Children in Nairobi', paper presented at the Pan African Association of Anthropology, Nairobi, Kenya.

Muraya, J. (1993) 'Street Children: A study of street girls in Nairobi, Kenya', Centre for Development Studies, University College of Swansea, Wales.

Njeru, E. (1993) 'Female-headed Households: Consequences for child survival and development', University of Nairobi, Kenya.

Njeru, E., Kariuki, P.W. and Kilbride, P. (1996). 'Nairobi Street Children: Adolescent health', in *Social Behaviour and Health*, Monograph No. 3, pp.64–69.

Nowrojee, V. (1990) 'Juvenile Delinquency and an Exploration of the Laws Governing Children in the Criminal Process in Kenya', unpublished M.A. thesis, Bryn Mawr College, P.A.

Onyango, P. and Kariuki, P.W. (1992) *Urban Poverty: Research and evaluation of street children and their families in Kenya*, Ford Foundation, Nairobi, Kenya.

Onyango, P., Orwa, K., Ayako, A. and Kariuki, P. (1991a) *A Summary Study of Street Children in Kenya*, ANPPCAN, Nairobi, Kenya.

Onyango, P., Suda, C., and Orwa, K. (1991b) 'Report on the Nairobi Case Study on Children in Especially Difficult Circumstances', UNICEF.

Suda, C. (1994). 'Report of a Baseline Survey on Street Children in Nairobi', Institute of African Studies, University of Nairobi.

Wainaina, J. (1981) 'The Parking Boys of Nairobi', *African Journal of Sociology*, Special Edition, University of Nairobi.

Chapter 15

Obbo, C. (1992) *Needs, Demands, Resources in Relation to Health Care Demands in Kampala*, Save The Children Fund, Kampala.

Parkin, D.J. (1969) *Neighbours and Nationals in an African City Ward*, Routledge and Kegan Paul, London.

Panos (1990) 'Triple Jeopardy: Women and AIDS', The Panos Institute, London.

Society for Women and AIDS in Africa (SWAA) (1989) 'Report on the First International Workshop on Women and AIDS in Africa', Harare 10–12 May.
UNAIDS (1997) 'Women and AIDS', Geneva.
UNAIDS (1998) 'Women and AIDS', Geneva.
Williams, G. and Tamale, N. (1991) 'The Caring Community: Coping with AIDS in urban Uganda', Action Aid, Strategies of Hope no. 6.

Chapter 16

Beall, J. (ed.) (1997) *A City for All: Valuing difference and working with diversity*, Zed Books, London.
Becker, C.M. and Morrison, A.R. (1996) 'Public Policy and Rural-urban Migration', in Gugler, J. (ed.) *Cities in the Developing World: Issues, theory and policy*, Oxford University Press, Oxford.
Bozzoli, B. (1991) *Women of Phokeng, Consciousness, life strategy and migrancy in South Africa, 1900–1983*, Ravan Press, Johannesburg.
Burman, S. (1994) 'Intergenerational Family Care: Legacy of the past, implications for the future', paper presented at the Journal of Southern African Studies Conference, York, September.
Caces, F., Arnold, F., Fawcett, J. and Gardner, R. (1985) 'Shadow Households and Competing Auspices: Migration behaviour in the Philippines', *Journal of Development Economics* vol. 17 (1), pp. 5–25.
Cohen, A. (1969) *Custom and Politics in Urban Africa, A study of Hausa migrants in Yoruba towns*, Routledge and Kegan Paul, London.
Crehan, K. (1992) 'Rural Households: Making a living' and 'Rural Households: Survival and change', in Bernstein, H. (ed.), *Rural Livelihoods*, Oxford University Press in association with Open University Press, Oxford and Milton Keynes.
Drakakis-Smith, D. (1992) 'Strategies for Meeting Basic Food Needs in Harare', in Baker, J. and Pedersen, P.O. (eds.) *The Rural-Urban Interface in Africa: Expansion and adaptation*, Scandinavian Institute of African Studies.
Evans, J.E. (1997) 'Growth Prospects Study: Rapid assessment of the impact of policy changes on rural livelihoods in Malawi', a report prepared for the World Bank and financed by UNDP, Lilongwe.
Gorman, M. (1996) 'Older People and Development: The last minority?' in Anderson, M. (ed.) *Development and Social Diversity*, Oxfam, Oxford.
Grown, C.A. and Sebstad, J. (1989) 'Introduction. Toward a Wider Perspective on Women's Employment', *World Development*, vol. 17 (7).
Jamal, V. and Weeks, J. (1988) 'The Vanishing Rural-urban Gap in Sub-Saharan Africa', *International Labour Review*, vol. 127 (3).
Jones, S. (1994) *Assault on Childhood*, Witwatersrand University Press, Johannesburg.
Kanji, N. (1993) 'Gender and Structural Adjustment Policies: A case study of Harare, Zimbabwe', unpublished Ph.D. thesis, University of London.
Kanji, N. (1995) 'Gender, Poverty and Economic Adjustment in Harare, Zimbabwe', *Environment and Urbanization*, vol. 7 (1), April.
Lee-Smith, D., Manundu, M., Lamba, D. and Gathuru, P.K. (1987) 'Urban Food Production and the Cooking Fuel Situation in Urban Kenya –

National Report: Results of a 1985 national survey', Mazingira Institute, Nairobi.

McKay, A. et al. (1997) 'Trade Liberalisation and Agricultural Supply Response: Issues and some lessons', *European Journal of Development Research*, vol. 9 (2), pp. 129–147.

Mabin, A. (1990) 'Limits of Urban Transition Models in Understanding South African Urbanisation', *Development Southern Africa*, vol. 7 (3), August.

Mbiba, Beacon (1995) *Urban Agriculture in Zimbabwe*, Avebury, Aldershot.

Mlozi, M.R.S., Lupanga, I.J. and Mvena, Z.S.K. (1992) 'Urban Agriculture as a Survival Strategy in Tanzania', in Baker, J. and Pedersen, P.O. (eds.) *The Rural-Urban Interface in Africa: Expansion and adaptation*, The Scandinavian Institute of African Studies, Uppsala.

Moser, C. (1996) *Confronting Crisis: A comparative study of household responses in four poor urban communities*, Environmentally Sustainable Development Studies and Monograph Series No. 8, The World Bank, Washington DC.

Moser, C. (1998) 'The Asset Vulnerability Framework: Reassessing urban poverty reduction strategies', *World Development*, vol. 26 (1), pp. 1–20.

Murray, C. (1981) *Families Divided: The impact of migrant labour in Lesotho*, Ravan Press, Johannesburg.

Potts, D. (1995) 'Shall We Go Home? Increasing urban poverty in African cities and migration processes', *The Geographic Journal*, vol. 161 (3), pp. 245–264.

Potts, D. with Mutambirwa, C. (1998) 'Basics are a Luxury': Perceptions of ESAP's impact on rural and urban areas', *Environment and Urbanization*, vol. 10 (1), pp. 55–76.

Rakodi, C. (1991) 'Women's Work or Household Strategies?' *Environment and Urbanization*, vol. 3 (2).

Rees, W. (1992) 'Ecological Footprints and Appropriate Carrying Capacity: What urban economics leaves out', *Environment and Urbanization*, vol. 4 (2), pp. 121–130.

Robertson, C. (1984) *Sharing the Same Bowl: A socio-economic history of women and class in Accra, Ghana*, Indiana University Press, Bloomington.

Seppala, P. (1996) 'The Politics of Economic Diversification: Reconceptualizing the rural informal sector in Southeast Tanzania', *Development and Change*, vol. 27, pp. 557–78.

Tacoli, C. (1998) 'Beyond the Rural-urban Divide', *Environment and Urbanization*, vol. 10 (1), pp. 3–4.

Todes, A. (1998) 'Gender, Place, Migration and Regional Policy in South Africa', in Mapetla, M., Larsson, A. and Schlyter, A. (eds.), *Changing Gender Relations in Southern Africa, Issues of urban life*, Institute of Southern African Studies, National University of Lesotho.

Wood, C. (1982) 'Equilibrium and historical-structural Perspectives on Migration', in *International Migration Review*, vol. 16 (2), pp. 298–319.

Wratten, E. (1995) 'Conceptualising Urban Poverty', *Environment and Urbanization*, vol. 7 (1).